W9-ABB-487

Gardening in the Upper Midwest

Gardening in the Upper Midwest

By Leon C. Snyder

University of Minnesota Press, Minneapolis

Copyright © 1978 by the University of Minnesota.
All rights reserved.
Printed in the United States of America
at the North Central Publishing Company, St. Paul.
Published by the University of Minnesota Press,
2037 University Avenue Southeast, Minneapolis, Minnesota 55455,
and published in Canada by Burns & MacEachern Limited,
Don Mills, Ontario

Library of Congress Catalog Card Number 77-88650

ISBN 0-8166-0833-4

The University of Minnesota is an equal
opportunity educator and employer.

Second printing, 1978

This book is dedicated
to my wife, Vera A. Snyder,
for her encouragement
and for her tolerance
of the many hours spent
in the preparation
of this manuscript.

Acknowledgments

The author wishes to acknowledge the assistance of and thank Helen Bean and Nancy Roberts, secretaries in the Department of Horticultural Science, for typing the manuscript; Linda Sanford, naturalist at the arboretum, for drawing the art work; June Rogier, librarian at the arboretum, for helping with the index; Louis and Helen Fisher of Hastings for permitting the photographing of their yard, and the Visual Aids Department of the Agricultural Extension Service for providing four color photographs.

Table of Contents

Color photograph section follows p. 118

Gardening in the Upper Midwest

Introduction

Many excellent books have been written on gardening. Most of the authors of these books are from the eastern states, the South, or the West Coast. Except for George Luxton's *Flower Growing in the North*, published in 1956, no books cover the garden problems faced by gardeners in the Upper Midwest.

The climate of Minnesota and its surrounding states and Canada is different from that in other parts of the United States. In the winter, the temperature can drop to −40°F. or colder. In the summer, temperatures can climb to 100°F. or higher. Not only does this area have extremes of temperature but it also has a fluctuating rainfall. Summer droughts are not uncommon. Generally, the rainfall decreases as one moves in a northwesterly direction. Average annual rainfall in our area ranges from about 28 inches in the southeast to about 16 inches in the northwest. Fortunately, most of this rainfall comes during the growing season.

The severity of our winters places the greatest limitation on the plants that can be grown. Winter injury on plants takes many forms:

Tip kill and dieback on woody plants may be the result of an early heavy freeze that occurs before plants have fully hardened,

3

thus killing the late growth. Plants must be selected that mature earlier in the fall, and cultural practices must be modified to hasten this maturity.

Lack of flower bud hardiness is another problem with many kinds of plants. Peaches, flowering quince, and many azaleas cannot be grown successfully here because they lack flower bud hardiness. Breeding to develop hardier varieties offers the best solution to this problem.

Winter burn on evergreens is common. We have all seen yews and hemlocks turn red and brown in late winter. The plant hardiness laboratory in the Department of Horticultural Science at the University of Minnesota has shown that one cause of winter burn is a sudden drop in temperature. The sun, reflected from a white snow surface on a still day in February, may cause the temperature in the leaves to rise as much as $50°$ or $60°$ F. above the air temperature. If the sun goes behind a cloud or a building, the temperature drops suddenly and tissues within the leaves are killed. By planting sensitive varieties on sites where they will receive some winter shade, the problem of winter burn can be reduced. Another practical approach is to plant species and cultivars (see p. 9 for definition) that are naturally resistant to winter burn. The University of Minnesota Landscape Arboretum and Horticultural Research Center, both located on State Highway 5 west of Chanhassen, are evaluating thousands of species and cultivars of ornamental plants for winter hardiness and landscape qualities such as texture, foliage, color, bloom, and resistance to insects and diseases. We have identified a number of winter burn-resistance selections in evergreen species that typically show winter burn.

Sunscald on the southwest side of the trunk is still another type of winter injury that occurs on thin-barked trees especially during the first few years until they have developed a crown that shades the trunk. The Norway maples are particularly sensitive to this type of injury. Wrapping the trees in the fall with a tree wrap made of weather-resistant paper minimizes sunscald.

Soils are also highly variable, in both texture and pH. Heavy clay soils and sandy soils are intermixed in certain areas. In the same yard great differences in soil texture may exist. The gardener should understand the effect of soil texture on soil moisture and plant growth. Some plants do well on clay soils, others on sand. In northern parts of the area it would be unwise to attempt to grow apples on sand because of problems of winter injury. On heavier soils nearby, apples thrive.

The pH of the soil is another important consideration. Iron chlorosis, a yellowing of the foliage caused by a lack of available iron, can be a problem on alkaline soils, which are common in the Red River Valley and throughout the western parts of the region. Members of the rose family are extremely susceptible to iron chlorosis. Some plants, like ashes and lilacs, tolerate alkaline soils and these should be planted. Few soils in the region are extremely acid. Adding lime to such soils corrects any acidity problem.

If one recognizes the limitations, gardening in the North can be a rewarding experience. Some plants like peonies, lilacs, and flowering crabapples grow to perfection. We may never have a cherry blossom festival like that held in Washington, D.C. each spring, but we can have displays of flowering crabapples that are every bit as spectacular. In addition, we have the lovely fruits to attract birds to our yards during the winter. Fruit and vegetable growing can also be rewarding experiences.

This book is written to help new gardeners and those who may have moved here from a milder climate. It is also hoped that experienced gardeners may find information that will make them even better gardeners.

The book is organized to give gardeners a ready reference to the many gardening problems that arise. The first 6 chapters are devoted to a general discussion of plants and how they grow and to cultural practices like soil management, pests and their control, and the pruning and training of plants. Chapters 7 and 8 cover the growing of fruits and vegetables in the home garden. The rest of the book is devoted to the aesthetics of gardening, including landscape design, the lawn, and the selection of ornamental plants. Lists are included to help gardeners select the right plants to make their yards more beautiful and useful. (Plants are listed alphabetically by scientific names, with common names in parentheses.) There are chapters on the selection and care of deciduous trees, deciduous shrubs, evergreens, vines, ground covers, perennial and annual flowers, bulbs, and garden roses. Ferns are included in

Chapter 17. A hardiness zone map, keyed to the individual plants, is provided in Chapter 11, p. 99.

The information is based on my years of practical experience as a gardener, superintendent of the University of Minnesota Horticultural Research Center, and director of the Minnesota Landscape Arboretum, which is administered by the University of Minnesota's Department of Horticultural Science and Landscape Architecture.

Chapter 1

Classification of Plants

Gardeners should have some knowledge of how plants are classified. The plant kingdom includes many kinds of plants ranging in size from microscopic bacteria to giant redwoods. The science of taxonomy deals with the orderly classification of these plants.

The taxonomist divides plants into three major groups: the Thallophyta, the Bryophyta, and the Tracheophyta.

The word "Thallophyta" means "Thallus plants." These plants are primitive and undifferentiated into roots, stems, and leaves. The bacteria, fungi, and algae belong to this group. Bacteria and fungi are important to the gardener because they cause many diseases of garden plants. Algae are sometimes a problem in greenhouses and in wet, shady locations.

The word "Bryophyta" means "moss plants." This group contains the mosses and the liverworts. Mosses are primitive plants that like shade and moist sites. Liverworts are flat, creeping plants that grow in moist, shady sites. They are frequently found growing along a stream. In Japan mosses are grown for their landscape effect. In the moist Japanese climate mosses make a fine ground cover under pines. We use mosses in terrariums, but for the most part we make little use of these charming plants in outdoor gardens. When mosses grow in a shady lawn, we try to get rid of them.

The Tracheophyta have well-differentiated roots, stems, and leaves and well-developed tissues for conducting food and water. The group contains the ferns and their allies as well as the seed-producing plants. This group of higher plants is the one that the gardener is primarily concerned with. The Tracheophyta are sub-divided into three classes: Filicinae, Gymnospermae, and Angiospermae. The Filicinae include the ferns and the fern allies like the horsetails and lycopodiums, or ground pines. These reproduce by spores and do not bear seeds.

The Gymnospermae and the Angiospermae are the seed plants and are considered the highest forms of the plant kingdom. The Gymnospermae include the conifers, cycads, ginkgoes, and so on. The word "Gymnospermae" means "naked seed." In this group the seeds are not enclosed in a fruit. In the conifers the seeds are borne at the base of the scales that constitute the cones. As the cones mature, the scales separate and the seeds drop to the ground.

In the Angiospermae the seeds are produced inside fruits which assume a variety of forms and may be either dry or fleshy. The Angiospermae are divided into two subclasses: Monocotyledoneae (monocots) and Dicotyledoneae (dicots). These names refer to the number of seed leaves, or cotyledons. The Monocotyledoneae have other distinguishing characteristics besides the single cotyledon: The leaves are parallel veined. The vascular bundles (water and food conducting tissues) are often scattered as in corn, and there is no well-differentiated cambium (a single layer of cells capable of cell division. The flower parts (sepals, petals, stamens, and carpels) usually occur in 3's or multiples of 3. The Dicotyledoneae is the largest group of seed plants. In addition to having two cotyledons, or seed leaves, the leaves are netted veined, the vascular bundles form a cylinder and develop a well-defined cambium, and the flower parts do not occur in 3's or multiples of 3.

Below the class and subclass categories, plants are classified into orders and families and finally into the correct genus and species. It is important that the gardener know both the scientific and common name of a plant. Knowing the family to which a plant belongs can also help since many of the plants in a family have similar cultural requirements.

The scientific name always consists of the genus and the species names and sometimes the name of the botanical variety. The common name may be easier for some people to remember, but, unfortunately, different common names are used for the same plant in different parts of the country and occasionally in the same locality. For example, the several species of *Amelanchier* are variously known as serviceberry, sarvisberry, Juneberry, saskatoon, shadbush, snowy mespilus, and so on.

The scientific name for a given plant, once the taxonomists have agreed upon it, is the same throughout the world. Scientific names are not difficult to pronounce and are easy to remember. We have no trouble remembering names like petunia, zinnia, tradescantia, and impatiens, which are generic names that are also used as common names.

Every plant has a genus and species identification. This system of classification was devised by Linnaeus in the eighteenth century and is called the binomial system. Let us take a familiar group of plants like the maples. All maples belong to the genus *Acer*. The species name is often descriptive: *Acer rubrum* is the red or swamp maple, *Acer saccharum* the sugar maple. In the oaks the genus name is *Quercus*. *Quercus alba* is the white oak, *Quercus coccinea* the scarlet oak.

Minor differences in plant form or color are common within a plant species. A naturally occurring population that differs from the species is called a botanical variety. An example is the Black Hills strain of white spruce. Native across the northern United States and Canada, white spruce have denser foliage in the Black Hills of South Dakota than elsewhere. The scientific name of the white spruce is *Picea glauca*. The strain growing in the Black Hills is *Picea glauca* var. *densata*. Another example of a botanical variety is the Colorado blue spruce. The Colorado spruce is normally green, but occasionally trees with a bluish cast are found in nature and in nurseries. The scientific name of Colorado blue spruce is *Picea pungens* var. *glauca*.

To distinguish a horticultural variety from a botanical variety, the term "cultivar" is used. A single plant in a seedling population may differ from all the rest. If this plant has characteristics that would make it a desirable plant to grow for ornamental or food purposes, it is given a cultivar name and usually propagated vegetatively either from cuttings or by grafting (see Chapter 3). A few examples will help clarify the difference between a botanical variety and a cultivar. Let us first consider *Picea pungens* var. *glauca* (Colorado blue spruce). In a seedling population containing blue forms, a single plant may be distinct in form or color. This plant can be selected, propagated vegetatively, and introduced as a named cultivar. A cultivar name is always capitalized and either enclosed within single quotation marks or prefixed with the letters "CV." The Moerheim Spruce is a compact form of Colorado blue spruce that has very blue foliage. This is properly designated *Picea pungens* 'Moerheimi' or *Picea pungens* CV Moerheimi. Several seedlings of Norway maple develop a bloodred foliage. One of these is the Crimson King Norway maple. This is properly designated *Acer platanoides* 'Crimson King'. Most cultivars of trees and shrubs are increased from a single, selected parent plant by vegetative means.

In efforts to create new and better horticultural plants, man has often crossed two or more species of the same genus. The seedling population from a cross between two species is sometimes given a specific name. To distinguish this interspecific hybrid from a natural species, the species designation is preceded by an "x." *Spiraea* x *bumalda* (Bumalda spirea) is a hybrid species derived by crossing *S. japonica* x *S. albiflora*; *Syringa* x *chinensis* (Chinese Lilac) by crossing *S. laciniata* x *S. vulgaris*. Of the hundreds of other hybrid species that exist, some are natural hybrids and others were created by man. Usually, a seedling population of a hybrid species is somewhat variable. Individual plants that stand out as being superior to their sister seedlings may be vegetatively propagated and given a cultivar name. *Spiraea* x *bumalda* 'Anthony Waterer' (Anthony Waterer Spirea) is such a cultivar.

In the development of new cultivars in many genera of plants, several species are sometimes involved in the ancestry of a single selection. This is true with garden roses and many flowering crabapples. In such instances only the genus name precedes the cultivar name. *Malus* 'Sparkler' is the proper designation for the recently introduced Sparkler crabapple. *Rosa* 'Peace' is the proper designation for the Peace rose, one of the Hybrid Tea roses.

Not all cultivars are vegetatively propagated. Some are grown from seed. This is particularly true of annual flowers and vegetables. F_1 hybrid seed is the result of crossing two inbred lines. The seedlings resulting from such a cross will be very uniform and are given a cultivar name. Seeds saved from such hybrid plants will not produce uniform plants; seedlings in the second generation will revert to parental types. This is why one should not save seeds from F_1 hybrids.

Cultivar names are also given to plants grown from open-pollinated seeds, provided the resulting seedlings are uniform and distinctive. Such seeds are generally the result of several generations of inbreeding to fix the desired characteristics. Seeds must then be produced in isolated fields to prevent cross-pollination from some other cultivar.

With commonly grown plants like the tomato and marigold, it is permissible to use the common rather than the scientific name. Tomato 'Big Boy' is as acceptable as Lycopersicum 'Big Boy'. In the chapters that follow, many species and cultivar names will be used; the preceding explanation should help gardeners understand the nomenclature.

Chapter 2

Plant Structure and Growth

A knowledge of the structure and growth of plants is an aid to understanding some of the problems that develop when growing plants. All seed-producing plants have vegetative organs (roots, stems, and leaves) and reproductive organs (flowers, fruits, and seeds). Ferns have vegetative organs and reproduce by spores.

Vegetative Organs

ROOTS

Roots anchor the plants. They also absorb water and plant nutrients from the soil and carry these upward to the stem. Some roots are modified for food storage. Carrots, peonies, and rhubarb are familiar examples. Although most roots grow under the surface of the soil, aerial roots develop on some plants, most often on those that grow in tropical rain forests. The form of the root system can vary greatly. A plant is said to have a taproot when a single root grows straight down and lateral roots develop from this main root. The taproot may or may not serve the additional function of food storage. Taproots modified for food storage as in the carrot and beet are called fleshy taproots. Some plants develop

12

fascicled roots, with many roots of about the same size radiating from the base of the plant. In most plants these fascicled roots are slender and are referred to as fibrous roots. Such members of the grass family as corn have a fibrous, fascicled root system. In other plants, like dahlias and peonies, the fascicled roots are modified for food storage and the main roots are fleshy.

STEMS

Most stems develop above ground and are variously branched. The functions of the stem are to support the leaves in such a manner that they are exposed to the maximum amount of sunlight and to transport water and minerals upward to the leaves and the manufactured foods downward from the leaves to the roots. Food storage is another function of certain stems. Other stems develop underground. The rhizome of quack grass is a creeping, underground stem. The fleshy rhizome of the iris plant develops at the ground surface and may be partly below ground. The edible tuber of the Irish potato is a fleshy stem that develops underground at the end of a slender rhizome. In the gladiolus, the corm is a modified fleshy stem. In the lily and onion, food is stored in bulbs consisting of a conical stem and fleshy leaf bases. The fleshy stems of the cactus are green and carry on photosynthesis, or food manufacture.

LEAVES

Leaves are generally flat and green. They may be rather small and scalelike in some plants, as in the arborvitae, or needlelike, as in the pines. The major function of leaves is photosynthesis. Some leaves are modified for food storage, and the scales of the lily bulb are modified leaf bases.

Leaves assume a variety of forms. These leaf forms and the arrangement of leaves on the plant can be very useful in identifying plants. Leaves are opposite when two leaves arise opposite each other on the stem, alternate when only one leaf develops at a node, and whorled when three or more leaves arise at a node. The blade of a simple leaf is in one piece. In compound leaves the leaf blade is divided into a number of leaflets. Normally, a leaf has a

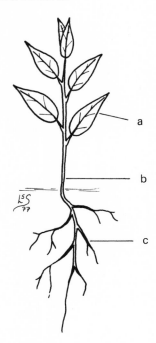

Diagram of a plant: *a.* leaf, *b.* stem, *c.* root.

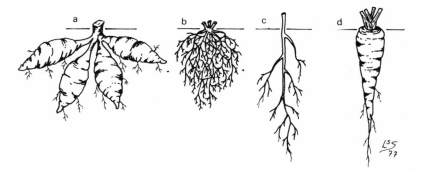

Types of root systems: *a.* fleshy fascicled, *b.* fibrous fascicled, *c.* fibrous taproot, *d.* fleshy taproot.

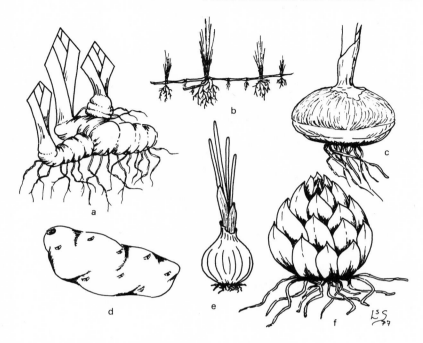

Modified stems: *a.* rhizome (iris), *b.* rhizome (quack grass), *c.* corm (gladiolus), *d.* tuber (potato), *e.* bulb (onion), *f.* bulb (lily).

petiole that supports the leaf blade. In some plants there are two bractlike stipules at the base of the petiole.

The venation of leaves is either parallel or netted. Parallel venation is characteristic of most monocots; netted venation, of most dicots. A simple, netted-veined leaf has either a single midrib from which lateral veins radiate (pinnate venation) or several veins of about equal size radiating from the base of the blade (palmate venation). The elm and the maple respectively illustrate these two types of venation. A compound leaf may be pinnately compound (as in the green ash), twice pinnately compound (as in the Kentucky coffee tree), or palmately compound (as in the Ohio buckeye and Virginia creeper).

There are several kinds of leaf margins. An entire leaf margin has no indentations and is straight or curved. A jagged leaf margin with teeth that point outward is dentate. If the teeth point for-

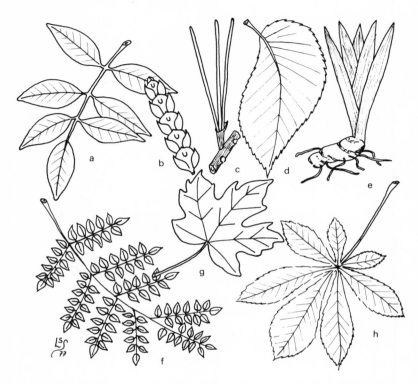

Types of leaves: *a.* pinnately compound, *b.* scale, *c.* needle, *d.* pinnately simple, *e.* simple, parallel veined, *f.* twice pinnately compound, *g.* palmately simple, *h.* palmately compound.

ward, the margin is serrate. A scalloped margin with rounded teeth is crenate. Leaves can also have different kinds of lobes. The oak leaf is pinnately lobed, the maple leaf palmately lobed.

Reproductive Organs

FLOWERS

The typical flower is composed of modified leaves (sepals, petals, stamens, and carpels) attached to a swollen stem tip, or receptacle:

Sepals. Lowermost leaves, usually green. Collectively called the calyx.

Petals. Attached above the sepals. Usually colored to attract pollinating insects. Collectively called the corolla.

Stamens. Pollen-producing organs located above the petals. Each stamen has a stalk portion, the filament, and a pollen-producing part, the anther. Collectively called the androecium.

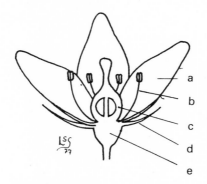

Diagram of a flower: *a*. petal, *b*. stamen,
c. pistil, *d*. sepal, *e*. receptacle.

Carpels. Located in the center of the flower. One or more carpels make up the pistil. There may be one or more pistils per flower. The basal portion of the pistil is the ovary, the neck portion the style, and the upper, flattened or feathery portion the stigma.

Types of flowers

Complete flower. Has all four kinds of modified leaves.

Incomplete flower. Lacks one or more kinds of modified leaves.

Perfect flower. Has both stamens and pistils and may or may not have sepals and petals.

Imperfect flower. Has either stamens or pistils, not both. May or may not have sepals and petals.

A monoecious plant has imperfect flowers and bears both staminate and pistillate flowers on the same plant. (Examples: corn and cucumber.) A dioecious plant has imperfect flowers but bears sta-nate and pistillate flowers on separate plants. (Examples: bitter-sweet and cottonwood.)

Inflorescences

An inflorescence is a group or a cluster of flowers. The following are examples:

Spike. An inflorescence in which the flowers are unstalked and borne along a long axis. Examples: timothy and plantain.

Raceme. The flowers are borne on short stalks, or pedicels, along an elongated axis. Example: chokecherry.

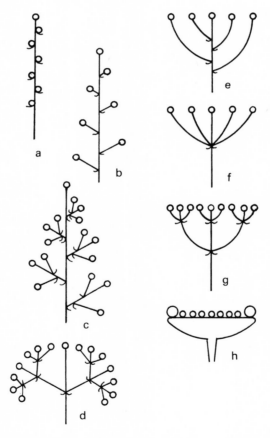

Types of inflorescences: *a.* spike, *b.* raceme, *c.* panicle, *d.* cyme, *e.* corymb, *f.* umbel, *g.* compound umbel, *h.* head.

Panicle. An open type of inflorescence with branching and re-branching. Oldest flowers are near the base. Examples: brome grass and PeeGee hydrangea.

Cyme. Similar to the panicle except the oldest flowers are at the tip of the stem and lateral branches. Example: baby's breath.

Corymb. Similar to the raceme but the lower pedicels are elongated, resulting in a flat-topped flower cluster. Example: cluster roses.

Umbel. Has several elongated pedicels that arise from a common point. Example: onion.

Compound umbel. Produces a simple umbel at the end of each pedicel. Example: carrot.

Head. Has unstalked flowers clustered at the end of the stem. In certain members of the sunflower, or composite, family, the marginal (ray) flowers have strap-shaped corollas. The center flowers are called disk flowers when they differ from the ray flowers. Examples: clover and sunflower.

FRUITS

Fruits are formed from the fertilized ovary and sometimes include other parts of the flower such as the receptacle. Fruits are of many types and often prove useful in plant identification. Fruits are either dry or fleshy at maturity.

Dry Fruits

Grain, or caryopsis. Has a single seed that is fused with the ovary wall. Examples: wheat and corn.

Achene. A single-seeded, dry fruit in which the ovary wall is distinct from the seed coat. Example: clematis.

Samara. Similar to the achene but has a winged portion which aids in seed dispersal. Produced in pairs (as in the maple) or separately (as in the ash).

Schizocarp. A specialized type of fruit produced by members of the carrot family. Its ovary separates at maturity into single-seeded segments. Example: parsnip.

Legume. A podlike fruit with a single row of seeds. When the pod opens, it separates along two sutures. Examples: garden pea and snap (string) bean.

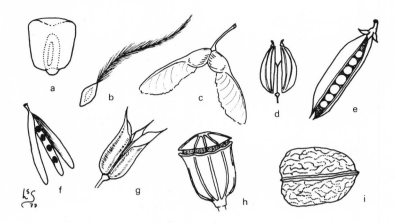

Types of dry fruit: *a.* caryopsis (corn), *b.* achene (clematis),
c. samara (maple), *d.* schizocarp (carrot), *e.* legume (pea),
f. silique (mustard), *g.* follicle (delphinium),
h. capsule (poppy), *i.* nut (walnut).

Silique. May be either elongated and round or flattened and disk-
like in cross section. Has a central partition dividing the fruit into two equal parts. Usually opens to shed the seeds. Example:
mustard.

Capsule. A multicarpelled fruit that usually opens near the tip to
discharge the seeds. Examples: lily and poppy.

Nut. Has a hard shell surrounding the seed or seeds. Some nuts
have a pulpy covering on the shell. Example: walnut.

Fleshy Fruits

Pome. Has several seeds borne in compartments at the center, or
core, of the fruit. The fleshy part is really the receptacle of the
flower that has grown up around the ovary. Examples: apple,
Juneberry, and hawthorn.

Aggregate. A collection of fleshy carpels resembling small drupe-
lets. The fruits separate from the receptacle (as in the raspberry)
or the receptacle breaks off with the fruit (as in the blackberry).

Drupe. Has a hard shell enclosing the seed or seeds. The shell is
surrounded by fleshy pulp, which in turn is surrounded by a
thin skin. Examples: cherry and peach.

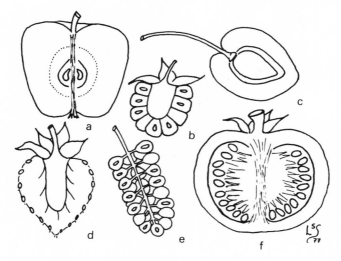

Types of fleshy fruits: *a.* pome (apple), *b.* aggregate (raspberry),
c. drupe (cherry), *d.* accessory (strawberry),
e. multiple (mulberry), *f.* berry (tomato)

Accessory. Edible portion is the enlarged receptacle in which are
embedded the achenes, or "seeds." Example: strawberry.

Multiple. Formed from several flowers borne along a short axis.
Examples: mulberry and pineapple.

Berry. A many-seeded fruit in which the seeds are embedded in
pulp. Examples: tomato and grape.

The Plant Cell: Structure and Function

The plant cell is the unit of structure in plants. Some primitive
plants may consist of a single cell or a chain of cells. In higher
plants there may be millions of cells of various shapes and sizes.

The typical cell consists of a cell wall and a living protoplast
that practically fills the cell. The outer membrane of the protoplast is called the plasma membrane. The vacuole is a cavity in the
center of the cell and is filled with water, various nutrients, and
sugars. The living protoplast is composed of the nucleus (with nucleolus) and cytoplasm. Chloroplasts, starch grains, and other cell
components are embedded in the cytoplasm.

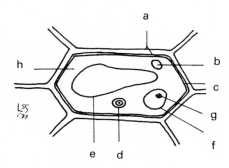

Parts of a plant cell: *a*. cell wall, *b*. plastid (chloroplast),
c. plasma membrane, *d*. plastid (starch grain), *e*. vacuolar
membrane, *f*. nucleus, *g*. nucleolus, *h*. cytoplasm.

Cells near the root and stem tips, the apical meristems, are compact, dense with protoplasm, and capable of repeated cell division.
These cells are responsible for the terminal growth of both roots
and stems. The cambium is a cylinder of cells, one layer thick, that
lies between the bark and the wood. The cells of the cambium divide, adding thickness to the stems and roots.

Cells formed by the apical meristem and cambium differentiate
into a variety of cell types that perform different functions. The
outermost layer of cells on young root tips, young stems, and
leaves are the epidermal cells. These have a layer of cutin, a waxy
substance deposited on the outside to protect the plant from water loss. Directly under the epidermis the cells are thin walled and
usually hexagonal in cross section. Such cells are living and often
are filled with starch grains. These and the cells in the center of
the stem, the pith, are called parenchyma cells, and function in
food storage.

Sieve tubes and their companion cells are formed by the cambium toward the outside of the plant and carry food from the
leaves to the roots. The sieve tubes are elongated, with perforated
end walls. Cytoplasm streams through the pores, carrying dissolved
sugars, amino acids, and so on. The companion cells are shorter
than the sieve tubes and form a vertical row parallel to the sieve
tubes. The vessels are also formed from the cambium and are located inside the cambium. These are elongated in a continuous

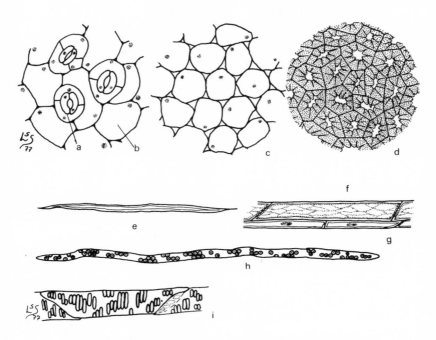

Types of cells: *a.* stomate with guard cells, *b.* epidermis, *c.* parenchyma, *d.* stone, *e.* fiber, *f.* sieve tube, *g.* companion cell, *h.* tracheid, *i.* vessel.

row. As the vessels mature, the end walls dissolve and the walls thicken, usually with spiral thickenings. The mature vessels form continuous tubes connecting the root tips with the leaves. The function of these vessels is to transport water and plant nutrients from the root tips to the leaves. In conifers and ferns the water-conducting cells are called tracheids. These are elongated cells with thickened walls and connected by lateral pores. The water and plant nutrients move upward in a zigzag manner.

Other cells that are differentiated include the fibers and stone cells. The fibers are elongated, taper pointed, and have thick, lignified cell walls that provide strength and support. Stone cells are irregular in form, with thickened cell walls. They have no special function.

Plant tissues are composed of various kinds of cells. Simple tissues, with one type of cell, include the epidermis, cortex, pith, cork, and meristems. Complex tissues contain several different types of cells. The phloem and xylem are examples. Cells deposited by the cambium toward the outside of the stem or root constitute the phloem, which is made up of sieve tubes, companion cells, parenchyma, and fibers. Cells deposited by the cambium toward the center of the stem or root constitute the xylem, which contains vessels or tracheids, parenchyma, and fibers.

The manner by which water and plant nutrients enter and move through the plant is of great interest to the gardener. First, let us understand the role of water in the plant. Water is a constitutent of all living cells and may constitute 95 percent or more of cell weight. Water filling the cells and pushing against the cells walls keeps the plant tissues turgid. Water is a raw material in the process of photosynthesis (see p. 26) and serves as a solvent for plant nutrients that enter from the soil and for foods manufactured by the plant. The evaporation of water from the plant has a cooling effect on the plant and its immediate surroundings.

Water enters the plant primarily through the roots and to a lesser extent through the leaves. The root hairs, which are extensions of epidermal cells and located directly behind the root tips, have direct contact with soil particles. These hairs greatly increase the water-absorbing surface of the plant.

A film of moisture surrounds each soil particle. The outer portion of this film is capillary water, which is free to move in the soil and enter the root hairs. The root hair is a living cell within which the protoplast presses tightly against the cell wall. In the center is the vacuole filled with cell sap containing sugars and minerals in solution. Water and nutrients enter the cell by the process of osmosis through the plasma and vacuolar membranes. If the water concentration in the capillary water surrounding the soil particles is higher than the water concentration in the cell sap, water enters the root hair. This in turn causes water to move into adjoining cells of the cortex. Each mineral element in the soil enters by the same process, depending on relative concentrations of the element and always moving from high to low concentrations.

At the opposite end of the plant, water is evaporating from the leaves by a process called transpiration. This water loss is influ-

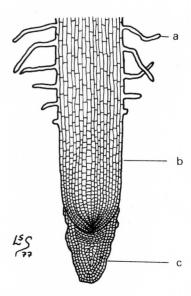

Root tip: *a.* root hair, *b.* meristem, *c.* root cap.

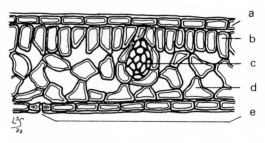

Cross section of a leaf: *a.* upper epidermis, *b.* palisade layer,
c. vein, *d.* mesophyll, *e.* stomate.

enced by temperature, relative air humidity, and wind. Water
moves from the leaf into the air through tiny holes in the leaves
called stomates. Loss of water through guard cells surrounding the
stomates lowers the concentration of water in these cells. By osmosis, water moves from adjoining cells to replace that lost by evaporation. Cells nearest the veins of the leaves draw on water in the
vessels of these veins. This in turn creates a suction known as tran-

spiration pull that draws on water entering from the root hairs. Water continues to enter the plant and move upward so long as the transpiration pull exceeds the adhesive forces holding water in the soil. During periods of drought and high evaporation, water intake may not keep up with water loss and temporary wilting can occur. If such conditions of stress persist, permanent wilting and death of the plant results.

PHOTOSYNTHESIS

Photosynthesis has been called the most important chemical reaction in nature. Without this process, no life on this planet would exist. The process is essentially a chemical one in which carbon dioxide combines with water to form a simple sugar. Photosynthesis requires light as an energy source and the presence of chlorophyll. It occurs only in living, chlorophyll-bearing cells that are exposed to light. The process can best be compared to a manufacturing process. The leaves are the factory, the palisade and mesophyll cells the rooms, and the chloroplasts the machines. Carbon dioxide, which comprises .03 percent of the air we breathe, and water are the raw materials. Sunlight or artificial light supplies the energy to run the machines. Simple sugars constitute the main manufactured product and oxygen is a by-product. The sieve tubes and the vessels are the transportation system, and special storage organs serve as warehouses. From the simple sugars complex carbohydrates, fats, and proteins are synthesized.

RESPIRATION

Respiration is a process that takes place in all living cells, both plant and animal. Chemically, the process is the reverse of photosynthesis. Simple sugars are oxidized to form carbon dioxide and water, and energy is released in the process. Respiration occurs all the time. The rate of respiration is directly proportional to the temperature.

Growth of Plants

Growth in plants can be divided into four steps: cell division, cell enlargement, cell differentiation, and cell maturation. Cell division occurs in the apical meristems of stems and roots and in the cambium. Cell enlargement includes the stretching of the cell wall and the dispersal of the protoplasm. Differentiation may involve the thickening of the cell walls and the disappearance of the protoplast in cells like vessels and fibers. In cell maturation the cells become part of the mature tissues. Growth in length occurs at the stem and root tips; growth in diameter, on either side of the cambium. In certain leaves the base of the leaves remains meristematic, and elongation occurs at the base of the leaf blade. This is true of grasses.

Plant growth may be either vegetative or reproductive. In annuals, vegetative growth takes place early in the growth cycle, followed by flowering and fruiting and finally death. In trees and shrubs, vegetative growth may continue for several years before reproductive growth begins. In perennials, vegetative growth generally precedes reproductive growth each season, except in certain wild flowers that flower early in the spring. Maintaining a proper balance between vegetative and reproductive growth requirements is essential to successful gardening. Shade and high nitrogen levels in the soil favor vegetative growth, full sun and high phosphorus levels reproductive growth.

Chapter 3

How Plants Are Propagated

Propagation of plants occurs by sexual or asexual means. Sexual propagation involves growing plants from seeds; asexual (vegetative) propagation, from a part of the plant.

Seed Propagation

It is important to understand that a seed is produced as a result of sexual union. The seed contains genetic characteristics of both parents. Unless both parents are genetically similar, the seedlings that result can be variable. Most vegetable and annual flower seeds are produced by seed companies whose practices ensure that such seeds will yield uniform seedlings.

Seed companies are producing F_1 hybrid seeds of many kinds of vegetables and annual flowers. These hybrid seeds are produced by crossing two inbred lines. The seedlings from such seeds are very uniform and exhibit hybrid vigor. If seeds are collected from F_1 plants and planted, the resulting seedlings will be variable. It is important, therefore, not to save the seeds of F_1 hybrids for planting.

A seed contains an embryo plant surrounded by a supply of

stored food and is protected by a seed coat. A mature seed stored in a cool, dry place retains its ability to germinate for some time. This time varies with different seeds. It is generally best to buy new seeds each year. Before planting seeds that you have carried over from a previous year, a germination test should be run. This is accomplished by placing a wet blotter in the bottom of a covered dish. Count a number of seeds and scatter them over the surface of the blotter. Replace the cover and put the dish where the temperature is about 70° F. Watch for germination and determine the percentage of seeds that grow. It is important that the resulting seedlings show vigor. Seeds that send out weak sprouts may not produce healthy seedlings.

Moisture, proper temperature, air, and viable seeds are requirements for germination. A few seeds, like Kentucky bluegrass and lettuce, require some light. During the germination process, the seed coat absorbs water and the seed swells. The moisture entering the seeds activates digestive enzymes, and the resulting soluble foods move from the storage tissues to the embryo. The embryo grows rapidly. First, the radicle emerges from the seed and grows

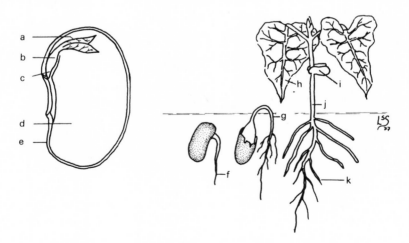

Bean seed and germinating seedling: *a.* epicotyl, *b.* hypocotyl, *c.* radicle, *d.* cotyledon, *e.* seed coat, *f.* radicle, *g.* hypocotyl, *h.* true leaf (from epicotyl), *i.* cotyledon, *j.* stem (from hypocotyl), *k.* root (from radicle).

downward into the soil to form the root system. In most seeds of dicotyledonous plants, the hypocotyl elongates to elevate the cotyledons, or seed leaves, above the soil. The epicotyl, which develops between the cotyledons, grows upward to form the leafy stem. In monocotyledonous plants like corn and onions, there is a single seed leaf.

Most garden vegetables and some annual flowers are seeded directly in the garden. The depth of planting and the proper time for planting are important considerations. There are no fixed rules for ascertaining the correct depth of seeding. Generally, the depth is dependent on seed size. Small seeds should not be covered with more than ½ inch of soil. Large seeds can be planted from 2 to 3 inches deep. The amount of moisture in the soil also determines the depth of seeding. In early spring, when the soil is cool and moist, shallow seeding results in faster germination.

The proper time for planting seeds varies with the location and the season. Usually, for each 100 miles north or south of the Twin Cities, there is about a week's difference in timing. Seeding can be done earlier on sandy soils that warm up quickly in the spring than on heavy clay soils. Frost-tolerant plants may be seeded as soon as the soil can be worked in the spring. Warm-season plants should not be seeded until the soil has warmed up and the danger of frost has passed.

Some plants that have a long growing season should be started indoors or purchased from a commercial grower. Growing healthy plants indoors is a challenge and requires skill and attention to details. Plants of most flowers and vegetables can be grown in approximately 6 to 8 weeks. Seeds should not be started too early or plants will be tall and leggy. Knowing when each kind of plant can safely be planted outdoors in your area is essential to success in growing plants.

The most common problem when growing plants is lack of light. Unless you have a greenhouse or ample sunny windows, fluorescent light in the basement provides the answer to the light problem. "Damping off" of seedlings, another problem when growing plants, is caused by soil fungi and can be transmitted on dirty containers. It is best controlled by starting seeds in new containers or clean, used ones and by using sterile growing mediums like Jiffy

Mix. If you use soil, the soil should be sterilized by baking it in a 200°-250°F. oven for 30 minutes. Treating the seed with a good fungicide may help, too.

Seeds can be started in shallow flats or flowerpots. Fill the container with the growing medium to within about ¼ inch of the surface. Plant the seeds in shallow rows if you are using a flat or scatter the seeds on the surface if you are using pots. Cover the seeds lightly with the growing medium. Water by partly submersing the container in water. When moisture shows on the surface, remove the container from the water and place it in a warm place where the temperature will be about 70°F. Cover with a sheet of glass or plastic to conserve moisture during the germination period. As soon as the seedlings start to emerge, the cover must be removed and the seedlings given adequate light. Water with a fine spray or mist. In about two weeks, or as soon as the first true leaves form, the seedlings should be transplanted, giving every seedling about a 2 × 2 inch space. Some growers use individual containers for each seedling.

Seedlings should be hardened before being planted in the garden by putting them outdoors about 7 to 10 days before planting them in the garden. Select a sheltered location and be prepared to cover the plants or move them inside if a storm or frost is predicted. A cold frame is an ideal place to harden plants.

Vegetative Propagation

Many garden plants are propagated vegetatively rather than from seeds. The method ensures trueness to type for plants that do not grow true from seeds, for example, most cultivars of woody fruits and ornamentals and many perennials, and includes propagating plants that do not produce viable seeds. Vegetative propagation is accomplished by cuttings, layering, grafting, and division or separation.

CUTTINGS

Propagation by cuttings is the simplest and most rapid method. Various parts of the plant can be utilized. For the majority of

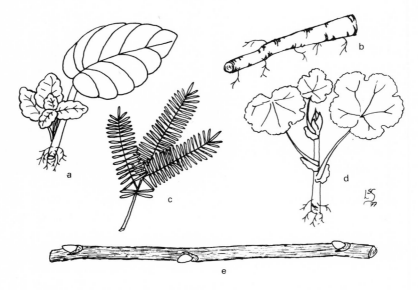

Types of cuttings: *a.* leaf (African violet), *b.* root (horseradish), *c.* evergreen (yew), *d.* herbaceous stem (geranium),
e. hardwood stem (grape).

plants, stem cuttings are employed. Herbaceous and softwood
stem cuttings are taken during the active, growing season, and
evergreen and hardwood stem cuttings are secured from mature
growth usually in early winter. For some plants a leaf or even a
portion of a leaf is used; for a few plants, root cuttings give the
best results.

All cuttings are best rooted in suitable, sterile mediums. Washed
sand, like that used in making concrete, is excellent for most
plants. Perlite and vermiculite are also employed. For acid-loving
plants, like blueberries and azaleas, a mixture of sand and acid
peat is used. Some means must also be provided to ensure high humidity during the rooting process. Misting is used in commercial
greenhouses, with good results. Plastic-covered frames and containers also help increase the humidity.

Cuttings should be taken from healthy stock plants that are true
to type. Herbaceous and softwood cuttings should be obtained
when new growth is fully developed but before tissues become
hard and woody. Terminal cuttings are generally best, but if prop-

agating stock is scarce, cuttings can be made from a section of the stem. The length of the cutting is variable, depending on the type of plant and its rate of growth. Most cuttings are from 3 to 5 inches long. Using a sharp knife or razor blade, make a clean basal cut, preferably at a slant and through a node. Remove the lower leaves but retain two or more leaves at the tip. Cuttings that are difficult to root should be dipped in a hormonal powder like Rootone. With a knife or a narrow board, make a narrow trench in the rooting medium. Insert the cuttings, spacing them about 2 inches apart. Firm the medium against the cuttings. Rows should be about 4 inches apart. Water the cuttings and repeat as required to keep the medium moist but not wet. For best results, the temperature of the rooting medium should be a few degrees warmer than the air temperature. This can be accomplished by placing the propagating container over a radiator or by using a light bulb in a box below the container. If you are planning to make only a few cuttings, a flowerpot can be used and a plastic bag placed over the pot and held in place with a rubber band. The plastic allows light to enter and keeps the air moist around the cuttings. During the rooting period the plants should be located in good light. As soon as the roots have developed, the cutting should be removed and potted in soil that is high in organic matter. The time required for rooting can vary from a few weeks to 6 or more.

Evergreen cuttings are normally taken in early November and placed in a greenhouse bench filled with sand. They will usually be rooted by spring. Hardwood cuttings, also obtained in November, should be 8 to 12 inches long, with several internodes. The cuttings are tied in bundles and stored over the winter in a cool, moist place. As soon as the soil can be worked in the spring, the cuttings are inserted into the soil at an angle, with the uppermost bud at soil level. The soil is then firmed to provide close contact with the cutting. Roots form along the basal part of the cutting, and leafy stems develop from the uppermost buds. Grapes, willows, and honeysuckle are often propagated in this manner.

Leaf cuttings are used on a limited number of plants. The African violet is the best example. A clean cut is made through the petiole about 1 inch below the attachment to the leaf blade. The leaf and petiole are inserted in the rooting medium at an angle, with the petiole covered to the base of the leaf. Roots form at the base of the petiole, and an adventitious bud develops at the base and produces several small plants. Certain large-leaved begonias can also be propagated from a leaf or even a portion of a leaf. A cut is made through the vein on the underside of the leaf, which is then placed flat on the rooting medium. Roots form above the cut, and an adventitious bud develops a new plant. Some plants like the kalanchoes form young plants along the edges of the leaf.

Blackberries, horseradish, and garden phlox are usually propagated from root cuttings. A section of root is placed horizontally in the rooting medium. Adventitious buds develop that produce new plants.

LAYERING

Layering is another method of vegetative propagation. A tip layer is made by taking a young stem of a shrub like the Vanhoutte spirea and bending it over until it touches the ground directly behind the stem tip. A notch is made on the underside of the stem at this point and the stem held down with a mound of soil placed over it. This is done in late summer. Roots form above the notch. When the tip is well rooted, which should be by the following spring, the stem can be cut below the point of rooting and the young plant moved to a new location. This method has the advantage of supplying water and nutrients from the parent plant to the new plant during the rooting process.

Mound layering involves notching stems right above the soil line and mounding the soil around the base of the plants. Roots form above the notches and grow into the soil in the mound. Timing is the same as for tip layering. Currants and the rootstocks for dwarfing apple trees are propagated in this manner.

Serpentine layering is used for vines like English ivy that trail on the ground. A stem is notched at several points on the undersurface. Soil is placed over the notched portion of the stems. Several plants are thus produced from a single stem while it is still attached to the parent plant.

Air layering is often used for reproducing large houseplants like the rubber plant and dumb cane which often grow too tall for the

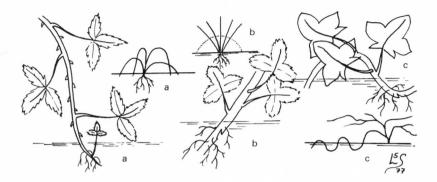

a. Tip layering (black raspberry), *b.* mound layering (currant), *c.* serpentine layering (English ivy).

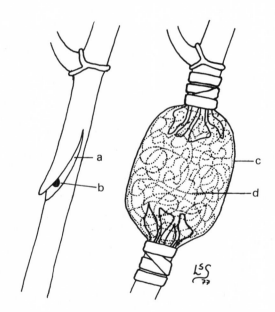

Air layering (rubber plant): *a.* slit in stem, *b.* pebble, *c.* plastic covering, *d.* sphagnum moss.

average home. A new plant can be started from the top of these plants. With a sharp knife, make a diagonal cut about two-thirds through the stem. Put a small pebble in the slit so that the surfaces do not grow together again. Wrap the stem at this point with moist sphagnum moss and hold the moss in place with a wrapping of clear plastic. Roots form above the slit and grow into the moist sphagnum. When the sphagnum moss is filled with roots, the main stem can be cut below the roots and the new plant potted in a suitable soil mixture.

<h2 style="text-align:center">GRAFTING</h2>

Grafting is another technique used to increase the number of plants. Most fruit trees and most cultivars of shade and ornamental trees are propagated by grafting, as are cultivars of conifers that prove difficult to root from cuttings.

In grafting, a scion (a section of stem or a bud) is grafted on either a seedling root or a vegetatively propagated root. Seedling roots are most commonly employed. With dwarf fruit trees, selected rootstocks are vegetatively propagated by mound layering. In making a stem graft, it is very important that the stem portion be completely dormant. The scions to be grafted are cut in late fall or early winter from vigorous, young stems that are unbranched. The parent tree should be healthy and true to variety. The scions should be stored in a cool, moist place until it is time to make the graft. The temperature must be right above freezing. The scions are usually tied in bundles and buried in moist sawdust to keep them from drying out. Scions can also be wrapped in aluminum foil or in plastic and stored near the freezing unit in a refrigerator. Nurserymen usually make the grafts in March on roots that were dug the previous fall. Gardeners often make their grafts in April on seedling roots that are growing in the garden. Various types of grafts are used to join the stock and the scion. The whip graft is employed where the stock and the scion are approximately the same diameter. A diagonal cut is made on both the stock and the scion. The angle of the cut should be the same on each. A slit is then made parallel to the longitudinal axis about two-thirds the distance from the base to the top of the slanted cut. Next, the two

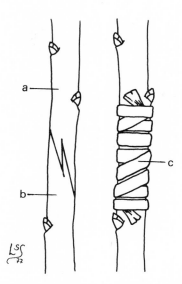

Whip graft: *a.* scion, *b.* stock, *c.* rubber grafting tape.

pieces are joined by sliding the "tongue" of one into the "slit" of the other. It is important that the cambium of both stock and scion be in contact at least along one side. Grafting wax is often used to seal the union, but good results can be obtained by using rubberized electricians' tape or special grafting tape. Grafts made in the nursery cellar are usually covered with moist sawdust until it is time to line them out in the nursery. The roots should not be allowed to dry out.

Grafting from a bud is normally done in early fall. The buds should be mature, but the bark should separate easily from the wood on the stock. In budding, a bud stick is cut from the desired cultivar. The leaf blades are cut off, leaving a short portion of the petiole, which serves as a handle. When cutting the bud from the bud stick, a small shield of bark is removed. A t-shaped cut is usually made in the north side of the stem of the stock at or near the ground line. The bark is folded back and the bud slipped into place. The upper portion of the shield is cut along the line of the top of the "t." A rubber budding strip is used to hold the bud in

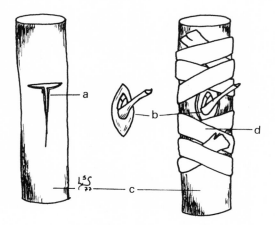

Bud graft: *a*. t-shaped cut, *b*. stock, *c*. rubber budding strip.

place, but the band must not cover the bud. By winter the cambium of the bud shield has united with the cambium of the stock. In the spring the seedling stem should be cut directly above this bud at about the time that the bud begins to open. Stone fruits, roses, and certain shade trees are normally propagated by budding.

Grafting is successful only when the stock and the scion are closely related. If possible, one should use the same species for both the rootstock and the scion variety. Grafts between closely related species are usually successful. Intergeneric grafts can sometimes be made, but the results are less likely to be successful. Grafts between two families are seldom successful.

Plants propagated by stem or bud grafts are more expensive than seedling plants of the same size. This is because of the extra labor and time required to produce the plant.

DIVISION

Division is another method of propagation that is often used on herbaceous perennials. Most fibrous-rooted perennials that develop a multiple crown, like garden phlox, daylilies, and chrysanthemums, can be dug in the early spring and separated into a number of divisions. Some can be pulled apart. Others must be cut with a sharp knife. Perennials with fleshy roots and rhizomes, such as peonies and irises, are best transplanted in late summer or early fall. The clumps are dug, divided, and replanted.

Many garden plants produce fleshy storage organs called bulbs or corms. These increase naturally by offsets. Hardy kinds like garden lilies and alliums can be dug in the fall, divided, and replanted. Tender kinds like gladioli and Peruvian daffodils are dug in the fall, stored over the winter, and replanted in the spring.

Chapter 4

Soil and Soil Improvement

A fertile, productive soil is essential to successful gardening. A knowledge of soils and soil fertility should help improve one's gardening.

Soil Composition

The typical mineral soil is composed of rock particles, organic matter, water, and air. The solid particles make up about 50 percent by volume, and the water and air each occupy about 25 percent. The exact percentages vary, depending on the nature of the soil and on whether the soil is wet or dry. In addition there are soil microorganisms and plant nutrients in solution.

The rock particles differ greatly in size and are classified as sand, silt, or clay. Sand particles are visible to the unaided eye, and their size ranges from 2.0 to .05 mm. Silt particles are visible under an ordinary microscope and range from .05 to .002 mm. Clay particles are extremely small, less than .002 mm., and can be seen only under an electron microscope.

The term "loam" is applied to a mixture of ingredients, and the terms "sandy loam," "silt loam," and "clay loam" are applied, depending on the texture.

Clay soils are likely to present the greatest problem for gardeners. The very small particles are platelike and become extremely sticky when wet. If such soils are cultivated when wet, large, hard clods result. If the soils are properly handled, the small clay particles adhere in granules or crumbs. This increases the penetration of water and air. Fall plowing or rotovating improves the granular structure, for freezing and thawing action during the winter causes the large clods to break down into granules.

Organic soils are derived from the decomposition of organic matter. If they contain 65 percent or more of organic matter, they are called peat soils; if 20 to 65 percent, muck soils. Peat soils are termed sedge or sphagnum, depending on the source of the organic matter. Compared with mineral soils, highly organic soils are usually low in plant nutrients.

Soil Improvement

Gardeners must generally start with disturbed soils of low fertility, because the topsoil, characteristic of farm fields, was removed or covered with subsoil during the construction of the home. Fortunately, the productivity of any soil can be improved.

ADDITION OF ORGANIC MATTER

Adding organic matter is the key to soil improvement. This increases the granulation and aeration of clay soils and improves the moisture and nutrient retention of sandy soils. It is difficult to add too much organic matter, especially if it is partly decomposed.

Almost any kind of organic matter can be used. Tree leaves, straw, hay, sawdust, wood chips, and ground corncobs are generally available and relatively inexpensive. Manures and peat are also effective.

Composted materials are better than raw, undecomposed organic matter. Various methods of composting exist. A compost pile can be made by alternating layers of organic refuse like tree leaves, straw and hay with activating layers containing decay organisms like soil and manure. The organic layers should be about 12 inches thick. Adding a high-nitrogen fertilizer to the activating layer also helps hasten decomposition, since the decay organisms require nitrogen for their metabolism. As the pile is being built, the materials should be watered and at the center of the top of the pile there should be a depression to catch rainwater. After about 6 weeks of composting, the pile should be turned over with a fork to provide a more uniform compost. The length of time required to make compost is very variable; it depends on the size of the pile, the organic materials used, the season of the year, and the quantity of fertilizer and activator used. Under favorable conditions good compost can be made in a few weeks. In other cases it may take a year or longer. Special, manufactured compost containers are available and come with instructions. Some gardeners have a pit for making compost; others use concrete blocks or boards to enclose the compost.

The quantity of compost or organic matter to be used varies with the soil problem. Ordinarily 3 to 4 bushels per 100 square feet is recommended. This should be incorporated into the soil by spading, rotovating, or plowing. Organic matter continues decomposing after it is added to the soil, so for best results, one must continually add organic matter to the soil each year.

Green manure crops are also used to add organic matter to the soil. Rye can be planted in the fall after most garden crops have been harvested, and turned under in the spring in time for spring planting. If Sudan grass or soybeans are used as green manure crops, part of the garden must be taken out of cultivation for an entire season.

ESSENTIAL ELEMENTS

A knowledge of plant nutrients is essential to successful gardening. Of all the elements present in the soil, only about 15 are needed for plant growth: carbon, hydrogen, oxygen, nitrogen, phosphorus, potassium, calcium, magnesium, manganese, iron, sulfur, boron, zinc, copper, and molybdenum.

Carbon, hydrogen, and oxygen are involved in photosynthesis. Carbon dioxide is a gas present in the atmosphere. It is used in photosynthesis and restored in the atmosphere by the oxidation of carbon-containing compounds, respiration, and the burning of fossil fuels. Water contains both hydrogen and oxygen. Except in dry seasons, the quantity of water in the soil is normally sufficient for plant growth. Irrigation makes it possible to supply adequate amounts of water.

Substantial quantities of nitrogen, phosphorus, and potassium are used by plants. Soils are often deficient in these elements, which are usually added in the form of commercial fertilizers. It is important that the gardener understand the function of each of these major elements.

Nitrogen is a constituent of amino acids and proteins as well as of the chlorophyll molecule. Adequate levels of nitrogen ensure normal vegetative growth and a healthy green color. A deficiency of nitrogen results in stunted plants of a yellowish green color. An excess causes rank, vegetative growth.

To maintain the proper nitrogen level in the soil, one should understand how nitrogen enters the soil. Approximately 80 percent of the air we breathe is gaseous nitrogen. This nitrogen is inert and cannot be used by higher plants. During electrical storms lightning fixes this gaseous nitrogen, and as much as 5 to 6 pounds of nitrogen per acre can fall in the accompanying rains. Bacterial nodules on the roots of certain legumes also fix the nitrogen in the soil air and convert it to protein in the cells of the bacteria. Certain free-living bacteria in the soil fix nitrogen, too. Called nitrogen-fixing bacteria, these function best in warm, well-aerated soils. Organic matter in the soil also releases available nitrogen as it decomposes. In the protein molecule, nitrogen is in the amine (NH_2) form. This NH_2 is further reduced in the soil to ammonia, NH_3. Most higher plants cannot utilize the ammonia, which must be oxidized to the nitrate (NO_3) form before the nitrogen becomes available. Soil bacteria are involved in this conversion of proteinaceous nitrogen to the nitrate form. In a cold, wet spring, denitrifying bacteria can reverse this process and convert nitrates to ammonia. The amount of available nitrogen in the soil is very variable. Under natural conditions where no crops are removed from the soil, the nitrate level remains more or less constant. Where crops are removed, as in gardening, fertilizer is needed.

Phosphorus, a component of nucleic acid, is considered essential for flowering and fruiting. In soils it is usually present in a stable form as salts of calcium, magnesium, iron, and aluminum. At low and high pH's the phosphorus is tied up as insoluble salts. In the pH range from 5 to 7, which includes the pH of most garden soils, some phosphorus is soluble and available to plants. In such soils the available phosphorus is in the acid phosphate (HPO_4) form.

Potassium serves a catalytic function in respiration and in carbohydrate metabolism. It is essential for healthy development of roots and stems. Levels of potassium are low in organic soils and fairly high in mineral soils. Potassium is present as soluble salts like potassium chloride. Continuous cropping necessitates adding phosphorus and potassium in the form of fertilizers.

The other elements are usually grouped as minor, or trace, elements. They are used in small quantities and are normally present in sufficient amounts to ensure normal plant growth, although deficiencies do occur occasionally. Some fertilizers contain these trace elements.

Calcium is a cementing substance that holds cells together. Most soils contain sufficient calcium to meet the requirements of plants grown, but sometimes on acid soils lime must be added to decrease the acidity.

Magnesium, manganese, and iron are all associated with chlorophyll. Magnesium is a constituent of the chlorophyll molecule, and both manganese and iron are catalysts in chlorophyll synthesis. Iron is usually present in adequate quantities, but in high lime soils it forms insoluble salts and is not available to plants. A chlorotic condition (yellowing of the leaves) known as iron chlorosis can develop in some plants grown on such soils. Clematis, planted near a house foundation, occasionally shows symptoms of iron chlorosis, because lime leaching from the mortar of the house foundation binds the available iron in an insoluble form.

The functions of the other essential elements are not too clearly understood. They are known to be essential for normal cell division and differentiation.

FERTILIZERS

The use of commercial fertilizers in both farming and gardening has increased steadily. In the past these fertilizers have been relatively cheap and have been the most economical means of maintaining soil fertility and productivity. When properly used, they give excellent results.

The analysis of the fertilizer is indicated on the bag. The percentage of nitrogen (N), phosphorus (P_2O_5), and potassium (K_2O) must be shown. A 10-10-10 fertilizer indicates that the fertilizer contains 10 percent each of N, P_2O_5, and K_2O. The higher the numbers, the more concentrated the fertilizer. The selection of a fertilizer should be based on the crop to be grown. If you desire vegetative growth, a fertilizer high in nitrogen should be used. If you are growing a crop like tomatoes where fruits are the main concern, a fertilizer high in phosphorus is best. For potatoes, which store a great deal of starch in their tubers, a fertilizer high in potassium should be used.

In the vegetable garden, where one grows a variety of crops in a relatively small space, it would be impractical to use a different analysis of fertilizer on each crop. In my garden I apply a 10-10-10 fertilizer over the entire garden when the soil is being tilled in early spring. By rotating the crops within the garden, the needs of each kind of vegetable are supplied. In a flower border, where bloom is the primary concern, or in a vegetable garden that has received liberal quantities of decomposed organic matter, a 5-10-10 fertilizer may be best. Lawn fertilizers are generally high in nitrogen.

More important than the analysis is the rate of application. A safe rule is to apply the fertilizer at a rate that will supply a pound of actual nitrogen per 1,000 square feet of soil surface. For a 10-10-10 analysis, one would use 10 pounds; for a 5-10-10 analysis, 20 pounds; and for ammonium nitrate (33-0-0), only 3 pounds per 1,000 square feet. It is the nitrogen in the fertilizer that "burns": too much nitrogen in the soil water causes reverse osmosis and the plant loses water, resulting in a "burned" appearance. By controlling the quantity used, the danger of "burning" is virtually eliminated.

A whirlwind type of spreader applies the fertilizer quickly and uniformly. With a little practice the proper setting can be determined in order to apply the right amount of fertilizer.

A soil test, which can be made by any soil-testing laboratory, gives a clear picture of the fertility level of the soil and serves as a guide for determining the analysis and quantity of fertilizer needed.

Some gardeners express much concern about the relative merits of so-called organic and inorganic fertilizers. Generally speaking, fertilizers derived from natural products like bone meal, blood meal, fish emulsion, soybean meal, rock phosphate, etc. are considered organic. Manufactured fertilizers like ammonium nitrate, super phosphate, potassium chloride, and blends of such ingredients are called inorganic. Fortunately, plants are less concerned about the source of the nutrients than gardeners are. For most plants, nitrogen is nitrogen so long as it is in the nitrate (NO_3) form. In the soil most nitrogen regardless of source is converted to nitrate nitrogen, although some plants can use nitrogen in the ammonia form. Phosphorus enters the plant only in the acid phosphate form. The phosphorus in super phosphate is immediately available to plants. The phosphorus in rock phosphate must be acted on by soil acids before becoming available.

The chief advantage of organic sources of nitrogen is their longer period of availability. This may be an advantage or a disadvantage, depending on the season of the year. In early spring, when the soil is cold and wet, plants can suffer from a lack of nitrate nitrogen even with ample reserves of organic nitrogen present, because nitrifying bacteria are inactive. In the fall, organic sources of nitrogen keep trees and shrubs growing vegetatively and thus interfere with normal hardening processes that prepare the plants for winter.

The idea that chemical fertilizers poison the soil and kill earthworms and beneficial soil organisms is not well founded. If such fertilizers are properly used, with liberal applications of organic matter, the number of earthworms and beneficial organisms should actually increase. Earthworms are abundant in my garden, where I have used chemical fertilizers for years.

Mulching

The purpose of mulching varies. A summer mulch is used primarily to control weeds and to keep the soil moist and cool. A winter mulch is used to protect plants from extreme cold and to avoid sudden changes in temperature. Mulches are also used to delay the start of growth in the spring, to lengthen the growing season, to keep fruits clean, and to reduce leaf diseases of roses.

Many materials are used for mulches. Plastic and paper mulches have the advantage of being relatively inexpensive and easy to apply. Clear plastic helps warm the soil in the spring and get plants off to an earlier start. Special weed control treatments are needed where clear plastic mulches are used, or weeds will grow and thrive under the plastic and push it up. Black plastic excludes light and is effective in controlling weeds. Plastic mulches are used in northern parts of the region to lengthen the growing season for a wide variety of vegetables like sweet corn, melons, and tomatoes. Plastic is commonly used for everbearing strawberries to keep the berries clean.

Organic mulches are usually applied in early summer after the soil has warmed up. These organic mulches hold moisture and prevent high soil temperatures. They also help control annual weeds by excluding light needed for germination and reduce the spread of diseases carried by splashing rain. An organic mulch should be relatively cheap, readily available, and attractive looking. Many materials are used. Compost made from tree leaves is ideal. Chopped hay and straw are also good. Shredded tree bark is attractive and usually available from garden centers. Sphagnum peat is good looking but may be blown by the wind and once it dries out it is difficult to moisten. Coffee and tea grounds, peanut shells, and coconut fiber are also occasionally used. The advantage of organic mulches over plastic mulches is that they can be worked into the soil at the end of the growing season to improve the physical structure of the soil.

For a winter mulch, clean straw and marsh hay are commonly employed. Insulating materials in roll form can also be used, but these are rather expensive.

Chapter 5

Plant Pests and Their Control

A good gardener must learn to recognize plant symptoms associated with insects and disease and take whatever measures are necessary to control the insects and diseases involved. Injury to garden plants is caused by a variety of agents. Animals of various kinds feed on plants. Some inject toxic substances that result in gall-like formations (abnormal growths). Plant diseases can be caused by bacteria, fungi, and viruses. Some disease symptoms may result from physiological disorders. Symptoms of mineral deficiency, various types of winter injury, and injuries caused by air and soil pollution are nonparasitic. Weeds take their toll by lowering crop production.

Rodents

Rodents feed on roots and stems of woody plants and occasionally on fleshy, underground storage organs like lily and tulip bulbs. Field mice often girdle the base of tree and shrub stems. Members of the rose family and winged euonymus are favorite sources of food for mice. When hungry enough, mice also girdle pines and many other woody species. When the bark is chewed all around the stem and through the cambium to the wood, the tree gradually dies from starvation of the roots, since food manufactured by the leaves moves downward to the roots through the inner bark. Mice are most likely to feed on bark during the winter months, when food is scarce. They work under the snow. Sometimes, when grass and weeds are allowed to grow up around the trees and mice can be protected from their enemies under this cover, girdling occurs in the fall of the year. The safest method of protecting trees and shrubs from mouse damage is to put a cylinder of ¼ inch mesh hardware cloth around the base of the tree. The top of the cylinder should be high enough so that mice will not enter if snow becomes deep. Tramping the snow around the base of the tree when snow is deep keeps the top of the cylinder above the snow line.

Rabbits, both cottontail and jack, also feed on the bark of trees and shrubs, especially during the winter months, when other food is scarce. They feed above the snow line and often cut off entire branches. It is more difficult to protect plants from rabbits than from mice. A cylinder of chicken wire can be used, but this must project well above the snow. Repellents, such as Goodrite Zip, sprayed on the trunk and lower branches in the fall help too. Dried blood in mesh bags hung from branches of the tree also repels rabbits.

Pocket gophers kill trees by feeding on roots. Fairly large trees up to 4 or 5 inches in diameter sometimes die rather suddenly. When this happens, the tree can easily be lifted out of the soil, with all its roots chewed off. The mounds of pocket gophers give warning of their presence.

Woodchucks, striped gophers, and chipmunks also cause problems. These rodents are fond of fresh foliage and often eat tender vegetables and young flowering plants.

Moles produce another type of injury. They feed on soil insects and push up ridges of soil, thus making the surface unsightly. Getting rid of the soil insects is the most effective method of ridding your yard of moles.

The best control for rodents of all kinds is to encourage and protect their natural predators: fox, owls, and hawks. Sometimes, when the natural predators have been killed by man, the gardener must resort to trapping and poison baits to protect garden crops from rodents. Your county Agricultural Extension Service can give you advice on how best to keep the rodents under control.

Deer

One hates to think of deer as being destructive but occasionally, when deer populations have become too high, they cause considerable damage. Not only do they feed on tree branches, but they also destroy trees by polishing their horns on the trunks of young trees. They seem to pick the choicest young trees to work on. There is no practical control against deer other than keeping their population down by controlled hunting. Fences are of little help since deer can easily jump most of them. Repellents may be effective for short periods, but these must be replenished at frequent intervals.

Birds

Birds are especially destructive on ripening fruits of all kinds. In the home garden they can strip the fruits from a cherry tree in a few hours. Robins are among the worst offenders. The only practical solution to this problem is to cover plants with bird netting as the fruits start to ripen. Devices to scare birds away may work for a while, but birds soon become accustomed to them.

Insects

Insects cause serious damage to garden plants and trees. Canker worms can defoliate large elm trees in a few days. Cabbage worms perforate heads of cabbage and make them worthless. Striped cucumber beetles perforate the leaves of cucumbers and other vine crops in a few hours. Learning to recognize these troublesome insects should assist you in preventing serious damage to your plants.

Insects are classified according to the damage they inflict on plants. Chewing insects eat parts of both vegetative and reproductive organs. These insects include worms, caterpillars, beetles, and grasshoppers. Sucking insects pierce the plant organs and suck juices from the plant. A curling and distortion of the affected part of the plant results. Aphids, leaf hoppers, and plant bugs have sucking mouthparts. Rasping insects, the most common of which are thrips, scrape the surface of the leaves and other plant organs. And some insects cause gall formations.

Troublesome insects can be controlled in a variety of ways. Rotation of crops and sanitation greatly reduce insect problems. Natural enemies of insects also aid in insect control. Predatory insects like lady beetles and praying mantis help, and many birds also feed on insects. Spraying to control insects should be kept to a minimum. Sometimes, when nothing else works, a timely spray application saves a crop or plant from serious damage. Consult your county Agricultural Extension office for recommended chemicals to use for each insect problem.

Red Spiders

Red spiders, or spider mites, can be very troublesome during hot, dry periods. Most plants are susceptible, but damage is usually greatest on evergreens and members of the rose family. In the house, red spiders affect a large variety of plants including ivies and roses. An off-color or rusty appearance of the foliage usually indicates the presence of red spiders. To confirm this, take a sheet of white paper and hold it under a plant branch. Tap the branch. The red spiders will fall on the paper and can readily be seen as tiny specks. If these specks move, your plant assuredly has red spider. Washing the foliage with a spray of water helps remove the red spider. This method does not kill the spiders and they will return to the plant. Spraying with a good miticide generally provides satisfactory control. Again, consult your county Agricultural Extension office for recommended controls.

Slugs

In a wet season slugs may be a real problem. They resemble snails without shells, have soft bodies and are coated with a slimy substance. Slugs hide during daylight hours and move about at night. They have voracious appetites and feed on most garden plants.

Good air circulation between plants and exposure to sunlight reduce slug problems. Slugs are particularly troublesome to plants with large leaves and to plants with dense foliage close to the ground, such as strawberries. During the daytime slugs can be found under boards and large leaves, and in mulch material. Occasionally, boards are used to trap slugs. By turning the boards over, the slugs can be killed by dusting them with lime. Stale beer is also used to attract slugs. A shallow pan of beer is sunk in the ground to its rim. Slugs are attracted by the beer, fall in, and are drowned. Sometimes in a wet year when slugs are numerous, slug baits are used to attract and kill the slugs. Read the label to see if the bait is safe for your plants. Some baits may be used around flowers but not around fruits and vegetables.

Diseases

Diseases in plants are caused by a parasitic organism or physiological disorder. Bacteria, fungi, and viruses produce diseases in plants. Symptoms vary, depending on the host and the causal agent. Leaf and fruit spots, blights, wilts, galls, soft rots, mildews, and rust are common symptoms. Learning to recognize the disease in early stages of development is important. Protective bacteriacides and fungicides can prevent infection from occurring but are generally ineffective once the disease organism has entered the plant. Sanitation, rotation, and planting disease-resistant varieties also aid in disease control. Consult your county Agricultural Extension office for the correct diagnosis of a disease and for recommended chemicals.

Reducing losses from virus diseases is aimed at controlling insects that transmit the disease. Removing diseased plants is also helpful in reducing infection. Protective sprays are of little or no value in controlling virus diseases.

Physiological diseases are treated by first determining the cause and then taking measures to correct the condition or conditions causing the problem. Symptoms of nutritional deficiency are not difficult to recognize; adding the proper fertilizer plus minor elements usually corrects the problem. Winter protection and the proper choice of plant species and cultivars can reduce winter injury. Air pollution poses a more difficult problem. Avoid planting varieties that are highly susceptible to air pollutants.

Weeds

A weed is defined as a plant out of place. Not only are weeds unsightly but they also reduce yields by robbing crop plants of essential water and plant nutrients. Frequent cultivation is the best control for weeds in the home garden. Some of the preemergence weed killers can be safely used to kill annual weeds that come up after the crop plant is well established. Read instructions on the package to be sure that the weed killer is safe to use around the plants you are growing. Lawn weeds like dandelions can be safely killed by using selective weed killers.

In controlling weeds by cultivation, cultivate shallow and as often as necessary to kill the weeds. Kill the weeds while they are small and before they compete with your crop plants. Never let weeds go to seed in your garden. Failure to control weeds is the most common cause of not having a successful garden.

Chapter 6

Pruning and Training

Pruning is both an art and a science. No garden practice is less understood than pruning. Most gardeners recognize the need for pruning, but most are hesitant to start. There are no simple steps to follow for becoming an expert pruner, but knowing how a plant grows and the reasons for pruning should help.

Reasons for Pruning

If a plant has any dead wood, such dead wood should obviously be removed. This improves the appearance of the plant and lessens the chances of decay. Narrow-angled crotches are weak crotches that are likely to split as the tree or shrub matures. Wide-angled branches are strong branches. In pruning, leave wide-angled branches whenever possible and remove narrow-angled branches. Lower tree branches that interfere with traffic around the yard should be removed as soon as they start to interfere. Trees that are very dense exclude light from the lawn and should be thinned to permit light to filter through. Occasionally the leader (main stem) of a tree, like a spruce, is injured. Several lateral branches usually grow upward to replace the leader. Allowing these to grow results in a multiple-stemmed tree. All but one of these leaders should be removed or cut back as soon as possible. Sometimes trees and shrubs are planted in limited spaces. Such plants must be pruned to limit their size. Flowering and fruiting are better on relatively young branches. Fruit trees that have not been pruned may become overly reproductive. Because too many fruits set for the limited vegetative growth, they do not receive an adequate supply of the nutrients needed to develop fruit size and quality. Pruning to stimulate vegetative growth would improve the size and quality of the fruit. The same rationale for pruning applies to flowering shrubs. Removing some of the older stems favors the development of young, vigorous growth and thus improves the size and quality of bloom.

Pruning Tools

To do a proper job of pruning, it is important to purchase tools of high quality. They cost more but last longer and enable you to do an excellent job of pruning. Hand pruning shears are of two general types: the anvil with a single cutting blade that cuts against a flat plate and the shearing type with two cutting blades. The shearing type is best for woody plants. If pruning is done regularly most of it can be accomplished with a pair of good hand shears. The long-handled shears, or loppers, are good for larger branches up to 1 inch or more in diameter. A pruning saw is needed for removing larger branches and for renewal pruning of large shrubs (see discussion under How to Prune on p. 56). Many types of pruning saws are on the market. A saw with a blade that can be adjusted to get between crowded branches is useful. The type of pruning saw styled after the hacksaw but with coarser teeth is excellent for pruning. Avoid the type that has teeth on top and bottom.

When to Prune

The proper time for pruning depends on a number of factors like time of bloom, disease problems, and sap flow. Most shade and fruit trees are best pruned during late winter. Exceptions are trees that bleed, such as maples and birch, which should be pruned after the leaves have fully opened.

Shrubs that flower on new wood, like hydrangeas and summer-flowering spireas, should be pruned before growth starts in the spring. Prune spring-flowering shrubs as soon as the flowers have faded.

Trees and shrubs that have a disease like fire blight or oak wilt should not be pruned during the growing season. It is best to prune such trees when the temperature is below freezing to avoid spreading the disease. Hedges should be pruned several times during the growing season whenever new growth is sufficiently long. Evergreens like pines and spruce are best pruned when new growth develops in the spring. Junipers, arborvitae, and yews can be pruned anytime.

How to Prune

Knowing how to prune is something that one learns by experience and study. Each plant has a different habit of growth and requires special pruning. In general we practice two kinds of pruning: tip pruning and renewal pruning.

In tip pruning, the terminal growth is removed. The terminal bud has apical dominance: it synthesizes a growth-regulator substance which diffuses downward to inhibit the growth of lateral buds. By removing the terminal growth, the inhibiting effect is removed and lateral buds develop. Such pruning results in a dense plant. Formal hedges are pruned in this manner. We also practice tip pruning when we pinch back the new growth on chrysanthemums in the spring. Evergreens that must be grown in a limited space are often tip pruned. Tip pruning results in an unnaturally formed plant and should be practiced only where a formal effect is desired or where space is limited.

Renewal pruning involves removing entire stems or branches. It is a thinning-out type of pruning. For most flowering shrubs the best blooms occur on stems that are from 2 to 4 years old. On very old stems the flowers are small and overcrowded. By removing the oldest stems each year, the plant retains the maximum amount of high-quality flowering wood. Removing the old stems causes vigorous new growth to develop from the base of the plant.

Such pruning retains the natural form of the plant and keeps the plant young and productive. Renewal pruning is also practiced on fruit trees to encourage new growth and to let sunlight enter the trees.

Several things must be kept in mind when pruning. In pruning back a stem, use sharp pruning shears and make the cut about ¼ inch beyond a bud and parallel to it. In removing a branch, make a clean cut close to the main stem. Never leave a stub. In removing a large branch, undercut about 1 foot from the stem and then cut from above to remove the weight of the branch. Next make a cut close to the stem, holding onto the stub as you remove it to prevent the tearing of the bark.

Wound dressings are often recommended on cuts that are more than 2 inches in diameter. The value of wound dressings is somewhat questionable. Wounds seem to heal about as quickly whether they are treated or not. Wound dressings like Tree-Cote, orange shellac, and grafting wax are often used. Avoid using a paint containing lead.

Pruning Hedges

Hedges may be either informal or formal. The informal hedge receives little or no pruning. The formal hedge is sheared using the tip-pruning method. Hand or electric hedge shears are used for shaping the hedge. The pruning should start at planting time. The newly planted hedge should be pruned back to within about 6 inches of the ground. This will result in lateral branching close to the ground. When new growth is about 6 inches long, the hedge should be pruned. It may be necessary to prune 2 or 3 times during the season. In pruning a formal hedge, the sides should gradually taper inward toward the top. The top may be flat, rounded, or pointed. The important thing is to have the base broader than the top so that light can reach the base of the hedge.

Hedges are often trained to a shape that is the reverse of this ideal. The "umbrella" effect is achieved by not pruning at planting time and by pruning only the top. The result is a hedge that is open and narrow at the base, with a broad, flat top.

Formal hedges require much work, and similar results can be achieved by selecting the right plants to grow as an informal hedge.

Espalier Pruning

Espalier pruning involves training a tree or shrub in one vertical plane. Such plants are usually trained against a wall. Pruning must start when the plant is young and must be continued throughout its life. All the branches are removed except those that can be trained to grow in the one vertical plane that parallels the wall. To provide support, it is usually necessary to fasten the main branches to the wall. In Europe espaliered fruit trees are often grown on the south side of a wall to capture as much sunlight and warmth as possible to mature the fruits.

Topiary Pruning

Pruning is often done to achieve certain artistic effects. Yews are often pruned into shapes resembling animals like ducks and rabbits. This can be a fascinating hobby but it does little to enhance the beauty of the plants.

Pruning Herbaceous Plants

Certain herbaceous plants benefit from pruning. A tall, leggy coleus or geranium plant can be made full and rounded by pruning the tip of the stem, thus removing the apical dominance and forcing lateral buds to develop. By pinching the tips of the stems on a chrysanthemum plant in the spring, lateral branches form. This produces a fuller plant with more flowering stems. Larger blooms are produced on peonies and dahlias if lateral buds are removed. Tomato plants are often tied to stakes. This requires that lateral branches be removed as they form.

Chapter 7

Home Fruit Growing

Where space permits, growing quality homegrown fruits can be very rewarding. It is important that you know how much space is required and that you plant only hardy varieties recommended for your area. Tree fruits should not be planted unless you understand the problems of growing clean fruits and are willing to give the trees the required care.

Tree Fruits

APPLES AND PEARS

Apples and pears have about the same cultural requirements. Insects and diseases are real problems, and unless you are prepared to follow a rigid spray schedule, it would be best not to plant these tree fruits. Apple maggot, codling moth, curculio, aphids, spider mites, scab, rust, and fire blight are common on apples and to a lesser extent on pears. Commercial apple growers find they must spray weekly from petal fall to harvest in order to obtain clean fruits. This may mean spraying 16 or more times.

Unless you have adequate room and are equipped to spray and prune a standard size apple tree that may grow 20 or more feet

59

tall, you should plant dwarf trees. These trees produce fruits of standard size, but their mature size is reduced because the trees were grafted on dwarfing root systems. A number of different dwarfing roots are used, and each will produce a tree of a certain size. Malling IX will produce a mature tree that will not be more than 6 to 8 feet tall. Other Malling and Malling-Merton roots will produce trees of intermediate size. It is important to know the root system used and the size of the mature tree. Information can be obtained from your local nursery or from your county Agricultural Extension office.

One problem with the dwarf trees is they lack complete winter hardiness. Most of the rootstocks used are of English origin and are subject to winter injury when grown without mulch. Planting the trees in sod and using a winter mulch over the roots prevent loss from winter injury. The advantages of dwarf trees are early production of fruits and ease of maintenance. It is not uncommon to obtain fruits the third or fourth year after planting, and it is much easier to prune, spray, and harvest fruits from dwarf trees.

Because they are small, dwarf trees can be planted close together. Instead of the 30 × 30 foot space needed for standard trees, dwarf trees can be grown in a 10 × 10 foot space. Trees grafted on Malling IX roots should be staked to ensure a vertical trunk. Mice can be a problem so be sure to protect your trees with a cylinder of ¼ inch mesh hardware cloth. This is especially important where mulch is used for winter protection. Poison baits may also be needed if you have a high mouse population in your yard.

When selecting varieties, consider hardiness, time of harvest, and quality of the fruits. You should plant more winter varieties than summer and fall varieties. Your state Agricultural Extension Service has lists of recommended varieties for your area. It also has a spray guide with a schedule to follow for growing clean fruits.

STONE FRUITS

Stone fruits including plums, cherries, apricots, and peaches can be grown with fewer insect and disease problems. Clean fruits can be obtained with only a small number of spray applications. Plum curculio and brown rot are the major problems. For best results, stone fruits should be grown under cultivation. If grown in sod, they should be heavily mulched and fertilized in the spring with a high-nitrogen fertilizer.

Plums usually fruit on fairly young trees. Pollination may be a problem with hybrid plums like 'Red Glow' and 'Superior'. A wild plum can pollinate such varieties or a special pollinator like 'Toka' or 'South Dakota' can be planted. European plums such as 'Dietz' and 'Mount Royal' are self-fruitful. Cold weather which reduces bee activity, and late spring frosts can also reduce fruit set.

Pie, or sour, cherries can be grown in the North, but sweet cherries generally lack hardiness. The 'North Star' variety is a natural dwarf that grows to a height of about 8 to 10 feet. 'Meteor' is a larger tree. The main problem in growing pie cherries is birds. As soon as the fruits start to show color, robins and other birds move in; unless you have a number of trees, the birds will get all the fruits before they are fully ripe. The answer to this problem is to cover the tree completely with bird-proof netting. The netting can be draped over the tree and tightly secured at the base, or a removable wooden frame may be built around the tree to hold the netting. By covering the trees, the cherries can be left on the trees until fully ripe. This improves the size and quality of the fruits.

Apricots should be planted for their ornamental value. If you obtain a crop of fruit, this is a bonus. Apricots bloom very early in the spring, and pollination can be a real problem because of cold, wet weather. Do not expect a full crop of apricots every year. The commercial varieties of apricots are not hardy in the North Central states. Only apricots with the Manchurian apricot in their breeding, like 'Moongold', 'Sungold', and 'Scout', should be planted. These apricots are attractive ornamentals, especially in the spring when they are in bloom and again in the fall when the leaves turn golden yellow.

Growing peaches is not advised if the winter temperature in your area gets colder than −15°F. Sometimes peach trees survive a few years, and occasionally, following a mild winter, you may obtain some fruits. Such trees are generally short-lived and frequently die after they have produced their first crop.

Small (Bush and Vine) Fruits

Most gardeners can find room for a few small fruits. Strawberries and raspberries provide an excellent return for the space used. A few currants, gooseberries, and the Nanking cherry can be worked into the shrub border. Grapes should be grown on a trellis and can serve as a privacy fence.

STRAWBERRIES

Strawberries are universally liked and do well in all parts of the area except on alkaline soils. A clay loam is best, but quality strawberries may be produced on sand if you add enough organic matter and fertilizer and if you water during dry periods. Two types are planted: June-bearing and everbearing strawberries.

June-bearing strawberries produce one crop a year from flower buds that formed the previous fall. Rows should be spaced about 5 feet apart, and plants should be spaced from 18 inches to 2 feet apart in the rows. Plant in early spring using dormant or freshly dug plants. During the first growing season keep the plants cultivated and weeded. Do not let the rows get more than about 18 inches wide. Space the plants in a row. An ideal spacing would be about 8 inches apart. Keep in mind that among the worst weeds in a strawberry planting are excess strawberry plants. If the plants are crowded, the berries will be small and poorly formed. About the first of November a winter mulch should be applied. Clean straw or marsh hay should be placed over the rows to a depth of several inches. This will protect the flower buds from winter cold. These flower buds will be injured if the temperature falls much below 20°F. In the spring the mulch should be left on as long as possible to delay the start of growth. As soon as new growth begins, usually in late April, lift the mulch and place it between the rows. By holding back the growth in the spring, the blossoms are less likely to be injured by spring frosts. About the middle of July, after all the fruits have been harvested, the planting can be renovated for a second crop the following year. This is done by first mowing the planting and removing leaves and mulch. With a rotovator or hoe, narrow the rows to about 6 inches wide. The new row should be to one side of the original row so that only young runner plants remain. After narrowing the rows, thin the remaining plants to at least an 8-inch spacing. Apply a complete fertilizer like a 10-10-10 along either side of the row at a rate of 1 pound for each 25 feet or row. Cultivate and keep weed free for the remainder of the season. Remove surplus runner plants so that the row is no wider than 18 inches.

Everbearing strawberries are often grown using the hill system. A triple row with plants spaced about 1 foot apart is planted in early spring. If more plants are desired, leave a picking aisle at least 2 feet wide and repeat with a triple row. Remove runners as they form. Remove flower buds until July 1. By August 1 you should be getting a fall crop. A summer mulch helps conserve moisture and keep the berries clean. These plants can be carried over the winter and they will produce fruits the next spring and fall. With everbearers it is best to start a new planting each spring.

Varieties of strawberries are continually changing. Varieties popular a few years ago are no longer grown. Most states publish lists of recommended varieties, and these are revised annually. Consult your county Agricultural Extension Service to obtain such information. Varieties perform differently on different soil types. Experiment to find the variety best for your garden.

RASPBERRIES

Raspberries should be planted in rows spaced about 8 feet apart. The spacing in the row can vary, depending on the system of training used. For the hill system, space the plants about 30 inches apart. For the hedge-row system, a closer spacing may be used. The root system of the raspberry is perennial, but the stems live only two years. New stems form from adventitious buds that develop underground on the roots. These young shoots come up in the early spring and continue to grow all season. By fall they can be 5 or more feet tall. On everbearing varieties a crop of fruits is produced near the top of the new stems in the fall. On the summer-bearing varieties the stems remain vegetative the first year. The second year both the everbearing and the summer-bearing varieties produce a crop on the second-year canes. After they fruit, these canes die and should be removed.

In the staked-hill system of training, a stake is driven into the ground on each hill. If the original plants were planted 30 inches apart, the stakes should be spaced the same distance. Regular raspberry stakes cut from tamarack can be used. If these are not available, 1 X 2 inch redwood is acceptable. The stakes should be 7 feet long and should be driven into the ground so that they will not fall over. Pruning can be done either in the fall or early in the spring. Pruning involves removing all old, dead canes. These should be cut off at the ground level. The new, one-year-old canes should be thinned to leave about 6 canes per hill or 2 to 3 canes per running foot of row if the hedge-row system is used. The weaker canes should be removed. In the staked-hill system the selected canes are tied to the stake, using binder twine or some other heavy cord. Tie the stems tightly to the stake in two or more places. Do this early, before new growth starts. In the hedge row some means of support is needed. Posts are often spaced in the row about 1 rod apart, and a wire is run along each side of the posts and about 3 feet above the ground. The canes are trained in between these wires, and the two wires are tied at intervals to hold the canes in an upright position. The tips of the canes are then trimmed to a uniform height. Cutting back the tips helps force the development of lateral branches on which the fruits are produced. The advantage of staking is that the fruits are held off the ground and at a height that makes them easier to pick. Some growers use the tepee system of training, a method essentially the same as the staked-hill method except no stakes are used. The canes are tied usually with 2 ties for a tripod effect. Usually more of the tops must be removed when this method is employed. Some growers also use the hedge-row system with no supports. Such canes should be cut back to about 3½ feet so that each stem will be self-supporting.

With everbearing varieties that fruit in the fall on new canes, it is best to tie these new canes to a stake before the berries develop. If this is not done, the weight of the fruits will bend the canes to the ground.

As with strawberries, limiting the number of canes that develop is the secret to growing raspberries successfully. If canes have been allowed to grow without attention, a dense thicket develops in which the berries are small and difficult to harvest.

Raspberry mosaic, a virus disease, can stunt the plants and mottle the leaves. Berries on affected plants are crumbly. There is no cure for diseased plants, so they must be removed and destroyed. When making a new planting, start with virus-free plants.

There are fewer varieties of raspberries to choose from than there are of strawberries. You may wish to try different varieties and make your own selection. I have found the 'Boyne' variety of summer-fruiting raspberries to be best. 'Fall Red' has also done well. Its fall fruits start to ripen in early September.

CURRANTS, GOOSEBERRIES, AND THE NANKING CHERRY

If you like currants and gooseberries, a few plants will supply all the fruits you can use. 'Red Lake' currant is the best red-fruited currant. 'Welcome' and 'Pixwell' are good varieties of gooseberry. Pruning out the oldest stems at the ground line every spring and cultivation are virtually the only care these plants require. Occasionally, it may be necessary to spray for aphids on currants and for worms on gooseberries.

The Nanking cherry is a dual-purpose shrub that is often planted as an ornamental. The small, red fruits ripen in early July. They are tasty when eaten fresh and excellent for jelly and juice. As is required for the pie cherry, you will need to cover the plants with bird netting to keep birds from eating all the fruits.

BLUEBERRIES

Blueberries are also a favorite fruit. Highbush blueberries are commonly grown in mild climates and are sometimes planted in southern parts of this region (zone 4B — see hardiness zone map on p. 99). They are recommended only for trial in zone 4A (which includes the Twin Cities) and should not be grown north of the Twin Cities, because the plants are subject to winter injury. If you grow highbush blueberries, several varieties must be planted to ensure cross-pollination. The soil should be acid. Mixing acid peat moss with the soil and adding iron sulphate helps ensure proper acidity. The root system is shallow, and mulching to control weeds and conserve moisture is advised.

Crossing the highbush blueberry with the wild, lowbush blueberry has resulted in plants of intermediate size. The plants are low enough to be protected against winter injury. The berries are about as large as the highbush blueberry and are certainly equal or better in quality. The research on these half-high blueberries is being done by Dr. Cecil Stushnoff, Department of Horticultural Science at the University of Minnesota. Plants should soon be on the market in sufficient quantities to meet the demand.

GRAPES

There is a growing interest in grapes. The table, or European, grape is not fully hardy and must be removed from the trellis each fall and covered for winter. The native grape is used in grape breeding, and a few cultivars like 'Beta' and 'Worden' can be grown without winter protection. Grapes require a warm, sunny location to mature their fruits. A sandy loam soil on a south slope is ideal. For best results in northern parts of the area, plant on the south side of a wall. The support for grapes is usually two or three heavy wires stretched between posts. The lowest wire is about 30 inches above the ground. Plants are spaced from 8 to 10 feet apart, with a similar distance between rows. In early spring the plants should be pruned and the canes tied to wires. Fruiting occurs only on year-old wood. Forty buds per plant is an optimum number for maximum production. If you are using two wires, remove all but four branches of last year's growth. Fasten these four arms to the two wires and cut each arm back to 10 buds. This requires heavy pruning each spring, that is, you remove more than you leave.

Grapes should be harvested as soon as they ripen. Plant early-maturing varieties that ripen in early September. Late-maturing varieties are likely to be injured by fall frosts. The sugar content will be much better if the fruits ripen early, when the temperatures are high.

Wild Fruits

Numerous wild fruits can be found to supplement those grown in the garden. Wild strawberries, raspberries, and blueberries are of excellent quality. Their small size makes harvesting slow but well worth the effort. Wild blackberries and black raspberries can sometimes be found, and these, too, are of excellent quality. Chokecherries and Juneberries grow throughout the region. Birds usually get the fruits where plants are scattered, but sometimes, especially in northern areas, the fruits are harvested in abundance. Wild cranberries can be found in sphagnum bogs and occasionally are abundant enough to harvest. Pincherries make a fine jelly, but it takes many fruits to get much juice. Wild plums are often found growing in thickets. Our native highbush cranberry makes an excellent jelly and a refreshing drink; it is best to gather the fruits where they grow wild.

Chapter 8

Growing Vegetables

Growing vegetables can be a fascinating hobby as well as a way to supplement the family income. A vegetable garden need not be large to be practical. If properly planned and cared for, much produce can be grown in a limited space.

Selecting the Site

Most gardeners have little choice in selecting a site for vegetables. For best results the site selected should be in full sun and free of competing tree roots. The soil can be modified, but little can be done to reduce shade and competition from trees. Unless a suitable site is available near the house, it might be better to rent land in a community garden plot.

Planning the Garden

To get the most from a limited piece of land requires careful planning. Spacing to be left between the rows is determined by the size of the mature vegetables and the method of cultivation. In a small garden where cultivation is done by hand, the size of the mature plants should decide the space between rows. One must also be more selective in planting vegetables in a small garden. Space can be saved by not planting more of any vegetable than is needed. It is not necessary to plant the whole package of seeds. Rows of 6 to 8 feet may be sufficient for vegetables like leaf lettuce and chard. For ease in planting, group the cool-season vegetables and the warm-season vegetables. Sweet corn should be located where it will not shade other vegetables. More tomatoes can be grown in a limited space if the plants are trained on stakes.

Interplanting and succession planting help utilize space efficiently. Radishes can be seeded with parsnips in the same row. The radishes will be ready to eat in a few weeks and will not interfere with the slower-growing parsnips. Tomato plants can be started between rows of peas. The peas will be harvested before the tomatoes need the space. Sweet corn can be planted at two-week intervals until early July to provide a longer period of harvest. Cool-season vegetables that have a short growing season, like lettuce and radishes, should be planted in midsummer for a fall crop. Space occupied by early vegetables that have been harvested can be worked up, fertilized, and replanted to a fall crop.

Make a paper plan of your garden, drawing it to scale. First, list the vegetables you wish to grow. Decide on the length of row needed for each vegetable and on the spacing required. Arrange the vegetables according to the proper planting date so that you can plant from one side to the opposite.

Choice of Varieties

Part of the fun of gardening is testing new varieties. Your county Agricultural Extension Service probably has a list of recommended varieties which is usually revised annually. You can also consult experienced gardeners in your neighborhood to see what they are growing. Simply because a variety is new need not mean that it is superior to some of the older varieties. If you have been growing varieties that you like, continue growing them while you experiment with a few plants of a newer variety.

Order your seeds early to be sure of obtaining the varieties you would like to grow. Seeds can generally be purchased from a local

Planting Chart for Vegetables

Vegetable	Indoor Seeding	Transplant to Garden	Direct Seed in Garden	Spacing in Row (inches)
Asparagus		May 1		18
Bean, lima			May 20	4
Bean, snap			May 10	4
Beet			May 10	2
*Broccoli	April 1	May 10		18
Brussel sprout	April 15	June 1		18
*Cabbage	April 1	May 10		18
Carrot			May 10	2
*Cauliflower	April 1	May 10		18
Celery	February 1	May 10		15
Chinese cabbage			July 1	12
Corn, sweet			May 10	18
Cucumber			May 10	18
Eggplant	April 1	June 1		24
Kohlrabi			May 1	4
Lettuce, head	April 1	May 10		10
**Lettuce, leaf			April 20	2
Muskmelon			May 20	24
New Zealand spinach			May 10	8
Onion, seed	March 1	May 1	April 20	2
Onion, set		May 1		2
Parsley			May 10	6
Parsnip			May 10	2
Pea, garden			April 20	2
Pepper	April 1	June 1		18
Potato			May 10	15
Pumpkin			May 20	36
**Radish			April 20	1
Rhubarb		May 1		24
Rutabaga			June 1	4
**Spinach			April 20	4
Squash			May 20	36
Swiss Chard			May 10	4
Tomato	April 15	June 1		36
Turnip			April 20	2
Watermelon			May 20	24

Note: Dates are for the Minneapolis-St. Paul area. Plant 1 week earlier or later for each 100 miles south or north.

*May be direct seeded July 1 for a fall crop.

**May be direct seeded August 1 for a fall crop.

garden center. For some of the newer varieties, you may need to send away to a mail-order company. Be sure to buy seeds that are dated and show germination percentages.

Soil Preparation

For best results, the soil for vegetables should be well drained and moisture retentive. Adding organic matter improves both heavy clay soils and lighter sandy soils. Fall plowing is preferred to spring plowing, especially for clay soils. Avoid working clay soils when they are wet. Adding a complete fertilizer, like a 10-10-10, right before planting helps ensure that plants receive adequate nutrients to produce an optimum crop. You can use 1 pound of such fertilizer as a side dressing for each 25 feet of row, or 10 pounds per 1,000 square feet can be broadcast and worked into the soil.

Starting Plants Indoors

Many vegetables that require a long growing season must be started indoors to have transplants to set into the garden at the proper time. Growing these transplants was discussed in Chapter 3. Another choice is to purchase plants from a reliable grower or garden center. Head lettuce, early cabbage, sweet Spanish onions, tomatoes, peppers, and eggplant are examples of vegetables that should be started early. It takes from 6 to 8 weeks to grow transplants of most vegetables, so if you know the dates for outdoor planting in your area, you can judge the proper date for seeding. Do not start the seeds too early. Tall, overgrown plants are not as good as short, stocky ones.

Direct Seeding and Transplanting

Most vegetables can be seeded directly in the garden. Frost-tolerant vegetables like leaf lettuce, peas, and radishes should be planted as soon as the soil is workable in the spring. Usually, this is about April 20 in the Twin Cities area. Beets, carrots, chard, parsnips, potatoes, early sweet corn, and snap (string) beans can be planted about May 10. Transplants of broccoli, cabbage, cauliflower, and head lettuce can also be planted approximately May 10. As the soil begins to warm up about May 20, it is time to plant lima beans and vine crops. Eggplant, peppers, and tomatoes can be safely transplanted about Memorial Day. For each 100 miles north or south of the Twin Cities, vary the planting date by approximately 1 week.

Depth of planting and spacing of seeds in the row are also very important. Small seeds like lettuce and radish should be planted from ¼ to ½ inch deep. Larger seeds can be planted about 2 inches deep. Make a shallow trench with a hoe or hoe handle. Scatter the seeds lightly in the trench. Small seeds are difficult to space, but a little care in seeding can save much time later in hand thinning. Cover the seeds with finely pulverized soil and firm the soil by tamping with the back of the hoe or by walking down the row. Loose soil left over the seed soon dries out. If it does not rain within a few days of seeding, watering may be necessary to ensure a satisfactory stand.

Watering

Timely watering often means the difference between good production and poor production. About 1 inch of rainfall or an equivalent amount of water added by irrigation is needed each week during the growing season. When watering, it is best to soak the soil thoroughly to the depth of the root systems of crops being grown. This takes about 1 inch of water if the soil is dry. To test your irrigation system, place a pan with straight sides in the center of the spray pattern of the system. Keep track of the time it takes to accumulate 1 inch of water in the pan. Once a week is usually often enough to water, except possibly on sandy soils. A light sprinkling that wets only the surface soil is of little or no value.

Thinning

Small-seeded vegetables like lettuce, carrots, parsnips, direct-seeded onions, kohlrabi, etc. must be thinned before they start to compete with each other for light, water, and plant nutrients. A spacing of about 2 inches between plants is right for most root crops and leafy vegetables. There is no easy method of thinning. In most cases thinning involves getting down on your knees and pulling out the surplus plants.

Weed Control

A clean, weedless garden is the sign of a good gardener. The best method of maintaining such a garden is to start cultivating and hoeing before the weeds germinate. Frequent, shallow cultivation is most effective in killing the small weeds before they cause trouble. Most annual weed seeds germinate only if they are near the soil surface. Deep cultivation not only destroys crop roots but also brings a fresh crop of weed seeds to the surface, where they germinate and grow.

The best control for perennial weeds like quack grass, thistles, and milkweed is to eliminate them before starting a garden. This can be accomplished by spraying the previous fall with a weed killer like Dalapon. If perennial weeds do germinate in an established garden, they should not be allowed to grow. By keeping them hoed out, their underground storage organs will soon be depleted of stored food and they will die. A small patch of quack grass can be smothered by covering it with a black plastic sheet for a few weeks. Persistent small patches can be spot sprayed without too much danger to surrounding crops.

The best control for annual weeds is shallow cultivation. A pre-emergence weed killer like Dacthal can be used around established plants to keep weeds from germinating.

Mulching

Some vegetables benefit from summer mulch. Straw or clean hay can be used between the rows and under plants. The mulch not only helps smother annual weeds but also aids in conserving moisture and in keeping the soil cool. Vine crops and tomatoes that are unstaked are frequently mulched. The mulch helps keep the fruits clean and disease free. Some gardeners also use a mulch between rows of potatoes. The mulch reduces the sunburn problem on exposed potato tubers.

Mulches also cause some problems. They provide ideal habitats for slugs, which are often troublesome in a wet year. Mulches should not be applied until the soil has warmed up in the spring. If put on too soon, the soil remains cool and slows down the growth of warm-season vegetables.

Pest Control

Most vegetables can be grown with a minimum amount of pest control. The important thing is to become acquainted with the various diseases and animal pests and take appropriate action before serious injury occurs. (See Chapter 5.) In my garden I sometimes find I must spray to control flea beetles, striped cucumber beetles, asparagus beetles, cabbage loopers, aphids, and red spiders. Few of the vegetables require more than one or two sprays during the season, and some can be grown using no pest control. With our growing concern for our environment, it is important to use safe chemicals and to use them only when required to save a crop.

Your Agricultural Extension office has the latest recommendations for pest control. Always read the labels on chemicals and follow the manufacturers' recommendations. Since new chemicals appear on the market each year and some are removed for one reason or another, you should be sure that you are following up-to-date recommendations.

Harvesting

To realize the greatest nutritional value and good eating quality in vegetables, they must be harvested at the right time. One learns by experience the correct stage of maturity for each vegetable. Peas should be harvested as soon as the pods are filled. Snap beans taste best when the seeds in the pod are immature. Zucchini squash should be harvested while the fruits are still small, for if allowed to mature, the fruits are quite useless. Sweet corn must also be harvested at the right stage, as soon as the kernels are filled but while still tender and sweet. One reason for growing vegetables is to enjoy them at their peak of perfection.

Processing and Storage

Home processing of homegrown vegetables has increased greatly in recent years. For some vegetables home canning may be preferred, but for most vegetables freezing preserves the garden freshness better than canning. If you are in doubt about the best method to use, consult a home economist in the Agricultural Extension Service.

Winter storage is practical for certain root crops like carrots, beets, and parsnips as well as for potatoes. Such vegetables require a cool, moist storage. The temperature should be above freezing but below 40°F. For a few vegetables an ordinary refrigerator can be used. With larger quantities a root cellar or a specially insulated room in the basement is required. To maintain high humidity, crops should be stored in earthenware crocks or baskets lined with aluminum foil.

Onions should be stored in a cool, dry place. Hanging the onions in mesh bags from the ceiling in a cool room that does not freeze is ideal. Squash and pumpkins like a dry storage with a temperature of about 60°F. The furnace room in most homes is suitable.

Kinds of Vegetables

Space does not permit a discussion of all vegetables that can be grown. The following groupings contain most of the vegetables that are likely to be grown by the average gardener.

SALAD CROPS

Celery, lettuce, and parsley are the three most common salad crops. Celery requires a long growing season and is seldom grown in the home garden. It dislikes our hot, dry summers. If you grow celery, start the seeds indoors in February and transplant to the garden in early May. Keep plants watered during dry weather. Since quality celery is generally available on the fresh market, there is little incentive to grow it.

Leaf lettuce grows quickly to an edible stage. Seed can be planted early in the spring and again in late July or early August. The plants grow best during cool weather. As soon as the weather turns hot the leaves get bitter and flower stalks form. Some varieties like the 'Bibb' are more heat tolerant. Head lettuce is grown with difficulty. It is best to start the seeds indoors and transplant to the garden in early May. You may be successful in getting heads to form before the onset of hot weather.

Parsley can be seeded directly in the garden in early May. Thin the seedlings so that the individual plants are 4 to 6 inches apart. A few plants are sufficient for the average-sized family. Plants can be dug in the late fall and carried over the winter as houseplants, thus providing fresh parsley throughout the winter months.

GREENS

Swiss chard, New Zealand spinach, and spinach are the most common greens grown. Swiss chard tolerates hot weather and continues to produce until the first frost. Seed should be planted in early May. Harvesting can start as soon as the leaves are large enough and continue until late fall. Few insects or diseases affect chard.

New Zealand spinach is a hot-weather green and is not related to spinach. Seeds can be started in early spring. You must acquire a taste for New Zealand spinach. If you do not like it, do not bother to grow it.

Spinach is a cool-weather vegetable that must be grown either as an early spring crop or as a fall crop. It grows best in rich soil that is adequately supplied with water.

SOLANACEOUS FRUITS

Eggplant, peppers, and tomatoes belong to the potato family, *Solanaceae*. They have similar cultural requirements. For best results, the seed should be started indoors 6 to 8 weeks before it is time to set the plants outdoors. Since these are warm-season plants, little is gained by transplanting them much before Memorial Day. This means that the seed should be started during the early part of April. Short, stocky plants are best for transplanting to the garden. Tall, leggy plants are the result of either starting the seeds too soon or growing the plants in too little light. If plants are set out earlier than Memorial Day, be prepared to cover them if frost is predicted.

These fruits do best where they receive full sunlight. Peppers should be spaced about 18 inches apart in the row. Eggplants require a 24-inch spacing. Spacing to be left between tomato plants depends on the variety and the method of training. Staked tomato plants can be spaced about 18 inches apart. Unstaked plants need a 2- to 3-foot spacing. Tomato rows should be about 4 feet apart. A summer mulch helps conserve moisture and control weeds. Watering during dry periods contributes to producing a maximum crop of high-quality fruits.

Staking tomato plants requires much time. The chief advantage is closer spacing of the plants, which permits more plants in a limited space. The yield per plant is actually reduced by staking. A stake should be driven into the ground near each plant when it is set in the ground. As the plant grows, lateral branches are removed as they form, and the stem is tied to the stake, using soft cloth strips or raffia. Some gardeners allow only one stem to develop. Others may permit two or more to grow. The fruits on staked plants are cleaner and easier to pick than those on unstaked plants that are allowed to spread over the ground.

Tomato fruits should be picked as they ripen. When frost is predicted, the fully developed, green fruits should be harvested and allowed to ripen indoors. A temperature of 60°F. or above is needed to ripen the fruits.

Tomatoes are subject to several leaf diseases including septoria leaf spot and early blight. These diseases usually appear about the time the fruits start to ripen, and unless they are controlled by preventive sprays like Maneb or Zineb, they can seriously reduce the crop.

ROOT CROPS

Beets, carrots, parsnips, radishes, rutabagas, sweet potatoes, and turnips are the most commonly grown root crops. For a spring crop, radishes and turnips can be planted as soon as the soil is workable. They can be planted again, in late July or early August, for a fall crop. Rutabagas require a longer growing season and are normally not planted until late May or early June for a fall crop. They grow the most in late fall when the weather is cool. For this reason the best rutabagas are grown in the North. Beets, carrots, and parsnips should be planted in early May. Sweet potatoes are not grown to any extent in the North. On sandy soils and in warm years sweet potatoes can be grown. Plant only the early-maturing varieties and transplant rooted cuttings as soon as the danger of frost is past.

All root crops with the exception of sweet potatoes must be thinned to allow room for the roots to develop. Thinning of beets can be delayed until the tops are large enough to use for beet greens. Carrots, parsnips, rutabagas, and turnips should be thinned as soon as the plants are large enough to pull. The sooner the plants are thinned, the less the damage to the remaining plants. Unless radishes have been seeded very thick, thinning can be delayed until small, edible roots have formed. Thinning of carrots can proceed in two steps. The first thinning should space the plants about 1 inch apart. The second thinning should be made when the roots are large enough to use as baby carrots. A 2-inch spacing is adequate for the final thinning.

THE POTATO

The potato is the most widely grown and used vegetable. Most farm gardens and many city and small-town gardens have one or more rows of potatoes. There is nothing quite like new potatoes, freshly dug from your own garden. The quantity of potatoes to be grown depends on the size of your garden and the size and eating habits of your family. Unless you have good conditions for winter storage, you should not plant more than you can use during the summer and fall months. Early-maturing varieties, planted in late April or early May, should produce tubers of edible size by early July. Planting early and late varieties ensures a continuous harvest for nearly 4 months. Even with poor storage conditions you can store potatoes for several months. If soil and growing conditions are favorable, you should obtain at least a 10 to 1 increase from your seed potatoes. A peck of "seed potatoes" should produce 2½ bushels.

BULB CROPS

The common onion is grown for both green onions and mature onions that will be stored and used in the winter. Set onions of the globe type are usually planted for green onions, which are pulled and used as soon as they reach edible size. For winter use, the sweet Spanish type is usually grown from seed. Best results are obtained by starting seeds indoors under lights or in a greenhouse during early March. Transplant to the garden about May 1. Southern-grown transplants may also be purchased at most garden centers. Onions can be direct seeded but better results will be obtained with transplants. The onion maggot and thrip are the chief insect pests of onions.

THE COLE CROPS

Broccoli, brussels sprouts, cabbage, cauliflower, and kohlrabi are all members of the mustard family and have similar cultural requirements. Most grow best during cool weather.

Kohlrabi is normally seeded directly in the garden and thinned to a 4-inch spacing. A bulbous growth develops at the base of the stem, and this is harvested and used when 2 or more inches in diameter. The "bulb" is peeled and cut into sections and used fresh or boiled. If you have not eaten kohlrabi, you have missed a treat.

Brussels sprouts are not eaten until late fall. Start seeds indoors in mid-April and transplant to the garden around June 1. Small heads form from axillary buds along the base of the stem. These taste better after the first frost. 'Jade Cross' is the preferred variety to grow.

Cabbage, broccoli, and cauliflower are commonly grown. Plants are normally started indoors and transplanted to the garden. It takes about 6 weeks to grow the plants. For an early crop, transplant to the garden in early May. For a late crop, transplant to the garden in late June. Chinese cabbage, which also belongs to this family, should be grown only for the fall crop. Plants started in early July should mature before the onset of cold weather in the fall.

It is important to harvest at the right stage of maturity. Cabbage heads will split if left in the garden too long. Broccoli should be harvested before the yellow flowers develop. Cauliflower heads should be shaded by tying the leaves up around the head.

Aphids and the cabbage looper are the worst insect pests, and measures must be taken to keep these insects under control. The cabbage maggot can also be a problem.

VINE CROPS

This group includes cucumber, muskmelon, watermelon, pumpkin, and squash. Most people have difficulty distinguishing squash from pumpkins. The true pumpkins (*Cucurbita pepo*) have a hard stem attached to the fruit. The true squashes have a soft or spongy stem attached to the fruits. Unfortunately, some pumpkins are called squash and some squash pumpkins. The 'Table Queen', 'Butternut', and 'Zucchini' squashes are actually pumpkins. The 'Big Max' pumpkin is really a squash. Most canned pumpkin used for making pumpkin pie is made from winter squash.

Of the vine crops, cucumbers are a little more tolerant of cool soils and can be planted about May 10. Other vine crops should not be planted until the soil starts to warm up. It is generally safe to plant most vine crops by May 20. Starting plants indoors in separate containers may save a few days in time of ripening, and this could be an advantage in the North where the growing season is short. Vine crops normally trail along the ground, and this is no problem in large gardens. But where space is limited, they can be trained to a trellis. Bush types are also popular for small gardens. Know the needs of your family and do not plant more than you will use. A few hills of zucchini squash are enough for the average-sized family.

Muskmelons and watermelons prefer a sandy loam soil that warms up early to get the plants off to a good start. Other vine crops do well on the heavier soils.

Melons should be harvested at the right stage of maturity. With muskmelons a change in fruit color and the ability to separate the fruit from the vine with a slight twist indicate the proper maturity for harvest. With watermelons it is more difficult. Usually the underside of the fruit is greenish yellow and the fruit produces a dull thud when tapped. Experience is the best teacher in knowing when to pick watermelons. With cucumbers and summer squash, size is the determining factor. As indicated earlier, small fruits of a summer squash like 'Zucchini' are of much better quality than large ones. Winter squash and pumpkins must be picked before a hard freeze. A light frost that kills the vines seldom hurts the fruits.

The striped cucumber beetle can be a real problem on young vine crops. They seem to time their emergence with the germination of the seeds. When plants are small, the cucumber beetle can practically defoliate the plants overnight. Watch for this pest and take immediate control measures if you see the insect. Stalk borer can also take its toll once it is inside the stem. Sanitation reduces the problem.

SWEET CORN

Sweet corn is another vegetable that requires much space. It is best to plant several short rows of a given variety than a single long row. This is because of wind pollination: a short block of several rows ensures more even distribution of the pollen. Rows of sweet corn should be 30 to 36 inches apart. Spacing in the row is also important. If you plant 3 to 4 seeds per hill, space the hills about 18 inches apart.

To have a long season of harvest, one can either plant at one time several varieties with different maturity dates or make succession plantings using fewer varieties.

Sweet corn tastes best when harvested at the right stage of maturity and minutes before cooking and eating. There is no comparison between homegrown corn and corn that may have been on the grocer's shelf for a few days. High temperatures after harvesting convert the sugars to starch, so for a sweet taste, harvest right before eating.

LEGUMES

Snap beans, lima beans, and peas are the legumes most commonly grown. Peas are frost hardy and can be planted about as soon as the soil is workable. The earlier you plant peas the better, since the fruits should mature before the onset of hot weather.

Snap beans can be planted about May 10. Succession plantings can be made to provide for a longer period of harvest. Both the green pod and the yellow or wax pod are popular. There are flat and round-podded varieties of each. The bush types are most commonly planted, but pole types produce more beans in a limited space.

Lima beans require warm soil. They are normally not planted before May 20. Both large- and small-seeded varieties can be grown, but results are usually best with the small-seeded kind.

Harvesting at the right stage of maturity is the secret of getting quality legumes. Pea pods should be well filled, but they must be harvested while the peas are still tender and sweet. Snap beans should be harvested before the seeds develop in the pods; limas, as soon as the seeds are large enough.

PERENNIAL VEGETABLES

Asparagus and rhubarb are popular varieties. Asparagus is best grown in rows, where it can be cultivated and kept weed free. One- or two-year-old plants should be planted in early spring. Make a trench about 8 inches deep. Space the plants about 18 inches apart in the row. Cover the crowns and water to settle the soil and eliminate air spaces. Gradually fill in the trench as the young sprouts grow. No asparagus should be harvested until the third year after planting. After the plants are well established, the harvest period will be about 6 weeks long. You should stop harvesting each year about July 1 to allow time for vegetative growth and the storage of food in the fleshy crown. An asparagus planting remains productive for many years.

Rhubarb can be grown in a row in the vegetable or fruit garden, or it can be grown in the flower border. Fall and early spring are the best times to start plants. Like asparagus, rhubarb should not be harvested until the third year after planting. Then the stalks can be harvested each spring until about July 1. It is best to pull the stalks rather than to cut them. Discard the blade portion since it contains calcium oxalate crystals that are poisonous. Remove all flower stalks.

Asparagus and rhubarb should be fertilized each year. Applying topdressing with well-rotted manure in the fall and then a side dressing of a complete fertilizer in the spring should be adequate.

Chapter 9

Home Landscaping

A well-landscaped yard adds greatly to the enjoyment of one's home. It also adds to the value of the property. It is difficult to put a dollar value on the landscape, but most real estate agents agree that the value can be somewhere between 5 and 20 percent of the value of the property. An average value is about 13 percent. From this, you can see that landscaping is good business.

Most homeowners take several years to plan and plant their yards. They may seek the help of a landscape nursery or prefer to draw their own plans and buy the plants that are needed. Landscape architects occasionally design home landscapes, but they are usually kept busy on larger commercial and public projects. Books have been written on landscape design and persons planning to do their own landscaping should study the topic as much as possible.

Most yards can be divided into three more or less distinct areas: the public area, the private (outdoor-living) area, and the service area. No sharp lines separate these areas, and the amount of space devoted to each depends on the placement of the house on the lot and the size and interests of the family.

The public area is seen by the public and normally includes the part of the yard from the front of the house to the street or public road.

The private area, or outdoor-living area, is an extension of the living area of the house into the yard. Privacy can be achieved by border plantings. A patio may be an important part of this area.

The service area accommodates things like the clothesline, garbage cans, tool shed, dog run, garage, and so on. It should be compact and simply planted.

The first step in landscaping is drawing the plan. This is followed by selecting materials and finally by planting and maintenance. Each of these steps is interrelated and each is equally important. The best landscape plan in the world is not worth the paper it is drawn on unless the choice of plant materials is proper for executing the plan. Without adequate maintenance, no planting will look very good after a few years.

Planning

Let us start with the landscape plan. The purpose of a plan is to let us make mistakes on paper and to determine exactly the number of plants of each kind that will be needed.

To help you with your design, we should consider the proper use and positioning of certain plants and structural features:

Trees are used for framing the house, for shade, for background, and for ornament. Framing trees are usually planted in the public area. They should be planted out from the front corners of the house so that they frame the house rather than hide it as they grow to maturity. Trees planted for shade should be positioned only where shade is really required. Consider the angle of the sun during months when shade is needed. Remember that sunlight may be as welcome as shade; this is particularly true for about 9 months of the year. Background trees can be planted toward the back of the yard. They should be tall enough to be seen above the house when viewed from the front. Ornamental trees should be used as lawn specimens and planted where they can be enjoyed both from indoors and in the yard.

Existing trees should be carefully studied to see if their location is appropriate. The kind of trees present should also be known. If an undesirable tree is located where a tree should not be, it might be best to remove it. In a small yard two trees may be all that is required. If the front yard is large, a number of trees may be needed.

Shrubs and small evergreens are properly used around the edges of the yard to provide privacy and in the foundation planting to blend the house with the yard. Scattered shrubs in the lawn are a nuisance as far as maintenance is concerned; an open lawn is far more beautiful and easier to care for. A mixed shrub border adds interest to your outdoor living room. Planting shrubs in groups of three to five of a kind looks better than having a collection of individual plants of different varieties. Spacing of shrubs should allow room for the plants to grow to maturity: 6 to 8 feet between large shrubs, 4 to 6 feet for medium shrubs, and 2 to 4 feet for small shrubs. In designing the border, try to avoid a stepladder effect. Arrange the background shrubs to give a varied skyline. Use taller shrubs where you wish to hide an unsightly view, lower shrubs where you wish to frame a view. Arrange the shrubs so that all are visible from the yard side. If your shrub border is to serve as a background for a flower border, the front shrubs should not be shorter than the flowers.

The foundation planting requires care in planning. The purpose of the planting is to blend the house with the yard. For a one-story house the corner planting should reach about two-thirds the height of the eaves. Taller shrubs are needed at the corners for a two-story house. Plants under windows should never grow taller than the base of the window. Plants on either side of the entrance should be lower than the corner plantings. It is not necessary to hide the entire foundation of the house if the style of architecture is pleasing. Do not plant too close to the foundation. This is especially important with overhanging eaves.

Needle evergreens are often planted in foundation plantings. If this is done, select types not susceptible to winter burn and those that do not require much restrictive pruning. A combination of deciduous shrubs and evergreens is often more interesting than evergreens alone.

Flowers can be grown in a flower border or in a special cutting garden. The flower border should be located along one side of the yard, preferably in the private area and where it can be viewed from both indoors and out. A suitable background should be provided for the flower border. This background may be an informal shrub border, a hedge, or an ornamental fence. The depth and length of the flower border depends on the size of the yard and the interests of the family. A curved border is more interesting than one with straight lines.

Features like patios, trellises, sundials, walks, clotheslines, etc. should be carefully considered. The patio should be conveniently located near the kitchen. Trellises can be located by the house or garage, or they can serve as a screen. The use of sundials, pools, statuary, etc. depends on the interests of the family.

You are now ready to develop your plan. Make a scale drawing on paper, showing the location of the house, property lines, utilities like power and gas lines, drives and walks, and existing trees and mature shrubs. Use cross-section paper or draw in ½-inch squares on a sheet of white paper. Depending on the size of your plan and the size of your property, select a scale like 8 feet to the inch. It is good to indicate on the plan the size and height of all windows. Tracing paper should be used for preliminary designing. You will seldom be satisfied with your first effort, and by using tracing paper you can start over without having to relocate all the permanent features.

Locate the major areas by drawing circles or ovals on the tracing paper. In general the areas within the circles or ovals would be lawn areas and the areas outside would be used for the shrub and flower borders. Outline where shrubs and small evergreens will be positioned and locate all trees and special architectural features.

SELECTING SPECIFIC PLANTS

After you have decided on the plan that best suits your needs, you will need to select the plants that will give the desired effect. The selection of the right plants can be as important or even more important than the plan itself.

Before a plant can be used intelligently in the landscape, you should learn all you can about it. Some of the questions you should ask are:

1. Is the plant hardy? By this we mean, will it survive our northern winters in the soil and location where you wish to plant it? We ordinarily do not think of the Baltic ivy as being hardy, yet I have grown it successfully on the north side of a building where it receives protection from the winter sun and has dependable snow cover.

2. How large does it grow? The plant should be in scale with the grounds and the house.

3. What are the seasonal aspects? Does it have more than one season of beauty? A plant that combines good form and texture with good bloom is more valuable than one that has only attractive bloom. Colored fruits, fall color, and winter interest are other considerations.

4. Does the plant have any serious insect or disease problems? Avoid plants that require expensive spray programs to keep them healthy.

5. Will it become a serious weed? Many plants that would be acceptable as landscape plants can spread by seeds and underground rhizomes. Creeping Charlie, goutweed, and some of the polygonums are examples.

It is best to ask these questions before deciding to put a particular plant on the plan. We have plenty of good plants to select from. These plants are described later in this book.

With a dot indicate the exact location of every plant. Each group of plants should be delineated. Each kind of plant should be given a symbol and a planting list prepared giving the number of each kind needed. You can then order the right number and kinds of plants. Too often, we follow the reverse procedure. We buy plants on impulse and then try to find a place to plant them.

Another advantage of planning is that it allows an orderly development of the landscape. It is not necessary to do all the planting at once. The first year you may plant only the trees and the lawn. The shrubs and flowers can be added later, depending on your available time and budget.

Chapter 10

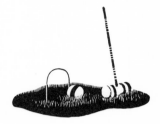

How to Have a Good Lawn

The lawn can be likened to the canvas on which an artist paints a picture. An attractive lawn adds much to the enjoyment of home ownership and outdoor living. Having an attractive lawn requires careful preparation of the soil before planting plus regular maintenance.

Kinds of Lawn Grasses

Kentucky bluegrass (*Poa pratensis*) is the most commonly planted and one of the best lawn grasses. A number of cultivars have been developed, most of which are improvements over the species. 'Park' and 'Newport', two cultivars used in lawn grass mixtures, are good for the average lawn. 'Park' was developed by the Agronomy Department of the University of Minnesota and exhibits especially good seedling vigor. It also turns green early in the spring. 'Newport' has a darker green color and broader leaves than common bluegrass.

For a really fine lawn that can be mowed to a height of ¾-1 inch, a number of elite types of bluegrass have been developed: 'Merion', 'Windsor', 'Prato', 'Fylking', 'Pennstar', 'Barron', and

'Nugget'. These should not be planted unless you are willing to give them extra care. For best results, use a blend of several cultivars.

Creeping red fescue (*Festuca rubra*) is more shade and drought tolerant than Kentucky bluegrass. Improved cultivars include: 'Illahee', 'Pennlawn', 'Ranier', and 'Ruby'. These and the common red fescue blend well with the Kentucky bluegrasses. Most commercial mixtures contain one or more cultivars of both Kentucky bluegrass and creeping red fescue.

Bentgrasses are of several types belonging to the genus *Agrostis*. Creeping bent (*A. palustris*) is used on golf greens. It should not be planted for the home lawn unless one has unlimited time and interest in giving it special care. Colonial bent (*A. tenuis*) is seed propagated. It makes a good lawn but requires more care than the bluegrasses and fescues. Bentgrasses do not blend well with other grasses. Redtop (*A. alba*) is often used as a nurse crop. It germinates quickly to produce a green lawn. It is relatively short-lived and gradually gives way to the more desirable grasses.

Ryegrasses belong to the genus *Lolium*. The perennial ryegrass (*L. perenne*) is relatively short-lived. It is often used as a nurse crop or where a temporary lawn is desired. New cultivars are being developed that have greater hardiness. 'Manhattan', 'NK-100', and 'Pelo' show promise. Italian ryegrass (*L. multiflorum*) is similar to *L. perenne* and is occasionally planted.

Zoysia (*Z. japonica*) is a warm-season grass that is widely advertised. It is slow to turn green in the spring and turns brown early in the fall. It has been slow to become established and has not been too winter hardy, especially in open winters with little or no snow. Lawn experts do not recommend it in our area.

Starting a Lawn

PREPARING THE SOIL

In starting a lawn one should consider the subsoil as well as the topsoil. The subsoil must be well drained. A sandy loam is best. If you have a heavy, clay subsoil, tile drainage may be required. The surface should be carefully graded to allow surface drainage away from the home. No pockets should be left where water will stand. Avoid unnecessary compaction of the subsoil.

At least 6 inches of topsoil should be added. This should be done in steps. First spread a 2-inch layer over the surface and roto-till it into the subsoil. This will help make a gradual transition between the topsoil and the subsoil. Next add the remaining 4 inches of topsoil and spread it evenly over the surface. Rake the surface to provide a uniform seedbed free of shallow depressions. If you saved the topsoil that was originally on the lot, reuse it. If you purchase topsoil to add to what you already have, be sure that it is a mineral soil of good quality. Black muck from old lake bottoms is not very satisfactory.

SEEDING

Before seeding, it is good to mix in some fertilizer. A fertilizer high in phosphorus and potassium, like an 0-20-20, should be added at a rate of 20-30 pounds per 1,000 square feet of surface. Work the fertilizer into the soil, using a rotovator. This gets the phosphorus and potassium into the soil, where the root system of your lawn will develop. Immediately before seeding, apply ½ pound of actual nitrogen per 1,000 square feet. This can be left on the surface. If you use ammonium nitrate, 33-0-0, it will take only 1½ pounds per 1,000 square feet of surface.

You are now ready to plant your grass seed. For a sunny lawn with few trees, your grass mixture should be high in the Kentucky bluegrasses. For a shady lawn, the mixture should be high in creeping red fescue. The proportion of bluegrass to creeping red fescue can vary from 80 to 40 percent for the Kentucky bluegrass depending on the degree of shade. The amount of grass seed to be planted varies with the kind of seed and the method of seeding. If you use a mixture, you need about 4 pounds per 1,000 square feet. Less could be used if you obtain an even distribution of your seed. Seeding can be done by hand, but a better job can be done with a whirlwind type of seeder or spreader. Seeding in two directions is best to ensure even distribution. Measure the lawn area. Purchase the correct quantity of seed. Divide the seed into two equal quantities and sow a half in each direction. After seeding, rake the seed in lightly. Do not cover too deeply since bluegrass seed requires light for germination. Rolling with a lawn roller partly filled with water helps firm the soil and place the seeds in close contact with the soil particles. Water immediately, using a fine mist. Repeat as necessary to keep the surface of the soil moist. Continue watering until the grass is well established. The length of the intervals between waterings can be lengthened after the lawn shows green.

If you do not have available water, a lawn can be started by using a mulch of straw or marsh hay applied at the time of seeding. The mulch must be evenly distributed and not more than 1 inch thick.

The best time to seed a lawn is in late summer, August 15 to September 10. The second-best time is in the spring as soon as the soil can be worked. The main advantages of late-summer seeding are fewer weeds and cool nights that favor development of vigorous grass seedlings.

Mowing should start as soon as the lawn is 3½ inches tall. Start mowing with the mower set at 2½ inches. Gradually lower the mower until you reach the desired height, which is about 1½ inches for an average lawn or 1 inch for an elite lawn.

SODDING

If you have a steep slope or need an immediate lawn, sodding may be preferable to seeding. It is more expensive and the choice of varieties is usually more limited. The same soil preparation is required whether you seed or sod. It is important to buy freshly cut sod and to lay it immediately. Watering during the first few weeks is critical. In laying sod on a slope, place the strips parallel to the slope. Adjoining strips should touch and be staggered like bricks on a wall. This prevents erosion of the soil. Take time to lay the sod carefully with no overlapping joints. On a steep slope the sod should be held in place by wooden pegs. Start mowing as soon as new growth develops.

Care of an Established Lawn

RAKING, MOWING, AND EDGING

In the spring any debris in the lawn should be cleaned up. Use a broom type of lawn rake. Avoid using a steel rake that digs into the soil and exposes the roots. Start mowing as soon as growth starts in the spring. A good rule is to mow whenever the grass has grown 1 inch above the height set for your mower. The frequency of mowing varies greatly depending on the fertility of the soil and the amount of watering. Continue mowing in the fall as long as there is grass to mow. Tree leaves should be raked and removed from the lawn before snow comes.

A well-groomed lawn is neatly edged. An edging tool or a sharp, square-nosed shovel can be used to make a clean vertical cut. A straight line can be made by stretching a strong cord between two stakes. For a curved border use a garden hose along the edge, with the desired curves serving as a guide. The grass beyond the vertical cut can be spaded into the soil where it will soon decompose, or it can be pulled out of the ground, the soil shaken from the grass roots, and the remains put on the compost pile. Grass along a sidewalk tends to grow over the edge, giving a ragged appearance; a special edging tool or a grass shears can be used to remove this overgrowth. Another place where edging improves the appearance is around trees and specimen evergreens. It is surprising how much the edging and trimming of the lawn can improve its beauty.

WATERING

Maintaining a green lawn all summer usually requires some watering. About 1 inch of water per week is needed. If it does not rain, watering to make up the deficit helps maintain a green lawn. If there is a water shortage, it is best to use the limited quantity of water available for trees, shrubs, flowers, and fruits and vegetables to keep them alive and growing. Your lawn becomes dormant during dry periods but will recover after the rains come. The important thing is to soak the soil to the depth of the grass roots each time you water. Frequent, shallow watering can be harmful by encouraging shallow rooting.

FERTILIZING

Maintaining a healthy lawn requires about 4 pounds of actual nitrogen per 1,000 square feet per year. This should be applied at rates that do not exceed 1 pound per application, that is, at least 4 applications per year are required. You should not fertilize during July and early August, since fertilizing during hot weather favors the growth of crabgrass and other warm-season weeds. The first application in the spring should be put on about the time the grass starts growing in late April; the other applications, at 4- to 6-week intervals. The last application, which should be made in mid-September, helps get the lawn started earlier in the spring.

Besides nitrogen, the lawn needs phosphorus, potassium, and the minor elements. Most lawn fertilizers are high in nitrogen, with lesser amounts of phosphorus and potassium. A 20-10-10 is an example of a good lawn fertilizer. For economic reasons you may prefer to use a farm fertilizer like a 10-10-10 for the first application in the spring and a straight nitrogen fertilizer for the other applications during the year. Ammonium nitrate and urea are examples of straight nitrogen. Check the percentage of nitrogen shown on the fertilizer bag and calculate the amount of fertilizer needed for your lawn. If your lawn area measures 10,000 square feet, you will need 10 pounds of actual nitrogen. If you are using a 20-10-10 fertilizer, this area would take 50 pounds. If you are using ammonium nitrate, which is approximately 33-0-0, it would take only 33 pounds or two-thirds of a 50-pound bag. Use a whirlwind type of fertilizer spreader and apply the right amount. Setting the spreader at a low rate and covering the lawn in two directions gives a more even distribution of the fertilizer. Keep track of the fertilizer setting so that it will not be necessary to calibrate it each time. If you follow the recommended rate and obtain an even distribution of the fertilizer, watering immediately after the application should not be necessary. I have used straight nitrogen fertilizers containing as much as 50 percent nitrogen, with no burning. If you get an uneven distribution or apply more than the recommended amount, watering can help prevent burning.

There has been a great deal of talk about phosphorus and its effect in polluting our lakes and streams. The best control for erosion is a healthy lawn. Unless you live near a lake or stream with a steep slope from your lawn to the water, there is little danger of phosphorus entering the water from your lawn. You may wish to have your soil tested to determine the level of available phosphorus. If the test shows adequate phosphorus, a phosphorus-free fertilizer should be used. If your soil is deficient in phosphorus, use a complete fertilizer to maintain a healthy, erosion-free lawn.

The form of the nitrogen may also be of concern to some gardeners. Organic sources of nitrogen like blood meal, sewage sludge, and soybean meal are more slowly available to plants and less likely to burn than inorganic sources of nitrogen. The release of nitrogen from organic sources is dependent on weather conditions. In cold weather the release is slow. Under warm, moist conditions the release can be rapid. Inorganic sources of nitrogen are immediately available to plants. Cost should be the determining factor in deciding the kind of fertilizer to be used. Some kinds of organic as compared with inorganic fertilizer cost as much as ten times more per pound of actual nitrogen.

WEEDING

The best control for lawn weeds is a healthy lawn. Sometimes, in spite of good care, weeds become a problem. Broad-leaved weeds like dandelions and plantain can be controlled by using a weed killer containing 2,4-D. Apply it on a still day when the weeds are actively growing and the temperature is above 60°F. Use a preparation that has a low volatility. Some broad-leaved weeds like creeping Charlie and mouse-ear chickweed are more difficult to control and may require a weed killer containing 2,4,5-TP. Crabgrass, a low, spreading annual grass, is often a problem. This is a warm-season grass that germinates about the time lilacs bloom. A preemergence crabgrass killer applied about the middle of May usually provides good control of crabgrass.

The perennial quack grass and other coarse grasses sometimes become established in the lawn. These are objectionable. Unfortunately, there are no selective weed killers that kill these grasses without also killing the desirable grasses. Close and frequent mowing favors the shorter and more desirable grasses. Over a period of

several years it is possible to starve the undesirable coarse grasses.
If your lawn is heavily infested with quack grass, it may be advisable to spray in the fall with a weed killer like Dalapon and to re-
seed or sod the next spring, as you would for a new lawn.

INSECT AND DISEASE CONTROL

Insects and diseases cause problems. White grubs often feed on
the roots, thus killing the grass. Several leaf-spot diseases affect the
color and appearance of the lawn; certain soil fungi can kill the
grass in small patches. These diseases are usually most prevalent in
warm, humid weather. Consult your county Agricultural Extension office for the latest recommended controls for these problems.

Renovating an Old Lawn

The kind of renovation needed depends on the condition of your
lawn. If weeds cover 40 percent or more of the area, complete renovation is required. Follow the recommendations for starting a
lawn. If the problem areas are small, vertical mowing and removal
of the dead grass or thatch followed by topdressing and overseed-
ing may be all that is necessary. Late August is the best time to do
this.

If the soil is compacted and feels hard underfoot, it should be
aerified; standing water after a rain may also indicate a compacted
soil. With problem lawns it may be necessary to aerify in alternate
years. Early spring or fall are the times to use aerifiers. These can
be rented. Use only the kinds that remove a plug of soil, for the
type that merely punches holes in the ground is of little value.

Chapter 11

Selection and Care of Deciduous Trees

Planting a tree is a longtime investment. No other gardening investment returns more satisfaction and value. If you make the right choices, these returns can be optimized.

When selecting a tree consider hardiness, rate of growth, mature size, form, and seasonal aspects like bloom, fruit, fall color, and winter appearance. Your choice can also be influenced by the type of soil you have. Select trees that will be in scale with the grounds and buildings when they reach maturity. Avoid overly large trees that may be expensive to remove or that require excessive pruning.

It is best to plant nursery-grown trees that have been properly root pruned. If you transplant a tree from a pasture or woodlot, do not attempt to move a very large one. Small trees up to 1 or 2 inches in diameter can usually be moved in the early spring with a reasonable chance of survival.

The cost of a tree purchased from a nursery is proportional to its size. When a tree is properly root pruned and moved with an adequate ball of soil, the only limits on size are the cost of the tree and the weight of the ball. For most purposes, little is gained by moving a tree much larger than 3 or 4 inches in diameter, because the larger the tree, the longer the recovery time. When moving a

96

tree with a tree spade, there is a temptation to move trees that are too large. For bare root trees that you plant yourself, 2 inches, trunk diameter, is about the upper limit to the size that can be safely moved.

For bare root stock, early spring as soon as the soil can be worked is the best time for planting. For ball and burlapped stock, for container stock, and for trees moved with a tree spade the planting season can be greatly extended. It is generally not advisable to plant in July and August. The best time to move birches and maples is in the spring as the leaves are opening.

When planting, always dig a hole of generous size. For bare root trees, the hole should be wide enough so that the roots can be spread without crowding and deep enough to accommodate the root system. For ball and burlapped stock or container stock, make the hole a little wider and the right depth for the ball or container. Put the topsoil in one pile and the subsoil in another. If the soil removed from the hole is not suitable to use as backfill, discard it and bring in good topsoil. Quality topsoil is as good or better than many of the soil amendments being used, such as peat moss. The subsoil, if used, should be added only on the surface above the root zone. Before planting container stock, remove the tree from its container so that its roots will come in direct contact with the soil. Always plant a tree to the same depth that it was when growing in the nursery. Fill in around the roots or ball with topsoil and tamp the soil to eliminate air pockets. For ball and burlapped stock, the burlap should be loosened and folded back to the sides of the hole when the hole is half-filled. Fill the hole to ground level, leaving a shallow depression around the tree. Soak the soil thoroughly with water and continue to water weekly until the tree is well established.

If your soil is reasonably fertile, little is gained by fertilizing during the first growing season. By the time new roots have formed, it is too late to fertilize. In future years fertilizers should be applied about May 1 and only as needed to maintain a healthy rate of growth.

Pruning trees at planting time can be important to their survival. Bare root stock requires heavier pruning than the other types. The pruning should preserve the natural form of the tree. It is better to thin the branches to reduce the leaf surface than to cut back all the branches. If necessary, cut back side branches directly beyond an outward-pointing bud or to a side branch that points outward. Removing some of the lower branches may also be advisable. Always make clean cuts and leave no stubs. For additional information on pruning, see Chapter 6.

An early, severe freeze in late fall can cause tip kill on trees and shrubs that have not been properly hardened. Withholding fertilizer and water after August 15 helps the plants harden properly.

Sunscald can be a problem on thin-barked trees like Norway maple and mountain-ash. The injury usually occurs on the southwest side of the tree, and probably happens in February and March when we have snow on the ground and bright, sunny days with little or no wind. The bark warms up from the direct sun and from the reflection of the sun on snow. A sudden temperature drop caused by clouds or by the sun going behind a tree or building can cause ice formation within the living cells, resulting in rupture and death of the cells. Shading the tree trunk by applying a tree wrap in the fall helps prevent this type of injury.

Kinds of Trees

This section is designed to help you select appropriate trees for your gardening situation. Brief species descriptions provide information on hardiness, native range, height, form, foliage, flowers, fruits, and culture. Comments on hardiness are keyed to the accompanying plant hardiness zone map. (The hardiness zones were established by the United States Department of Agriculture and are based on minimum winter temperatures.) New cultivars and varieties are suggested for trial when there is limited information on plant hardiness. By height of the plant we mean the normal growth that can be expected when it is planted in a landscape setting; the same species may grow much taller in its native region or under forest conditions. Presented at the end of the chapter are general tree lists (arranged by height) and special tree lists (trees with especially attractive foliage, flowers, form, etc., and trees for particular purposes and sites).

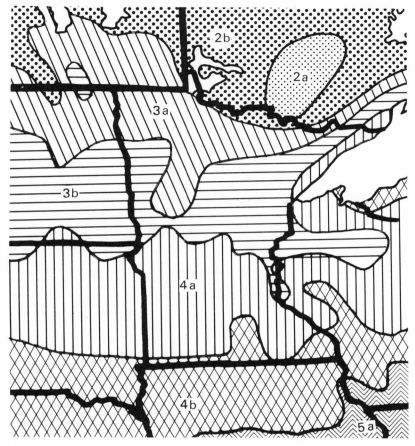

Plant Hardiness Zone Map

ACER (Maple). The maples include some of the better landscape trees and some that are not so desirable. All maples have opposite and palmately lobed leaves. Their winged fruits (samaras) are produced in pairs.

A. ginnala (Amur Maple). Hardy in all zones. Grown as a shrub and as a small tree that can be clumped or trained to a single stem. As a tree it often reaches a height of about 20 feet. Leaves are 3-lobed. Conspicuous, yellowish-white flower clusters are produced in May, and the fruits ripen in early August. The latter can turn from green to brown or they can be brilliant red. A selection with especially red fruits has been made at the University of Minnesota Landscape Arboretum. The fall color is outstanding, with various shades of orange and scarlet. This maple can be grown on most types of soil but does best on sandy loam. On alkaline soils the leaves are chlorotic.

A. negundo (Boxelder). Hardy in all zones. Brittle branches that break in ice storms and windstorms plus the presence of boxelder bugs are features that should discourage the use of this native species. It is mentioned because volunteer seedlings often start in yards and, if allowed to grow, soon develop into trees that are 40 or more feet tall. The species is drought resistant and is often planted in the western Dakotas in shelterbelts and even as a lawn tree.

A. platanoides (Norway Maple). Borderline hardiness in northern parts of zone 4a; hardy in zones 4b and 5a. Grows to a height of 50 feet and is easily recognized by the milky juice that exudes when a leaf or leaf petiole is injured. This round-headed tree has yellow, showy flowers in May. The fall color is golden yellow. The Norway maple and its cultivars grow on a variety of soils. The dense shade cast by the trees and their shallow root system may make it difficult to grow a good lawn under mature trees. The following cultivars are best for planting: 'Charles F. Irish', 'Cleveland', 'Emerald Queen', 'Jade Glen', 'Summershade', and 'Superform' are green-leaved cultivars with the characteristic rounded or oval crown. 'Cleveland' is perhaps the best of these cultivars. The leaves on 'Schwedleri' are red when new but soon turn green as summer approaches. 'Crimson King', 'Fassen's Red Leaf', and 'Royal Red' retain their bloodred to purple color all season. 'Variegatum' has variegated leaves of white and green. This cultivar is less vigorous and should be planted only in a sheltered location. 'Cucullatum' has a crinkled leaf. 'Columnare' and 'Globosum' are grown for their columnar and globe forms.

A. rubrum (Red Maple). Northern strains are hardy in all zones, but southern strains lack hardiness and should not be planted. This native maple grows from Florida to Ontario and from the East Coast to Minnesota. It is a medium-sized tree growing to a height of 40 or more feet and has a rounded crown. Trees are bisexual, producing reddish-colored flowers in early April before the leaves open. The red maple can be easily spotted when in bloom. The fall color varies from yellow to brilliant scarlet red. The red maple grows well on sandy and on wet soils where sugar maples fail. 'Armstrong' and 'Columnare' are eastern cultivars that are narrow and upright. 'Autumn Flame', 'Bowhall', 'October Glory', 'Red Sunset', and 'Schlesingeri' are eastern cultivars selected for their fall color; under growing conditions in this area, their fall color may be inferior to that of some of our native trees. When buying a red maple, make your selection in the fall from trees growing in the nursery when you can see the color of the fall foliage.

A. saccharinum (Silver Maple). Hardy in all zones. The silver maple is often planted for quick shade, because it grows rapidly to a very large size of 60 or more feet. The wood is brittle, and broken branches are common after windstorms and ice storms. Because it is large, this species should not be planted in small yards. The cut-leaved cultivars 'Beebe' and 'Blair' have narrow leaf lobes and are attractive when young.

A. saccharum (Sugar Maple). Hardy in all zones. Where soil conditions are proper, the sugar maple is an excellent large tree, 60 or more feet tall, with fall color varying from yellow to red. It grows best on heavy clay loam soils that are moisture retentive and on a north-facing slope. As with *A. rubrum* (red maple), selections should have good fall color. Several cultivars have been selected and named for their form. 'Newton Sentry' is very narrow and upright. 'Temple Upright' is columnar. 'Globosum' forms an upright globe that tapers at the top. 'Green Mountain' and 'Sweet Shadow' are cultivars of normal rounded shape.

A. spicatum (Mountain Maple). Hardy in all zones. A shrublike maple native along the North Shore of Lake Superior, where it is sometimes planted as an ornamental. By special pruning it can be trained to grow into a small tree that is 20 feet tall. The fall color is a beautiful orange-red. This species requires acid soil.

A. tataricum (Tartarian Maple). Hardy in all zones. Similar to *A. ginnala* (Amur maple), with which it often hybridizes, but is a little taller and the leaves lack conspicuous lobes. This is an excellent small tree, reaching a height of 25 feet.

AESCULUS (Buckeye, Horse Chestnut). Several species of buckeye are native to North America, but the horse chestnut is a species native to Europe. The genus is characterized by opposite, palmately compound leaves, large winter buds, and shiny brown nuts. Marginal leaf scorch can be a problem during a hot, dry summer, and the nuts are sometimes messy when they fall to the ground.

A. x *carnea* 'Briotii' (Ruby Horse Chestnut). Suggested for trial in zones 4a, 4b, and 5a. Selection resulting from a cross between *A. hippocastanum* (common horse chestnut) and *A. pavia* (red buckeye). Under growing conditions in our area, this will probably be a small tree under 25 feet. The large, bright red flowers borne in upright clusters make the tree striking when in bloom. This cultivar has flowered in a garden in North Oaks and at the arboretum.

A. glabra (Ohio Buckeye). Hardy in all zones. This native of the East Central United States is surprisingly hardy and can be grown throughout the North Central states and southern Canada. It forms a round-headed tree up to 40 feet tall. The greenish-yellow flowers are in 6 inch, upright panicles. The foliage is normally light green. A long-lived tree.

A. hippocastanum (Common Horse Chestnut). Trial in 4a; hardy in zones 4b and 5a. Although some nice-looking trees can be found in southern Minnesota, hardiness is borderline in the Twin Cities area. This European species is taller and not as hardy as *A. glabra* (Ohio buckeye), with larger and showier flowers. It is a large tree in milder climates but seldom grows more than 45 feet tall in our area. The leaves turn rusty brown along the edges in midsummer.

A. sylvatica (Painted Buckeye). Hardy in all zones. Trees in the arboretum were grown from seeds obtained from the Morton Arboretum near Chicago. All have grown well and appear to be as hardy as and faster growing than *A. glabra* (Ohio buckeye), with a mature height of about 40 feet. One tree in particular shows unusual vigor, has dark green summer foliage, and turns brilliant red in the fall. It has been named 'Autumn Splendor.' This tree may be a hybrid. It is being propagated and will be tested under a variety of conditions.

AMELANCHIER (Serviceberry). A large genus grown for early spring bloom and attractive red to purple fruits which ripen in July. Because plants tend to sucker, it is best to grow them in clumps of several stems. Leaf diseases can be a problem, and birds usually eat the fruits as soon as they turn color.

A. arborea (Downy Serviceberry). Hardy in all zones. A small tree that normally grows in a clump, reaching a height of 25 to 30 feet. The young leaves are downy and silvery green. The small, white flowers are produced in small, nodding racemes. The fall color is yellow to red.

A. x *grandiflora* (Apple Serviceberry). Hardy in all zones. A natural hybrid resulting from a cross between *A. arborea* and *A. laevis*. Excellent when grown as a clump, this small tree reaches a height of 20 feet. The crown is usually rounded, with wide-spreading branches. The new growth in the spring has a purplish cast; then in early May showy, white flowers bloom that are 1 inch in diameter. Sometimes, in a cool spring, the flower buds and opening flowers have a pinkish cast. Many consider this the best *Amelanchier*.

A. laevis (Alleghany Serviceberry). Hardy in all zones. This native is the most widely planted of the tree-type *Amelanchiers* in this area. The mature height is 25 to 30 feet. The foliage is purplish in early spring, turning green as the leaves open fully. The flowers are white, showy, in drooping racemes. Summer fruits are red. In the fall the leaves turn yellow or red.

BETULA (Birch). The birches are popular lawn trees grown for their papery bark. In nature, injury to young trees often results in natural clumps. To produce this effect, nurserymen often plant 3 or more trees in the same planting hole. A better method is to cut a young tree back and allow several stems to develop from the same root system. The bronze birch borers are serious problems on most white-barked birches and often cause premature death of the trees.

B. lenta (Sweet Birch). Hardy in all zones. A medium-sized tree, to 45 feet, that is pyramidal when young and rounded at maturity. The golden-yellow fall color is striking. The dark, cherrylike bark contrasts with the white of the snow in winter. The bark of young twigs has a pleasant, wintergreen flavor when chewed. This species is highly resistant to the bronze birch borer.

B. nigra (River Birch). Hardy in zones 4a, 4b, and 5a. A clump birch growing to a height of 40 or more feet. It is native along river bottoms from Florida to southeastern Minnesota. The papery, exfoliating bark is reddish-brown and most attractive in winter. As the tree reaches maturity, the bark on the trunk turns black. Although native to wet soils, this birch shows a surprising degree of drought resistance; it has grown as well or better on upland soils as on low, wet soils. It also seems resistant to the bronze birch borer. Plant northern strains.

B. papyrifera (Canoe Birch or Paper Birch). Hardy in all zones. Our native, white-barked birch grows to 45 feet. In nature it usually grows on north-facing slopes or at the edge of swamps where the soil is cool and moist. When planted on an exposed lawn, it is subjected to moisture stresses. During periods of drought, it is very vulnerable to attack by the bronze birch borer.

B. pendula (European White Birch). Hardy in all zones. Resembles *B. papyrifera* (canoe birch) and is even more susceptible to injury from the bronze birch borer. The mature height is about 40 feet. The species is not planted as often as some of its cultivars. 'Tristis' is a weeping form with slender, pendulous branches. 'Gracilis' is similar, with dissected leaves. This is usually sold under the name cutleaf European birch. 'Youngii' has drooping branches and is picturesque. 'Purpurea' has purple leaves and twigs. 'Fastigiata' grows narrow and upright. 'Youngi', 'Purpurea', and 'Fastigiata' have not been very long-lived in the arboretum.

B. platyphylla var. *japonica* (Japanese White Birch). Hardy in all zones. In an effort to find a white-barked birch with resistance to bronze birch borer, a number of species have been planted and observed. So far this 40-foot-tall birch is the only species that shows much promise. A replicated experiment has been set up in the arboretum to determine the degree of resistance to the borer. If this species proves resistant, it should largely replace the other white-barked birches.

Carpinus betulus (European Hornbeam). Hardy in zones 4a, 4b, and 5a. A small to medium tree reaching a height of 25 to 30 feet. Trees are upright when young but become spreading as they mature. The branches are smooth and angular, giving a distinctive appearance, especially in winter. The nutlike fruits are produced on leaflike bracts in pendulous clusters resembling hops. Two upright cultivars are on the market: 'Columnaris' is dense and egg shaped, with a central trunk; 'Fastigiata' becomes vase shaped with age and has no central trunk.

Carpinus caroliniana (American Hornbeam or Blue Beech). Hardy in all zones. A native tree similar to *C. betulus* (European hornbeam) but smaller, 20 to 25 feet tall. It is usually found growing with several trunks and forms a broad, mound-shaped crown. It can be trained as a single-stemmed tree.

CARYA (Hickory). The hickories are native to North America. They have deep taproots which make them difficult to transplant, except when small. Nursery-grown trees that have been root pruned transplant more successfully than trees that have not been so pruned. The most successful means of starting a hickory is to plant a nut where you want the tree to grow. The hickories are long-lived and attractive ornamentals.

C. cordiformis (Bitternut). Hardy in all zones. This native tree grows to a height of 45 feet. It is easily recognized by its long, yellow winter buds. The fruits are small and bitter tasting. This tree is subject to an insect gall that forms on the twigs and which can be unsightly. One may wish to preserve this tree if it is growing on one's property, but it is not ordinarily planted.

C. laciniosa (Shellbark Hickory). Trial in zone 4a; hardy in zones 4b and 5a. A large tree, to 60 feet, that has not been widely planted in this area. Peter Gideon, founder of the 'Wealthy' apple, planted seeds of the shellbark hickory about 100 years ago near Excelsior, Minnesota. The trees are still living and in good health. Seeds from one of these trees were planted at the Horticultural Research Center about 30 years ago. Two of the resulting seedlings were moved to the arboretum soon after its founding and are now over 20 feet tall, with excellent form and healthy foliage. One of the better hickories for landscape planting.

C. ovata (Shagbark Hickory). Hardy in zones 4a, 4b, and 5a. Native to southeastern Minnesota and characterized at maturity by bark that flakes off in long, narrow strips, giving a shaggy appearance to the trunk. The rate of growth is comparable to that of *C. laciniosa* (shellbark hickory). The mature height is about 60 feet. Trees in the arboretum are now about 20 years old and have not yet developed the shaggy bark.

Castanea dentata (American Chestnut). Hardy in zones 4a, 4b, and 5a. Other chestnut species, including *C. mollissima* (Chinese chestnut) and *C. sativa* (European chestnut), have not proved hardy in this area. The American chestnut was all but eliminated by the chestnut blight that ravaged native stands within the natural range for this species. A few trees planted outside this range escaped the disease owing to their isolation. Mature trees in our area, which is beyond the natural range, are about 60 feet tall. The American chestnut is not recommended for general planting because of the danger from the chestnut blight, but it is nice to have the species represented in some of our public and private gardens. A number of fine specimens may be seen at the arboretum.

Catalpa bignonioides (Southern Catalpa). Similar to *C. speciosa* (northern catalpa) and appears to be about as hardy.

Catalpa speciosa (Northern Catalpa). Hardy in zones 4a, 4b, and 5a. This rather coarse, 45-foot-tall tree with large, heart-shaped leaves is not planted as much today as it was earlier in the century. The flowers are large (2 inches in diameter), creamy white with yellow stripes and brown dots, and arranged in upright panicles. When in bloom the tree is beautiful, but when the flowers drop a mess is left on the ground. For this reason, planting is usually limited to parks and large grounds.

Celtis occidentalis (Hackberry). Hardy in all zones. The most widely planted species of *Celtis* in the Upper Midwest. It is a large, stately tree 60 or more feet tall, with a prominently ribbed bark.

The fruits are round and berrylike, with a dry, pulpy shell that has a sweet taste—hence its common name sugar berry. Although long-lived and capable of growing on most soils, this tree develops two diseases: a nipplelike gall, caused by a midge, forms on the undersurface of the leaves, and a "witches broom," caused by a fungus, forms on the small branches. Neither of these problems seems to seriously affect the health of the tree.

Cercis canadensis (Eastern Redbud). Trial in zones 4a and 4b; hardy in zone 5a. This lovely, small tree is seldom planted much north of central Iowa. Nursery-grown trees from seed collected within its natural range, which extends into southern Iowa, usually lack hardiness when planted in this area. A few trees planted in the Twin Cities and Rochester, Minnesota have survived and flower nicely each year. A population of seedlings grown from one of these trees located at the Horticultural Research Center have survived and are now flowering and fruiting at the arboretum. It is hoped that these will serve as a hardy seed source for this area. The redbud is a spreading tree that grows to 25 feet, with purplish-pink, pealike flowers in early May. The leaves are heart shaped and turn golden-yellow in the fall.

Cladrastis lutea (Yellow-wood). Suggested for trial in sheltered locations in zone 4a; hardy in zones 4b and 5a. This southern tree, native from North Carolina to Tennessee, is seldom planted in our area. In a sheltered location it grows and flowers, and several trees are doing well at the arboretum. The tree is vase shaped with several main branches growing from near the base of the trunk. The mature height is about 20 feet. The white, pealike flowers are produced in long, pendant clusters. The pods are constricted between the seeds.

Cornus alternifolia (Pagoda Dogwood). Hardy in all zones. The only treelike dogwood that can be grown in this area. Most attempts to grow *C. florida* (flowering dogwood) have met with failure. The pagoda dogwood forms a small tree about 20 feet tall. The alternate branches are formed in horizontal layers, suggesting a Japanese pagoda. This tree normally grows as a clump in nature, but it can be trained as a single-stemmed tree. The small flowers are creamy white, in flat-topped clusters. They lack the 4 white bracts that surround the flowers of *C. florida*.

Crataegus crus-galli (Cockspur Hawthorn). Hardy in zones 4a, 4b, and 5a. Of the many species of hawthorn that can be grown in this area, this is the only one that appears to have much resistance to cedar-hawthorn rust disease, which causes defoliation. The cockspur hawthorn is a spreading, flat-topped tree that fits the prairie landscape. It grows to 20 feet, with small, rounded leaves that are dark glossy green. The white flowers are produced in flat-topped clusters in early June. The long, pointed thorns can be a problem for small children; those who object to the thorns may plant the thornless cultivar 'Inermis'.

Crataegus x *mordenensis* 'Toba'. Hardy in all zones. A 20-foot-tall hybrid developed by the Experimental Station at Morden, Manitoba from a cross between 'Pauls Scarlet', a cultivar of *C. oxycantha*, and *C. succulenta*, a native species of hawthorn. It combines the hardiness of the native species and the double flowers of 'Pauls Scarlet'. The flowers open white but turn pink as they age. This variety has some resistance to cedar-hawthorn rust disease. Small, orange rust spots may appear on the leaves, but these spots do not enlarge to involve much of the leaf surface. 'Snowbird', a 20-foot-tall, white-flowered cultivar from the same cross, also shows promise.

Elaeagnus angustifolia (Russian Olive). Hardy in all zones. This small tree, up to 20 feet tall, is grown for its silvery-green, willow-like foliage. When in bloom during early June, the small, yellow flowers give off a delightful fragrance in the evening. The Russian olive does best on well-drained soil. Use as a specimen tree or in the back of the shrub border.

Fagus grandifolia (American Beech). Trial in all zones. Within its natural range, which extends into eastern Wisconsin and the Upper Peninsula of Michigan, the American beech is a beautiful large tree, to 90 feet. In Minnesota it has not been grown very satisfactorily and its height does not exceed 50 feet. It may be that our winters are too dry as well as too cold. If grown at all, the American beech should be planted in a sheltered location where the plants will receive ample moisture. Several trees have been planted in the Twin Cities area, and some of these are growing nicely at the arboretum.

FRAXINUS (Ash). This is an important genus containing several species and cultivars that are widely planted as shade trees. The leaves are opposite and pinnately compound. The trees are slow to leaf in the spring and drop their leaves early in the fall.

F. americana (White Ash). Hardy in zones 4a, 4b, and 5a. This large tree is native to southern and eastern Minnesota and grows 60 feet tall. It differs from *F. pennsylvanica* (the native green ash) in the fall color of its foliage, which is usually a shade of purple. Efforts are being made to select superior clones for fall color. 'Autumn Purple' is one such cultivar.

F. nigra (Black Ash). Hardy in all zones. A native ash that reaches a height of 45 feet and is usually found growing on low, wet soils. It is susceptible to a gall-forming mite that attacks the male flower clusters. Some work is being done to develop superior clones of the black ash.

F. pennsylvanica (Green Ash). Hardy in all zones. Common, widely planted ash that grows to 45 feet. Male and female flowers are produced on separate trees, and the foliage is golden-yellow in the fall. The green ash is drought resistant and grows on most soils. Because the tree is resistant to alkali chlorosis, it is especially good on alkaline soils. If one objects to the fruits, a male tree like the 'Marshall Seedless' should be planted. 'Summit' is another superior cultivar, and new selections are being made.

F. quadrangulata (Blue Ash). Trial in zone 4a; hardy in zones 4b and 5a. A large tree within its natural range, which is from Michigan to Tennessee. In this area it is rather slow growing and forms a round-headed tree that is 40 feet tall. It is characterized by 4 parallel ridges on young twigs. The sap contains a bluish-colored dye (hence the common name), and the foliage is dark green. A promising, medium-sized tree.

Ginkgo biloba (Ginkgo). Trial in zone 4a; hardy in zones 4b and 5a. A most interesting tree because of its antiquity. The species is reported to have been native to North America 150 million years ago. Although it disappeared from the North American continent, remnants of the species persisted in China. The tree was reintroduced into the United States about 1784. It grows to 45 feet in this area. Because it has bilobed, glossy green leaves, it was given the common name maidenhair tree. The fruits are plumlike and when fully ripe give off an offensive odor. Therefore, only male trees should be planted. It is best to plant fairly small trees. 'Fastigiata' is a narrow and upright cultivar; 'Pendula' has drooping branches.

Gleditsia triacanthos (Honeylocust). Hardy in zones 4a, 4b, and 5a, but at Grand Rapids, Minnesota the trees have killed back nearly to the ground. Reaching a mature height of about 60 feet, the honeylocust has an open, spreading crown, with fine-textured, compound leaves and long, pointed, branched spines which can be hazardous. The seed pods are long and numerous, containing beanlike seeds. Usually, only male trees are planted. A number of thornless, male selections have been named: 'Imperial', 'Shademaster', and 'Skyline' are examples. 'Sunburst' is another cultivar; its leaves are golden when they open and turn green as they reach maturity.

Gymnocladus dioica (Kentucky Coffeetree). Hardy in zones 4a, 4b, and 5a. A large, picturesque tree that grows 60 feet tall and is a native as far north as the Twin Cities. Thre is some question about the origin of a few of the older trees in this area. These may have been planted from a more southerly source by the Indians. The species is characterized by very large, twice pinnate leaves. There are few small lateral branches, giving a stark appearance to the trees in winter. The bark is deeply furrowed, and the pods are large and thick. Some people consider the pods a nuisance, and if this is of concern, plant a male tree. Few insect or disease problems affect this species.

Hippophae rhamnoides (Russian Sea Buckthorn), Hardy in zones 3b, 4a, 4b, and 5a. A small tree or large shrub that grows to 20 feet, with long, slender, silvery-green leaves. The sexes are separate, so plants of both sexes must be grown to obtain fruit. The female plants produce bright orange berries which are attractive in the fall and early winter. Good drainage is required.

Juglans cinerea (Butternut). Hardy in zones 4a, 4b, and 5a. A medium tree that grows to a height of 45 feet, with pinnately compound leaves. The nuts are elongated, deeply ridged, and very hard. Young twigs are pubescent. Sometimes planted for its shade and edible nuts.

Juglans nigra (Black Walnut). Hardy in all zones. This large tree grows 60 feet tall and is often planted for its shade and edible nuts. Where squirrels are abundant, the nuts may be more a problem than an advantage. Caterpillars can cause defoliation.

MAGNOLIA (Magnolia). Although the magnolias are native to the southeastern states and the Orient, they have shown a surprising degree of hardiness in this area. Most magnolias have big, showy flowers that open before the leaves unfold in the spring and large, dark green leaves.

M. acuminata (Cucumber Tree). Trial in zone 4a; hardy in zones 4b and 5a. One of the hardier magnolias and the largest that can be grown in this area. Under favorable conditions it grows into a large tree, but in this area it seldom exceeds 40 feet. It is upright when young but forms a wide-spreading crown at maturity. The flowers are greenish-yellow and about 3 inches across, opening after the leaves develop. The fruits are pink to red, embedded in a cucumber-shaped shell.

M. x *loebneri* 'Merrill'. Trial in zone 4a; hardy in zones 4b and 5a. A cross between *M. kobus* and *M. stellata*. Trees are upright when young, growing to a height of 15 feet. The flowers are white in early May and larger than those of *M. stellata*. A promising cultivar for sheltered locations.

M. salicifolia (Anise Magnolia). Trial in zone 4a; hardy in zones 4b and 5a. The bloom has been rather sparse, indicating a possible lack of flower bud hardiness. Crushed leaves of this magnolia give off a distinct anise fragrance. Young trees are compact and pyramidal, and the mature size is about 20 feet. The white flowers open before the leaves come out in the spring.

M. x *soulangiana* (Saucer Magnolia). Trial in zones 4a and 4b; hardy in zone 5a. This hybrid species and its numerous cultivars have not been very hardy in trials at the arboretum, although a few trees have survived and flowered in sheltered locations in the Twin Cities area. This is one of the more popular magnolias in eastern parts of the country. The height seldom exceeds 20 feet in our area. The flowers are large, saucer shaped, and white to purple. Plant only in sheltered locations.

M. stellata (Star Magnolia). Trial in zone 4a; hardy in zones 4b and 5a. One of the better magnolias to be planted. It is a small, spreading tree under 15 feet. The showy, white flowers are produced in abundance in early May but are sometimes destroyed by frost. 'Waterlily' is an excellent cultivar.

M. tripetala (Umbrella Magnolia). Trial in zone 4a; hardy in zones 4b and 5a. This species has been hardy at the arboretum, where the oldest trees are about 20 feet tall. The umbrella magnolia has the largest leaves of any magnolia that can be grown in this area. Leaves that are 18 inches long and 6 inches wide are not uncommon. Like *M. acuminata* (cucumber tree), this magnolia blooms after the leaves are fully open.

MALUS (Flowering Crabapples). Hardy in all zones. Many cultivars of flowering crabapples can be grown in this area. Over 150 of these may be seen in the arboretum collection. The arboretum staff is interested in cultivars that retain their attractive bloom as long as possible and those that have good-looking fruits which do not drop to the ground when ripe. Cultivars with small fruits adhering to the trees provide excellent winter food for birds and other wildlife. The arboretum staff is also most interested in cultivars that are resistant to apple scab, fire blight, and cedar apple rust. Few cultivars combine all these desirable traits. However, after a number of years of observation at the arboretum, the following species and cultivars are rated excellent: *Malus baccata* (Siberian crabapple), 'David', 'Flame', 'Golden Hornet', 'Henry F. Dupont', 'Liset', 'Pink Spires', 'Profusion', 'Red Splendor', 'Ringo', 'Sparkler', and 'Spring Snow'. There are many others that might be used for specific purposes: 'Red Jade' is planted for its weeping appearance, *M. baccata* 'Columnaris' for its upright form, and 'Royalty' for its red foliage.

Morus alba var. *tatarica* (Russian Mulberry). Hardy in zones 4a, 4b, and 5a. The hardiest mulberry and the only one commonly planted. It is a small tree reaching a height of possibly 25 feet. The fruits provide food for birds, which supposedly prefer mulberry fruits to cherry, raspberry, and strawberry fruits. I have not observed this to be necessarily true. If you have a single cherry tree, it is best to protect the fruits with a bird netting regardless of the number of mulberries you have planted. Birds plant the mulberry seeds, and seedlings volunteer for some distance around the parent tree. There are better small trees to plant than the mulberry.

Nyssa sylvatica (Sour Gum). Trial in zone 4a; hardy in zones 4b and 5a. Native to the eastern United States, this small tree is being tested at the arboretum for hardiness. The height rarely exceeds 25 feet, and the form is pyramidal, with drooping branchlets. The leaves are dark green and leathery, turning brilliant scarlet to orange in the fall. Select a sheltered location since this tree is out of its natural range in this area, and plant on slightly acid soil.

Ostrya virginiana (Hop Hornbeam or Ironwood). Hardy in all zones. This medium-sized native tree has been largely overlooked as an ornamental. It often grows with multiple stems and makes an excellent clump tree. It is 45 feet tall, with a well-rounded crown. The hoplike fruits are effective in late summer, and the longitudinally ridged bark adds winter interest. The tree is reported to be difficult to transplant, but at the arboretum we have experienced no difficulty in establishing it. This species is quite free of insect and disease problems.

Paulownia tomentosa (Royal Paulownia). Lacks hardiness in all zones. Indeed, the species is not considered top hardy much north of St. Louis, Missouri, and in this area it is subject to winter die-back. It is mentioned only because of the national publicity it has received in recent years. Advertisers claim that it is root hardy in

Montreal, but they make no claim for the hardiness of the parts above ground, which is important when considering the hardiness of a tree. In areas where the royal paulownia can be grown, it is an attractive tree that grows rapidly to about 40 feet. It has large, coarse leaves and showy flowers produced in pyramidal clusters. The flowers are fragrant and violet colored.

Phellodendron amurense (Amur Cork Tree). Hardy in zones 4a, 4b, and 5a. Virtually the only cork tree propagated for landscape use. It grows to a height of about 30 feet and has a spread of 30 or more feet. The tree is characterized by deeply fissured, corklike bark and massive, wide-spreading branches. It is bisexual, producing clusters of black, berrylike fruits which persist into winter. There are few insect or disease problems. Other species of *Phellodendron* may also offer promise. One acquisition, obtained as seed of the *P. sachalinense* (Sakhalin cork tree), has grown much faster than the Amur and may prove to be of hybrid origin. This is being considered for introduction.

Platanus x *acerifolia* (London Plane Tree). Trial in zones 4a and 4b; hardy in zone 5a. Young trees planted in the arboretum are doing fine, but how hardy this hybrid will be remains to be seen. It would not be expected to be as hardy as *P. occidentalis* (the native sycamore) because of its origin: it is a cross between *P. occidentalis* and *P. orientalis* (Oriental plane tree). The London plane tree is widely planted in the East and in Europe to line streets and for shade. It grows 100 feet tall and develops a trunk diameter of 6 or more feet in milder climates but seldom exceeds 40 feet in this area. The bark exfoliates, showing patches of light-colored, often yellowish inner bark. The leaves are lobed like maple leaves.

Platanus occidentalis (Sycamore). Trial in zones 4a and 4b; hardy in zone 5a. This species is not considered fully hardy even in the Twin Cities area. There may be some tip kill after a severe winter and dead twigs along the main branches are not uncommon. The sycamore is native throughout the eastern part of the United States. A few trees have been planted in this area, and some have grown to a fair size, to 40 or more feet. The maplelike leaves and the light-colored, blotched trunk resulting from the exfoliation of the bark are characteristic features that make it easy to recognize this species. Although it is not fully hardy, you may wish to plant the sycamore because of its interesting bark. Plant in a sheltered location and maintain ample soil moisture.

POPULUS (Aspen, Cottonwood, Poplar). A large genus containing many fast-growing species. As ornamentals, most species are not satisfactory because they grow too big for most yards. Cytospora canker can be a problem, and the "cotton" that blows around when the seeds of female trees are dispersed is objectionable.

P. alba (White Poplar). Hardy in all zones. This poplar is a medium-sized tree reaching 45 feet, with grayish-white bark and maple-shaped leaves that are silvery-white underneath. The tree is sometimes falsely called silver maple or white maple. Since it has the objectionable habit of sending up numerous root suckers, it is not recommended for landscape use in residential areas. The cultivar 'Pyramidalis' is often planted for its upright form, but it is not very long-lived and often starts dying after 5 to 10 years. This cultivar requires much water, and its roots can be a problem when growing a lawn or flowers.

P. deltoides (Cottonwood). Hardy in all zones. Frequently planted in the past as a fast-growing tree and still planted in shelterbelts in drier parts of the region. The cottonwood grows to be a very large tree, to 80 feet, which is out of scale in most yards. Because the cotton from female trees can be a nuisance, many communities now ban the use of this species for street planting. Where leaf rust disease is a problem on cottonwoods, you might plant the male cultivar 'Siouxland', which is resistant to the disease.

P. maximowiczii (Japanese Poplar). Hardy in zones 4a, 4b, and 5a. One of the best of the poplars, in arboretum trials and according to Dr. Donald Wyman's book *Trees for American Gardens*. The tree grows to 60 feet. The light green leaves develop early in the spring and turn golden-yellow in the fall.

P. nigra 'Italica' (Lombardy Poplar). Hardy in zones 4a, 4b, and 5a. Reaching a height of 45 feet, this narrow, upright cultivar of the black poplar is often planted as a fast-growing screen. Unfortunately, it is often short-lived because it is susceptible to the "cytospora canker" disease that affects the base of the lateral branches.

P. tremula var. *erecta* (Upright European Aspen). Trial in zone 4a; hardy in zones 4b and 5a. Plants are being tested to determine whether this tree might be used in place of the short-lived *P. albus* 'Pyramidalis' and *P. nigra* 'Italica'. Preliminary results appear favorable. This narrow, upright tree, growing 40 feet tall, is native to Sweden.

P. tremuloides (Quaking Aspen). Hardy in all zones. A native aspen 45 feet tall, with small, quivering leaves. It is of interest mainly for naturalizing. The whitish bark provides winter interest, and the golden autumn foliage is also very attractive. This aspen sends up many root suckers and should not be planted where these would be objectionable.

PRUNUS (Apricot, Cherry, Plum). Several species of *Prunus* are planted as ornamentals. All have showy, white flowers in early May and colorful, red to purple fruits in summer. The fruits are fleshy drupes.

P. americana (Wild Plum). Hardy in all zones. The common wild plum often forms thickets along American roadsides. It grows to 15 feet and is most attractive in spring with its numerous white flowers. It also produces small, reddish fruits which are prized for making preserves. This plum is often used as a rootstock for cultivated plums. The root suckers can take over and crowd out the cultivated plum. These suckers must be removed as soon as they appear.

P. armeniaca var. *mandshurica* (Manchurian Apricot). Hardy in all zones. This is the only hardy apricot that can be grown in our region. It is a small, spreading tree that reaches 20 feet at maturity. The white to pink flowers in early May, the colorful yellow fruits in July, and the golden-yellow fall color make this an attractive ornamental. The fruits can be used for preserves.

P. maackii (Amur Cherry). Hardy in all zones. Often develops several stems from the base and hence is best grown as a small, clump tree. The mature height is about 30 feet. The bark is the most interesting feature of this tree: the reddish-brown color and papery, exfoliating nature of the bark make it very attractive in winter, when color is needed. The flowers and fruits resemble those of *P. virginiana* (the native chokecherry). It is hoped that this species will become generally available.

P. 'Newport'. Hardy in zones 4a, 4b, and 5a. A hybrid developed at the Horticultural Research Center by crossing the 'Omaha' plum with *P. cerasifera* 'Atropurpurea'. This small tree, which is 15 feet tall, is grown for its reddish purple foliage. Often short-lived.

P. padus var. *commutata* (Mayday Tree). Hardy in all zones. Obtained its common name from the bloom in early May. The tree grows to a height of 25 feet. The flowers are larger and showier than *P. virginiana* flowers, and the fruits are black and sparsely produced. This species is very susceptible to the fungus disease known as "black knot."

P. pensylvanica (Pincherry). Hardy in all zones. This attractive native cherry, which is 25 to 30 feet tall, is seldom palnted. The double-flowered cultivar 'Stockton' is showier than the species and develops into a small, round-headed tree with bright red fall color.

P. serotina (Black Cherry). Hardy in all zones. The largest and best of the native cherries, often reaching a height of 45 or more feet and a trunk diameter of 1½ feet. The flowers resemble those of *P. virginiana*. The small, black fruits hang in pendant clusters and are messy when eaten by birds. These fruits are distinguished from *P. virginiana* fruits by a cuplike enlargement of the calyx at the base of each fruit. This tree is better for large grounds and parklike plantings than for small yards.

P. virginiana (Chokecherry). Hardy in all zones. Small tree or large shrub that is seldom planted except for naturalizing at the edge of a woods or for bird food. The leaves of the cultivar 'Shubert' (also sold as 'Canada Red') turn coppery red as they mature. The cultivar grows to a height of about 20 feet and makes an excellent screen. It can be trained as a small tree and is an attractive lawn specimen. Like all chokecherries, this cultivar sends up suckers which should be removed if it is being grown as a single-stemmed tree.

Ptelea trifoliata (Hoptree). Trial in zone 4a; hardy in zones 4b and 5a. This native of the eastern United States and Canada appears to be hardy at the arboretum. An open, spreading plant, the hoptree can be grown as a shrub or a small tree. The mature height is about 18 feet. The trifoliate leaves and the waferlike fruits add interest.

QUERCUS (Oak). A large and interesting genus containing many species of forest and landscape trees. The genus is divided into the white oak group, characterized by rounded leaf lobes, and the black oak group, with pointed leaf lobes. *Q. alba*, *Q. bicolor*, *Q. macrocarpa*, and *Q. robur* belong to the white oak group; *Q. palustris* and *Q. rubra* to the black oak group. Because they have taproots, oaks are generally considered difficult to transplant. However, nursery-grown stock that has been transplanted and properly root pruned can be moved successfully. Another mistaken idea is that oaks are extremely slow growing. This probably resulted from observing oaks on poor soils, where they often grow. When grown on fertile, well-drained soil and given proper care, oaks grow about as fast as other tree species. Avoid soil compaction. Oak wilt can be a problem on oaks, especially when they are grown close together. The disease spreads underground through the root systems from diseased to healthy trees. The symptoms are sudden wilting and death of the tree. Wide spacing and interplanting oaks with other tree species minimize the danger from oak wilt. Oaks should be pruned only during the winter months to reduce the chances of spreading the disease on pruning tools.

Q. alba (White Oak). Hardy in zones 3b, 4a, 4b, and 5a. The white oak is an especially fine, large tree with an oval shape at maturity. It grows 60 or more feet tall. The leaves have rounded and deep lobes and are light green; their fall color is purplish-red to violet-purple. Acorns may be a problem where squirrels are abundant.

Q. bicolor (Swamp White Oak). Hardy in zones 4a, 4b, and 5a. Another white oak with rounded leaf lobes. It is 45 feet tall and its leaves are dark green with a yellowish-brown fall color. This native of low, wet soils does not develop the prominent taproot that is characteristic of most oaks. It transplants readily and grows into a

Zinnias are one of the more popular garden flowers. The diameter of the flowers varies from less than 1 inch in the small button types to 5 inches in the large cactus-flowered types. Flower colors include orange, scarlet, purple, rose, salmon, and yellow.

An open gate with an inviting stretch of cool, green lawn connects two backyards. Roses are planted on either side, with an interesting foreground planting of annuals on the right.

A shade-loving ground cover, *Pachysandra terminalis*, borders the walk, and plants of *Impatiens wallerana* grow at the edge of the shaded terrace.

Above: Color is added to a foundation planting with roses, geraniums, and sweet alyssum. Below: A mixed flower border above a stone wall, featuring zinnias, sweet alyssum, and petunias.

Above: A new hybrid azalea, hardy to −40°F, is being developed at the arboretum and will be introduced in 1979. Below: An interesting dwarf conifer, *Chamaecyparis pisifera* 'Filifera', in the arboretum.

Above: *Forsythia ovata* (early forsythia) from Korea is the hardiest forsythia and blooms most years. Below: *Viburnum opulus* (European
highbush cranberry) is planted for its colorful fruits and showy flowers.

Above: *Syringa pekinensis* (Peking lilac), a small tree from China.
Below left: *Prunus maackii* (Amur cherry) with colorful winter
bark. Below right: *Carpinus caroliniana* (blue beech) in fall color.

Above: A colorful sunny flower border with a background of spider flowers and a foreground of coleus, helenium, and zinnias. Below: Shade-loving tuberous begonias, caladiums, and impatiens.

A foreground planting of the 'Peace' rose, one of the more popular hybrid tea roses, with a background of tall, pink dahlias.

beautiful tree. It has developed well on upland soils in the arbo-retum.

Q. macrocarpa (Burr Oak). Hardy in all zones. Seldom planted but an excellent, long-lived tree. Where growing native in a landscape planting, it should be preserved if possible. Mature trees are state-ly, 50 feet tall, with sturdy branches. Each leaf has a large, termi-nal lobe, and the bark is more deeply furrowed than on *Q. alba* (white oak). The cup at the base of the acorn resembles a burr.

Q. palustris (Eastern Pin Oak). Hardy in zones 4a, 4b, and 5a. Per-haps the most widely planted of all oaks. It grows with a central trunk to a height of about 50 feet. Lower branches on mature trees tend to droop, upper branches grow upright, and branches in the center grow at right angles to the trunk. The leaves are more deeply lobed than those of *Q. rubra* (red oak). The fall color is scarlet. The eastern pin oak likes slightly acid soil, and iron chloro-sis can be a problem on alkaline soils.

Q. robur (English Oak). Trial in zone 4a; hardy in zones 4b and 5a. Widely grown in the East and in Europe. Only a few trees have been planted in the Upper Midwest, where they reach a height of about 40 feet. Trees planted in the arboretum are growing well. The leaves are shaped something like those of *Q. macrocarpa* (burr oak) but are much smaller. The upright cultivar 'Fastigiata' is often planted. It has the same form as *P. nigra* 'Italica'.

Q. rubra (Red Oak). Hardy in zones 3b, 4a, 4b, and 5a. This oak has a deeply furrowed bark and grows to a height of 70 or more feet. It develops an attractive red to rusty-red fall color. Oak wilt disease is a problem with this species, especially in native stands. Red oaks are seldom planted, but where you have them growing in your yard, every effort should be made to protect them from the disease.

Robinia pseudoacacia (Black Locust). Hardy in zones 4a, 4b, and 5a. A medium-sized tree that seldom grows over 50 feet tall. The white, pealike flowers hang in pendant clusters in early June. Pre-fers well-drained soil. This would be a desirable tree except it is often killed by the stem borer. 'Umbraculifera' is a globe-shaped cultivar with a rounded head.

SALIX (Willow). A large genus containing over 300 species. Only a few are planted as landscape trees. Male and female catkins are produced on separate trees, and the "cotton" from female trees can be objectionable. Willows are generally fast growing and prefer moist soils.

S. alba (White Willow). Hardy in zones 4a, 4b, and 5a. This European species grows 45 feet tall and is sometimes used in shelterbelts. The cultivar 'Tristis' (Golden Weeping Willow) is often planted. Its golden twigs in early spring and its weeping appearance add interest. This tree is best planted near water. If located in the yard, its shedding branches can be messy and the drooping branches may be a nuisance when mowing the lawn. The bright red stems of the cultivar 'Chermesina' are especially attractive in late winter. Since the color is brightest on young stems, this cultivar is often grown as a shrub that is cut to the ground early each spring.

S. matsudana 'Tortuosa' (Corkscrew Willow). Trial in zones 4a and 4b; hardy in zone 5a. The corkscrew willow is not fully hardy and winter dieback is common. Introduced from China and Korea in 1923, the tree is small and upright, growing to 20 feet. The twisted, corkscrewlike branches are often used in flower arrangements. Plant in a sheltered spot and provide plenty of water.

S. pentandra (Laurel Willow). Hardy in all zones. One of the better willows that can be planted. It is a medium-sized tree, 40 feet tall, and its elongated, dark green leaves resemble *Kalmia latifolia* (mountain laurel) leaves. A good tree to use as a background or screen planting and in shelterbelts.

SORBUS (Mountain-ash). A large genus containing many species and cultivars. The pinnately compound leaves, the white, flat-topped flower clusters, and the bright orange to red fruits are characteristic of most species. All species prefer cool, moist soil and grow best in northern parts of our area. Fire blight and winter sunscald can be problems.

S. alnifolia (Korean Mountain-ash). Trial in zone 4a; hardy in zones 4b and 5a. This tree is growing well in the arboretum and in my yard at home. Unlike most mountain-ash trees, the Korean has simple leaves that resemble *Alnus* (alder) leaves. Young trees are upright and dense; mature trees are 25 feet tall. The lenticels (pores) on young branches are conspicuous, giving the tree a speckled appearance. The flowers and fruits are typical.

S. americana (American Mountain-ash). Hardy in all zones. Native to northern parts of our area, this small tree, 20 feet tall, is often found growing with multiple stems. The fruits are small and bright red. If possible, plant where the trees will be sheltered from the afternoon sun in winter.

S. aucuparia (European Mountain-ash). Hardy in all zones. The most commonly planted of all the mountain-ash species. It grows to a height of 30 or more feet. The small fruits are bright red, produced in large clusters, and remain on the tree well into winter. The cultivar 'Pendula' has drooping branches.

S. decora (Showy Mountain-ash). Hardy in all zones. Native to the North Shore of Lake Superior. This 25-foot-tall tree is similar to *S. aucuparia* (the European species) in general appearance. The fruits are readily eaten by birds in the fall and are usually gone before winter sets in. On the North Shore, where the fruit is abundant and winter birds are few, the berries remain and are an attractive feature of the winter landscape.

Staphylea trifolia (Bladdernut). Hardy in all zones. Usually a large shrub with several stems but can be grown as a small (15-foot-tall) tree with a single stem. The trifoliate leaves, the white, bell-shaped flowers, and the bladdery, yellow fruits are striking. The lenticels (pores) are also prominent and add interest in winter.

Syringa pekinensis (Peking Lilac). Hardy in zones 4a, 4b, and 5a. A small tree similar in size to *S. reticulata* (Japanese tree lilac) but more informal looking and finer textured. The brownish fruit clusters add interest in late winter. Unfortunately, no local source for this species exists.

Syringa reticulata (Japanese Tree Lilac). Hardy in zones 4a, 4b, and 5a. The only tree form of lilac on the market. A mature tree is about 25 feet tall with a rounded head. The large, white panicles of flowers in late June are of special interest.

TILIA (Linden, Basswood). The lindens are similar in appearance and are commonly planted as shade trees. They are characterized by heart-shaped leaves and berrylike fruits borne on structures that resemble wings and that separate from the tree to aid in seed dispersal. The flowers are fragrant and a good source of honey.

T. americana (American Linden or Basswood). Hardy in all zones. A native tree sometimes planted for its shade. It grows rapidly to 60 feet and is too large for a small yard. In the open, it forms a well-rounded crown and is long-lived. The fragrant flowers are the source of basswood honey. The leaves are large, heart shaped, and turn golden-yellow in the fall. Sprouts may grow up around the base of the tree, and these should be removed.

T. cordata (Littleleaf Linden). Hardy in zones 4a, 4b, and 5a. This small-leaved, European tree grows no taller than 45 feet. When young, the tree is pyramidal and dense, becoming open and spreading as it matures. 'Greenspire' is an improved selection with a central trunk and a dense, pyramidal form when young.

T. x euchlora (Crimean Linden). Hardy in zones 4a, 4b, and 5a. A hybrid resulting from a cross between *T. cordata* and *T. dasystyla*. 'Redmond' is a widely planted cultivar selected in Fremont, Nebraska by Plumfield Nurseries. It grows about 50 feet tall, has leathery, green leaves, and is dense and pyramidal when young.

ULMUS (Elm). Because of the prevalence of Dutch elm disease (a wilt disease that kills the trees). few elms are being planted. *U. americana* (American elm), *U. rubra* (slippery elm), and *U. thomasii* (rock elm) are native and very susceptible to the disease. *U. pumila* (Siberian elm) and *U. davidiana* var. *japonica* (Japanese elm) may have some resistance to the disease, but the extent of this resistance has not been determined. Most European species reported to have resistance are not dependably hardy. *U. glabra* 'Camperdownii' is sometimes planted for its weeping form, but it, too, is susceptible to Dutch elm disease. Because the disease is so widespread, elms are not included in the special tree lists. A list of replacements for elms is provided at the end of this chapter (see p. 126).

General Tree Lists

LARGE TREES
(over 50 feet)

Acer saccharinum
Acer saccharum
Carya laciniosa
Carya ovata
Castanea dentata
Celtis occidentalis
Fraxinus americana
Gleditsia triacanthos
Gymnocladus dioica

Juglans nigra
Populus deltoides
Populus maximowiczii
Quercus alba
Quercus rubra
Tilia americana
Ulmus americana
Ulmus rubra

MEDIUM TREES
(30 to 50 feet)

Acer negundo
Acer platanoides
Acer rubrum
Aesculus x *carnea* 'Briotii'
Aesculus glabra
Aesculus hippocastanum
Aesculus sylvatica
Betula lenta
Betula nigra
Betula papyrifera
Betula pendula
Betula platyphylla var. *japonica*
Carya cordiformis
Catalpa speciosa
Fagus grandifolia
Fraxinus nigra
Fraxinus pennsylvanica
Fraxinus quadrangulata
Ginkgo biloba

Juglans cinerea
Magnolia acuminata
Ostrya virginiana
Paulownia tomentosa
Phellodendron amurense
Platanus x *acerifolia*
Platanus occidentalis
Populus alba
Populus nigra 'Italica'
Populus tremula var. *erecta*
Populus tremuloides
Prunus maackii
Prunus serotina
Quercus bicolor
Quercus macrocarpa
Quercus palustris
Quercus robur
Robinia pseudoacacia
Salix alba

Salix pentandra
Sorbus aucuparia
Tilia cordata
Tilia x *euchlora*

Ulmus davidiana var. *japonica*
Ulmus pumila
Ulmus thomasii

SMALL TREES
(under 30 feet)

Acer ginnala
Acer spicatum
Acer tataricum
Amelanchier arborea
Amelanchier x *grandiflora*
Amelanchier laevis
Carpinus betulus
Carpinus caroliniana
Cercis canadensis
Cladrastis lutea
Cornus alternifolia
Crataegus crus-galli
Crataegus x *mordenensis* 'Toba'
Elaeagnus angustifolia
Hippophae rhamnoides
Magnolia x *loebneri* 'Merrill'
Magnolia salicifolia

Magnolia x *soulangiana*
Magnolia stellata
Magnolia tripetala
Malus (species and cultivars)
Morus alba var. *tatarica*
Nyssa sylvatica
Prunus americana
Prunus pensylvanica
Prunus virginiana
Ptelea trifoliata
Salix matsudana 'Tortuosa'
Sorbus alnifolia
Sorbus americana
Sorbus decora
Staphylea trifolia
Syringa pekinensis
Syringa reticulata

Special Tree Lists

TREES WITH SHOWY FLOWERS

Acer platanoides
Acer rubrum
Aesculus species
Amelanchier species
Catalpa speciosa
Cercis canadensis
Cladrastis lutea
Cornus alternifolia

Crataegus species
Magnolia species
Malus species
Prunus species
Robinia pseudoacacia
Sorbus species
Staphylea trifolia
Syringa species

TREES WITH COLORED SUMMER FOLIAGE

Acer platanoides 'Crimson King'
Acer platanoides 'Fassen's Red Leaf'
Acer platanoides 'Royal Red'

Acer platanoides 'Schwedleri'
Betula pendula 'Purpurea'
Elaeagnus angustifolia

Hippophae rhamnoides   *Prunus* 'Newport'
Malus 'Royalty'   *Prunus virginiana* 'Shubert'

TREES WITH BRILLIANT FALL COLOR

Acer ginnala   *Ginkgo biloba*
Acer rubrum   *Nyssa sylvatica*
Acer saccharum   *Populus deltoides*
Aesculus sylvatica   *Populus tremuloides*
Fraxinus americana   *Quercus alba*
Fraxinus pennsylvanica   *Quercus palustris*

TREES WITH COLORED BARK

Betula nigra   *Carpinus caroliniana*
Betula papyrifera   *Populus alba*
Betula pendula   *Populus tremuloides*
Betula platyphylla var. *japonica*   *Prunus maackii*

TREES OF COLUMNAR FORM

Acer platanoides 'Columnare'   *Carpinus betulus* 'Fastigiata'
Acer rubrum 'Armstrong'   *Ginkgo biloba* 'Fastigiata'
Acer rubrum 'Columnare'   *Malus baccata* 'Columnaris'
Acer saccharum 'Newton Sentry'   *Populus alba* 'Pyramidalis'
Acer saccharum 'Temple Upright'   *Populus nigra* 'Italica'
Betula pendula 'Fastigiata'   *Populus tremula* var. *erecta*
Carpinus betulus 'Columnaris'   *Quercus robur* 'Fastigiata'

TREES OF WEEPING FORM

Betula pendula 'Tristis'   *Malus* 'Red Jade'
Betula pendula 'Youngii'   *Salix alba* 'Tristis'
Ginkgo biloba 'Pendula'   *Sorbus aucuparia* 'Pendula'

TREES OF GLOBE FORM

Acer platanoides 'Globosum'   *Robinia pseudoacacia* 'Umbra-
Acer saccharum 'Globosum'   culifera'

TREES FOR MOIST SITES

Acer rubrum   *Quercus bicolor*
Betula nigra   *Salix alba*
Fraxinus nigra   *Salix pentandra*

TREES FOR DRY SITES

Acer negundo

Celtis occidentalis

Elaeagnus angustifolia

Fraxinus pennsylvanica

Hippophae rhamnoides

Quercus macrocarpa

Robinia pseudoacacia

TREES FOR STREET PLANTING
(replacements for *Ulmus* [elm] species)

Acer platanoides

Acer rubrum

Acer saccharum

Aesculus glabra

Aesculus sylvatica

Celtis occidentalis

Fraxinus americana

Fraxinus pennsylvanica

Gymnocladus dioica

Malus 'Red Splendor'

Ostrya virginiana

Tilia americana

Tilia cordata 'Green Spire'

Tilia x *euchlora* 'Redmond'

Chapter 12

Selection and Care of Shrubs

The selection and proper use of shrubs is very important: they are used in the foundation planting, in the border of the yard for screening and privacy, on a bank, at the edge of woods, and sometimes as a hedge along the driveway.

Plant only shrubs that will be hardy and long-lived. To use shrubs intelligently you must know their mature size and under what conditions they grow best. The following specie and cultivar descriptions plus general and special lists should help you select the right plants for your yard. Some of these plants can also be used as trees and have already been described in Chapter 11. When a shrub requires special care, specific comments are provided in the entry. See also Chapter 6 for a discussion of pruning.

Abeliophyllum distichum (Korean Abelialeaf). Trial in zones 4a and 4b; hardy in zone 5a. The flower buds may be injured in a severe winter, but the species has been more dependable than the closely related *Forsythia* x *intermedia* (border forsythia). This small shrub grows to 4 feet and has arching branches. The white flowers open in mid-April and resemble *Forsythia* flowers.

Acanthopanax sieboldianus (Five-leaved Aralia). Hardy in zones 4a, 4b, and 5a. The best of the *Acanthopanax* species. Mature

127

plants are about 6 feet tall. The flowers and fruits are inconspicuous, but the palmately compound leaves with 5 to 7 leaflets are attractive. The species does well in the shade and has few pests.

ACER (Maple). Contains mostly tree species described in Chapter 11), but a few are shrublike. These are repeated in this chapter.

A. ginnala (Amur Maple). Hardy in all zones. When grown as a shrub, this maple is an excellent screen or background shrub that grows to 15 feet. It can also be used as a formal hedge. An unnamed compact form that grows about 6 feet tall is on the market. 'Durand Dwarf', a bud sport discovered in Durand Eastman Park, Rochester, New York, is truly a dwarf, reaching a height of only about 4 feet.

A. spicatum (Mountain Maple). Hardy in all zones. A shrubby maple native to acid soils. Under proper conditions it reaches a height of 20 feet. The leaves are 3 lobed and heart shaped, the flowers yellow and produced in upright spikes, and the fruits red. The fall color is brilliant orange to red. Plant only on acid soils.

A. tataricum (Tatarian Maple). Hardy in all zones. Can be used for the same purposes as *A. ginnala* (Amur maple), but it is slightly larger, to 20 feet, and has leaves that are unlobed or nearly so.

Aesculus parviflora (Bottlebrush Buckeye). Trial in zones 4a and 4b; hardy in zone 5a. This wide-spreading, shrubby form of buckeye is of marginal hardiness and seldom exceeds a height of 6 feet. Dieback is common after a severe winter. The tall, slender flower spikes are striking in midsummer. Plant only in a sheltered location.

AMELANCHIER (Serviceberry). Described in Chapter 11. Two species are shrubs. These spread by underground stems to form dense clumps 4 or 5 feet across.

A. alnifolia (Saskatoon). Hardy in all zones. A shrub native to the prairie provinces of Canada, to the Rocky Mountains, and to northwestern Minnesota. It grows to a height of 6 to 8 feet. The shrub is attractive in bloom and in fruit. Often planted to attract birds to the yard.

A. stolonifera (Running Serviceberry). Hardy in all zones. The plants grow about 6 feet tall and their flowers are larger and showier than those of *A. alnifolia* (Saskatoon).

ARONIA (Chokeberry). Small to medium shrubs with white, pear-like flowers and small fruits that resemble tiny apples and are borne in flat-topped clusters. Excellent for bird food.

A. arbutifolia (Red Chokeberry). Trial in zone 4a; hardy in zones 4b and 5a. This species has not been as vigorous as *A. melanocarpa* (black chokeberry). Plants grow about 6 feet tall and are upright and open, with few stems. The fruits are bright red, and the foliage is red in the fall.

A. melanocarpa (Black Chokeberry). Hardy in all zones. Native to northern Minnesota and Wisconsin and hence the best chokeberry to be planted in our region. The shrub is dense and mound shaped, 4 feet tall, with dark green summer foliage that turns red in the fall. The fruits are jet black.

A. prunifolia (Purple Chokeberry). Hardy in all zones. Similar to *A. melanocarpa* (black chokeberry) but somewhat larger, 4 to 5 feet tall. The fruits are purplish black when ripe.

Berberis koreana (Korean Barberry). Hardy in all zones. This is the hardiest of the barberries, being fully hardy in the Winnipeg area. The plant grows to about 6 feet. It spreads by underground stems, and this can be a problem in a mixed shrub planting. It is best used in a mass planting. The racemes of yellow flowers in the spring, the red berries in late summer and fall, and the red foliage in the fall make this an attractive shrub.

Berberis thunbergii (Japanese Barberry). Hardy in zones 4a (only in sheltered locations), 4b, and 5a. The hardiness of this shrub is rather borderline and some dieback occurs after a severe winter. It is the most widely planted barberry. A mature shrub is about 4 to 5 feet tall, with a well-rounded form. The yellow flowers, red berries, and red fall color are attractive. A number of cultivars are on the market. 'Crimson Pygmy' is a dwarf form with red foliage. It grows to a height of about 1 foot and should be planted where it will have good snow cover, as it tends to develop tip kill. 'Atropurpurea' acquires a bright red color when grown in full sun but is less hardy than the species. 'Aurea' has golden-yellow foliage and is about as hardy as the red-leaved selections.

Buxus microphylla var. *koreana* (Korean Boxwood). Trial in zone 4a; hardy in zones 4b and 5a. This is probably the hardiest of the broad-leaved evergreens and is the hardiest boxwood. A variety of the littleleaf boxwood, the Korean boxwood is 2 feet tall, with variable hardiness and fall leaf color. 'Wintergreen' is a good selection. When planted in a protected area that receives some winter shade, it grows to a height of about 1½ feet and forms an attractive, mound-shaped plant. It can also be used as a formal hedge in protected sites.

CARAGANA (Pea Shrub). A large genus of hardy shrubs, producing yellow, pealike flowers that are showy in May. All species are drought resistant and do better in drier parts of the region.

C. arborescens (Siberian Pea Shrub). Hardy in all zones. A large shrub, to 15 feet, that is widely planted as a snow catch in field windbreaks. Leaf spot can be a problem in late summer. 'Pendula' is a good choice if a small, weeping tree is desired. This is grafted on an upright stem at the desired height. Suckers that develop at the base of the stem must be removed.

C. frutex (Russian Pea Shrub). Hardy in all zones. This suckering shrub grows 4 to 5 feet tall, and its leaves are dark green with 4 leaflets. 'Globosa', a nonsuckering cultivar developed in Dropmore, Manitoba, grows to a height of 3 feet and requires no pruning.

C. microphylla 'Tidy'. Hardy in all zones. This cultivar of the littleleaf pea shrub is one of the more graceful pea shrubs. It is a dense shrub that grows to about 8 feet. The light green leaves have very narrow lobes, and the flowers are lemon yellow.

C. pygmaea (Pygmy Pea Shrub). Hardy in all zones. A low shrub seldom more than 3 feet tall. Its resistance to iron chlorosis makes this a desirable shrub in the Red River Valley and other western areas where alkaline soils are a problem.

Caryopteris x *clandonensis* (Bluebeard). Plant in sheltered areas in zones 4a and 4b; hardy in zone 5a. It is unfortunate that this attractive shrub is not hardier; even under ideal conditions it is short-lived in our area. Often sold as blue spirea, the shrub is low, seldom over 3 feet, with showy spikes of blue flowers in late summer. It requires well-drained soil and full sunlight. Bluebeard can be treated as a perennial; since it blooms on new wood, it can be cut back nearly to the ground in early spring.

Ceanothus americanus (New Jersey Tea). Hardy in zones 4a, 4b, and 5a. Low, spreading, native shrub growing to a height of 2 to 3 feet. The white flowers are produced in upright, umbellike clusters in mid-June. The dry seed capsules add interest in late summer. The leaves were used by early settlers for tea—hence the common name. This shrub requires well-drained soil and prefers sandy soil. Young seedlings transplant readily, but established plants are moved with difficulty because they have gnarled roots.

Cephalanthus occidentalis (Buttonbush). Hardy in zones 4a, 4b, and 5a. Native along streams. Mature plants are 10 or more feet tall, and the round flower heads with protruding pistils are of special interest in late July. This shrub grows best on wet soils.

Chaenomeles speciosa (Flowering Quince). Trial in zones 4a and 4b; hardy in zone 5a. The shrub is not hardy. Its flower buds are killed at about −15°F., and flowers usually form only at the base of the plant where the buds were protected by snow. However, flowering quince can be very attractive: it is a low, mound-shaped shrub, seldom over 3 feet tall, which is often planted for its showy, orange to red flowers in early May. Numerous cultivars are on the market, but because they lack flower bud hardiness, few are sold in this area.

Chionanthus virginicus (White Fringetree). Trial in zone 4a; hardy in zones 4b and 5a. Plants in the arboretum are quite hardy and over 8 feet tall. The common name would suggest that this is a tree, and it does grow to a height of 30 feet in its native range from New Jersey to Florida. There are separate male and female plants. The male plants have larger panicles of white, delightfully fragrant flowers than the female plants, but the females have dark blue fruits produced in grapelike clusters. The rather coarse leaves are slow to open in the spring and turn golden-yellow in the fall. This relative of the lilac deserves to be more widely planted.

CORNUS (Dogwood). A large and useful genus of shrubs and small trees. The shrub dogwoods are valued for their colored winter stems, clustered flowers, colorful fruits, and fall color.

C. alba (Tatarian Dogwood). Hardy in all zones. A red-stemmed dogwood similar to *C. sericea* (the native red-osier dogwood) but seldom planted. The following cultivars are used in landscaping; all grow about 6 feet tall and have creamy-white flowers: 'Sibirica' is planted for its bright red winter stems; several selections sold under the name 'Argenteo-marginata' have leaves bordered with white; 'Gouchaultii' has a yellowish variegation; and 'Spaethii' has yellow leaf borders.

C. mas (Cornelian Cherry). Trial in zones 4a and 4b; hardy in zone 5a. This 8- to 10-foot-tall dogwood lacks hardiness and is not recommended. In arboretum trials it has shown considerable dieback and seldom flowers. The small, yellow flowers and the bright red, cherrylike fruits are attractive features where this dogwood is hardy.

C. racemosa (Gray Dogwood). Hardy in all zones. One of the better native dogwoods for ornamental use. The height varies with soil fertility and ranges from 8 to 12 feet. The gray stems, the creamy-white flowers in early June, and the white fruits borne on red pedicels in late summer are desirable features. Gray dogwood spreads by underground stems and is excellent for naturalizing at the edge of a woods.

C. sericea (Red-osier Dogwood). Hardy in all zones. This 10- to 12-foot-tall native grows abundantly in wet soils. Under cultivation it grows well in the shrub border. It has creamy-white flowers but is planted primarily for the effect of the red stems in late winter. Young stems have a brighter red color than older stems. Pruning out the oldest stems each spring encourages the development of new stems. Side branches often root where they touch the ground.

'Isanti' is a compact cultivar that forms a mound about 5 feet tall. The oystershell scale can be a problem if not controlled.

Cotinus coggygria (Smokebush). Root hardy in all zones. Frequently kills back nearly to the ground. For this reason, it seldom forms the smokelike flower panicles and rarely exceeds a height of 6 to 8 feet in our area. The fall color is yellow to orange. The cultivar 'Royal Purple' has been the best of the colored-foliage forms: its purplish-red leaves contrast nicely with the green of other shrubs. By cutting the shrub back to vigorous, live wood in the spring, a compact, upright shrub results. Should not be planted unless one is willing to prune out the dead wood in the spring.

Cotinus obovatus (American Smokebush). Hardy in zones 4a, 4b, and 5a. Plants have been hardy at the arboretum. A large shrub or a small tree, to 15 feet, with rather coarse foliage, this species is most beautiful in the fall when the leaves turn orange.

COTONEASTER (Cotoneaster). A large genus of shrubs. The size varies from low, creeping species to upright shrubs 6 or more feet tall. Fire blight, a bacterial disease, can be serious on cotoneasters in our area, thus limiting their usefulness.

C. apiculatus (Cranberry Cotoneaster). Trial in zones 4a and 4b; hardy in zone 5a. The hardiest of the low, spreading types of cotoneaster. Because the tips of the branches may kill back after an open (with little or no snow) winter, the height of the plant seldom exceeds 2 feet. Small, pinkish flowers in June are followed by bright red berries in August. It is best to plant this shrub where it will have good snow cover.

C. lucidus (Hedge Cotoneaster). Hardy in all zones. The most widely planted cotoneaster in this area. *C. lucidus* is used in the shrub border or as a clipped or informal hedge. The mature height is about 6 feet. Oystershell scale can be a problem.

C. multiflorus (Flowering Cotoneaster). Hardy in zones 4a, 4b, and 5a. A medium, mound-shaped shrub that grows 6 feet tall. It is virtually the only cotoneaster that has white flowers in May. The striking red berries are produced in late summer and early fall, and these are a favorite food of birds.

Cystisus hirsutus (Hairy Broom). Trial in all zones. Most of the brooms lack hardiness. This species is the only one that has performed satisfactorily. The shrub grows to about 2 feet and blooms in May with yellow, pealike flowers.

Deutzia x *lemoinei* (Lemoine Deutzia). Hardy in zones 4a, 4b, and 5a. The only species of *Deutzia* that has much hardiness, although some tip kill can occur after a severe winter. This hybrid resulted from a cross between *D. parviflora* and *D. gracilis*. The hardiness comes from the *parviflora* parent. The shrub grows about 6 feet tall and blooms in early June with showy, white flowers. The cultivar 'Compacta' is more compact and not as tall.

Diervilla lonicera (Bush Honeysuckle). Hardy in all zones. A low shrub, about 2 feet tall, native over much of this region. It has a tendency to sucker and can be used as a bank cover. The yellow, trumpet-shaped flowers in June are striking. The leaves have a reddish color in the fall.

Diervilla sessilifolia (Southern Bush Honeysuckle). Similar to *D. lonicera* and appears to be hardy.

Dirca palustris (Atlantic Leatherwood). Hardy in all zones. A native plant that makes an excellent landscape shrub. In the woods this shrub is open and may grow to a height of 8 feet. In the open the shrub is dense and grows about 6 feet tall. The small, yellow flowers in late April are especially welcome, and the leaves turn golden-yellow in the fall. The shrub grows best on slightly acid soil.

Elaeagnus commutata (Silverberry). Hardy in all zones. This native of northwestern Minnesota and the Dakotas has beautiful, silvery foliage which is prized for dry flower arrangements. It grows to a height of 6 to 8 feet, is very drought resistant, and should be planted on well-drained soil. Its suckering habit can be a problem in the shrub border.

EUONYMUS. A genus valued for its colored fruits and brilliant fall coloration. Most species have 4-angled stems and fruits that resemble *Celastrus scandens* (bittersweet) fruits. Scale insects can be a problem on most species.

E. alata (Winged Euonymus). Hardy in all zones. A large shrub, 8 or more feet tall. It is grown for its corky, winged twigs and beautiful, red autumn coloration. The cultivar 'Compactus' is often used but may show some winter dieback; it is hardy only in zone 5a.

E. europaea (European Spindle Tree). Hardy in zones 4a, 4b, and 5a. Another large shrub, often reaching a height of 15 or more feet. It is cultivated primarily for its colored fruits. 'Aldenhamensis' is the best cultivar, with brilliant pink, 4-lobed fruits.

E. fortunei (Wintercreeper). Trial in all zones. A variable species with plants ranging from low, creeping plants to upright shrubs. This species is evergreen and only low forms planted where they will receive good snow cover survive. These forms are discussed in Chapter 15.

Forsythia x *intermedia* (Border Forsythia). Trial in zones 4a and 4b; hardy in zone 5a. This yellow-flowered, hybrid species grows 6 to 8 feet tall and is the one most often planted. Numerous cultivars are on the market. Unfortunately, the flower buds are killed at −15°F. Most years the only bloom is on the lower branches that were covered with snow. I have seen good bloom in Minnesota only twice in over 30 years. This hybrid is not recommended unless one is willing to provide adequate winter protection.

Forsythia ovata (Early Forsythia). Trial in zone 4a; hardy in zones 4b and 5a. A severe winter may kill some of the flower buds, but good bloom can be expected most springs. This native of Korea is the hardiest *Forsythia*, reaching a height of about 6 feet. The flowers are smaller and lighter yellow than in *F.* x *intermedia* (border forsythia). Plant in a sheltered location.

Genista multibracteata. Trial in all zones. The only *Genista* that has bloomed in arboretum trials. Since the shrub blooms on new wood, it is best to cut back the plant nearly to the ground each spring; with this treatment it grows to a height of 2 to 3 feet. The yellow, pealike flowers are produced in late June or early July. The leaves stay green late in the fall.

Hamamelis virginiana (Witch-hazel). Trial in zone 3b; hardy in zones 4a, 4b, and 5a. This native shrub grows about 10 feet tall. When grown in the shade it is an open shrub, but in the open it is compact. Witch-hazel is the last shrub to bloom, producing yellow flowers in late September and October. The leaves turn golden in the fall.

Hippophae rhamnoides (Russian Sea Buckthorn). Hardy in zones 4a, 4b, and 5a. A large shrub or small tree, to 15 feet, with a narrow, silvery-green leaves. The sexes are separate. The female plants produce an abundance of small orange berries which can be very colorful. Plant on well-drained soil. Suckers sometimes grow up around the base of the parent plant.

Hydrangea arborescens (Hills-of-Snow Hydrangea). Hardy in all zones. A low shrub, seldom more than 3 feet tall, that produces white, flat-topped flower clusters with showy, sterile, marginal flowers and smaller, perfect flowers in the center. In the following cultivars all the flowers are sterile, resulting in showier flower clusters. 'Grandiflora' produces in early July large, rounded clusters of sterile flowers at the end of new growth. The cultivar 'Annabelle' has even larger flower clusters and has now largely replaced the older 'Grandiflora'. These shrubs like plenty of moisture. Although they can grow in shade, they flower better in full sun. Since they bloom on new wood, larger flower clusters are produced if the shrubs are pruned back nearly to the ground each spring.

Hydrangea paniculata 'Grandiflora' (Pee-gee Hydrangea). Hardy in zones 4a, 4b, and 5a. A coarse, 10-foot-tall shrub that produces big, showy clusters of sterile flowers in August. The flowers are at first white, then pink to purplish. They are produced in upright, pyramidal clusters. Pruning is different than for the cultivars of *H. arborescens*. Pruning back the lateral branches in early spring produces larger flower clusters. This shrub can also be trained as a small tree.

Hypericum kalmianum (Kalm St. John's-wort). Trial in zones 4a and 4b, hardy in zone 5a. One of the hardier St. John's-worts. It grows to about 2 feet and has yellow flowers in July. Since it blooms on new wood, it is best to prune it back in early spring before new growth starts.

Hypericum prolificum (Shrubby St. John's-wort). Trial in zones 4a and 4b; hardy in zone 5a. The time of bloom and the flowers are similar to *H. kalmianum*, but this species is slightly taller, to 3 feet, and more branched.

Ilex verticillata (Winterberry). Hardy in all zones. This native, deciduous holly is the only species of *Ilex* that has proved very hardy in our area. Mature shrubs are about 8 feet tall. The sexes are separate, so it is advisable to plant several seedlings in a group to be sure of getting fruiting plants. The bright red berries are produced in tight clusters along the stems and are most effective after the leaves drop and before the berries are eaten by winter birds Although winterberry is native to swamps, it flourishes on well-drained soils. Prefers slightly acid soil.

Kalmia poliifolia (Swamp Laurel). Hardy in all zones. A 1½-foot-tall, native laurel growing in acid bogs and most attractive when in bloom. The evergreen leaves are narrow and dark green on the top surface. The rosy-red to pink flowers open in mid-June. Unless you are in a natural boggy area, you will not grow this species very successfully. The popular eastern species *K. latifolia* (mountain laurel) has not proved hardy in arboretum trials.

Kolkwitzia amabilis (Beauty Bush). Trial in zones 4a and 4b; hardy in zone 5a. A medium shrub, 6 to 8 feet tall, of borderline hardiness and usually short-lived. The pink, vase-shaped flowers are especially lovely in early June. Plant on well-drained soil in a sheltered location.

Ledum groenlandicum (Labrador Tea). Hardy in all zones. This low shrub, 3 feet tall, is a native of acid bogs. The elongated, evergreen leaves are woolly underneath, with brownish hairs. The white flowers are produced in small, flat-topped clusters in May. Suitable for planting only on peaty, acid soils.

Lespedeza bicolor (Shrub Bush-clover). Trial in all zones. A dieback shrub that reaches a height of 6 feet and produces rosy-purple, pealike flowers on new wood in late summer. Cut back to live wood as soon as growth starts in the spring. Most effective in August and early September when few other shrubs are in bloom.

LIGUSTRUM (Privet). Common hedge plants in eastern and southern states. All species have marginal hardiness in this area, but the following species and cultivars are sometimes planted:

L. amurense (Amur Privet). Trial in all zones. One of the hardier privets, often planted as a clipped hedge. Dieback may occur after a severe winter, and this can mar the beauty of the hedge. The species can also be planted in the shrub border, where a little dieback is not very serious. Mature size is about 6 feet. The clusters of white flowers in mid-June add interest.

L. obtusifolium var. *regelianum* (Regel Border Privet). Trial in all zones. This low, spreading privet with horizontal branches grows 4 feet tall and is effective in the shrub border. It has about the same degree of hardiness as *L. amurense* (Amur privet).

L. vulgare (Common Privet). Trial in all zones. Most selections of common privet have not been hardy. Plants grow to 6 feet. The cultivar 'Cheyenne', introduced by the USDA from a plant grown at Cheyenne, Wyoming, has been about as hardy as the *L. amurense*, but dieback does occur after a severe winter.

Ligustrum (golden form). Trial in all zones. This unnamed selection of privet is reasonably hardy, although dieback occurs after a severe winter. It grows 3 feet tall and has bright golden-yellow leaves. Introduced by Hillside Nurseries of South St. Paul, this selection is now being propagated by several nurseries in the Twin Cities area and is sold by a number of garden centers.

LONICERA (Honeysuckle). A large genus of over 100 species. A few of these are grown for their showy flowers and brightly colored fruits. Leaf diseases can cause early defoliation.

L. maackii (Amur Honeysuckle). Hardy in all zones. Large shrub, to 10 feet, with cream-colored flowers in early June and bright red fruits ripening in late fall and persisting into winter. The variety *podocarpa* is often planted.

L. morrowii (Morrow Honeysuckle). Hardy in zones 4a, 4b, and 5a. A medium shrub, 6 feet tall, that is often planted as a clipped hedge. The flowers open white and turn pale yellow. The berries are dark red in midsummer.

L. tatarica (Tatarian Honeysuckle). Hardy in all zones. This tall honeysuckle grows to 15 feet and is widely planted as a screen and a clipped hedge. The color of the flowers varies from pink to white in late May, and the color of the berrylike fruits from orange to red in midsummer. This species is variable and numerous cultivars are on the market: 'Arnold's Red' and 'Zabellii' are widely planted for their dark red flowers; 'Zabellii' is also popular as a hedge plant.

L. x *xylosteoides* 'Clavey's Dwarf'. Hardy in all zones. A compact honeysuckle thought to be a hybrid between *L. tatarica* and *L. xylosteum*. This popular hedge grows to 5 feet. The foliage color is grayish green, and the flowers and fruits are not showy. Requires little or no pruning.

L. xylosteum 'Emerald Mound'. Hardy in all zones. A compact form of the European fly honeysuckle that grows 4 feet tall. Formerly known as the cultivar 'Nana', it was renamed a few years ago and is now widely grown for its dwarf, mound-shaped form. The foliage is dark green.

Magnolia stellata (Star Magnolia). Trial in zone 4a; hardy in zones 4b and 5a. The most shrublike of the magnolias. It is 7 feet tall and produces large, white flowers in early May. Because the shrub blooms early, frost may be a problem.

Myrica pensylvanica (Bayberry). Trial in zone 4a; hardy in zones 4b and 5a. Some dieback can occur after a severe winter. This seashore shrub, native from Newfoundland to Mayland, grows to about 5 feet and its leaves are semi-evergreen (they stay green until winter). The sexes are separate. The female plants produce gray-colored berries used for making bayberry candles. The plant does sucker, so it makes an excellent bank cover on well-drained soils.

Paeonia suffruticosa (Tree Peony). Trial in zones 4a and 4b; hardy in zone 5a. Not fully hardy. If given winter protection or planted where there is dependable snow cover, the plant grows to a height of about 3 feet and produces large, showy flowers in early June. Numerous cultivars are on the market.

PHILADELPHUS (Mockoranges). Trial in zones 4a, 4b, and 5a. Almost all species and cultivars of mockorange have borderline hardiness. Most of those that have proved hardy are tall and leggy, with bloom high on the plant. Many of the cultivars are of hybrid origin, so several species were involved in their breeding. *Philadelphus coronarius* 'Aureus' (golden mockorange) is widely planted and grows about 3 feet tall. It is attractive in the spring with its golden leaves and white flowers but is unattractive in late summer with its rusty green leaves. 'Enchantment' has been one of the better cultivars in arboretum trials. It grows to about 6 feet and has good bloom over the entire plant. 'Minnesota Snowflake' is about 6 feet tall and has double, white fragrant flowers, but the shrub tends to be leggy. 'Virginal', a 6- to 8-foot-tall cultivar of *P.* x *virginalis*, is widely sold but has not had reliable bloom in arboretum trials. Research continues at the arboretum to develop a better and hardier cultivar of mockorange, one combining ample bloom with attractive appearance.

Physocarpus opulifolius (Eastern Ninebark). Hardy in all zones. This medium shrub, 7 feet tall, is native to the North Shore of Lake Superior and to the bluffs along the Mississippi River in southeastern Minnesota. The small flowers are produced in flat-topped clusters and range from white to pink. The dried fruits can vary from brown to bright red, depending on soil and weather. On the North Shore they are especially red. Two cultivars are often planted: 'Luteus' is an attractive yellow color, especially in the spring. 'Nanus' is more compact and has smaller leaves than the species.

Potentilla fruticosa (Bush Cinquefoil). Hardy in all zones. The height of this shrub varies from about 2 to 4 feet. It is native around the world in the north temperate zone. There are numerous geographic strains and cultivars. Over 35 of these are growing in the arboretum collection. Flower color varies from white to tangerine, with some shade of yellow most common. 'Katherine Dykes' is a low, spreading shrub with lemon-yellow flowers. 'Jackmanii' is an upright shrub with deep yellow flowers. The flowers of 'Mount Everest' and 'Snowflake' are white. 'Tangerine' has orange flowers when grown in the shade or during cool weather and yellow flowers when grown in full sun and during the heat of summer. 'Coronation Triumph' has bright yellow flowers on a mound-shaped shrub.

Prinsepia sinensis (Cherry Prinsepia). Hardy in all zones. This medium, spiny shrub grows to a height of 7 to 8 feet and has dark green leaves. The small, yellow flowers in May are followed by bright red, cherrylike fruits in August. An excellent barrier plant.

PRUNUS (Almond, Cherry, Plum). Described in Chapter 11. The following species and cultivars are shrubs:

P. x *cistena* (Purpleleaf Sand Cherry). Trial in zone 3b; hardy in zones 4a, 4b, and 5a. Some tip kill can occur after a severe winter. This 6-foot-tall hybrid was produced by the late Dr. N. E. Hanson of South Dakota State University and resulted from a cross between *P. pumila* and *P. cerasifera* var. *atropurpurea*. It combines the hardiness of the native *P. pumila* with the red foliage color of *P. cerasifera* var. *atropurpurea*. The most widely planted of all purple- or red-leaved shrubs.

P. glandulosa (Dwarf Flowering Almond). Trial in zone 4a; hardy in zones 4b and 5a. Some dieback can be expected after a severe winter. This is a low, arching shrub that grows about 4 feet tall. The species has single, white flowers and red, cherrylike fruits. It is not planted as often as the cultivars 'Alboplena' and 'Sinensis', which have double, white and pink flowers in early May.

P. japonica (Japanese Bush Cherry). Hardy in all zones. Very hardy, low shrub from northern China. The mature height is under 5 feet. The pink to white flowers in May are followed by small, red cherries in July. These fruits make good preserves.

P. tenella (Russian Almond). Hardy in all zones. Another hardy, low shrub 4 to 5 feet tall. The flowers are pink and bloom early in May. The shrub has a tendency to sucker.

P. tomentosa (Nanking Cherry). Hardy in all zones. A 6-foot-tall shrub grown both for its ornamental qualties and for its fruit. The flowers are white to pink in early May. The fruits are rather small but produced in great abundance. Their color is typically red but white-fruited seedlings are not uncommon. Birds love the fruits so they must be protected with bird netting. The mild, sweet fruits are good to eat fresh and can also be used to make a refreshing drink and jelly.

P. triloba 'Multiplex' (Flowering Plum). Trial in zone 4a; hardy in zones 4b and 5a. Flower buds occasionally winter kill. This is a large shrub, 10 or more feet tall, with showy, double, pink flowers in early May. It is especially striking when in bloom but offers little landscape interest during the rest of the year. When grafted on wild plum roots, the shrub produces suckers, which should be removed.

P. virginiana (Chokecherry). Hardy in all zones. This large, suckering shrub, 15 or more feet tall, is sometimes planted for bird food and for naturalizing at the edge of a woods. The small, black fruits are prized for jelly. 'Shubert', a cultivar with coppery-red leaves, is widely planted as a specimen tree and can be used as a screen. It is one of the better colored foliage plants.

Rhamnus cathartica (Common Buckthorn). Hardy in all zones. A very large shrub or small tree, to 18 feet, that has been widely planted by birds. The glossy, green leaves with prominent veins make the plant easily recognizable. The black fruits are produced in abundance during late fall. The shrub was at one time used as a clipped hedge. It is the alternate host for crown rust of oats, a leaf disease that reduces oat yields, so it is not recommend for planting.

Rhamnus frangula (Glossy Buckthorn). Hardy in zones 4a, 4b, and 5a. Another large shrub, the glossy buckthorn grows 15 feet tall and is not a host for the crown rust. The species is not planted as often as two of its cultivars: 'Asplenifolia' has finely divided leaves and a rather lacy, fernlike appearance; 'Tallhedge' is columnar and often planted as a hedge.

RHODODENDRON (Rhododendron, Azalea). The genus *Rhododendron* contains both the evergreen rhododendrons and the deciduous azaleas. All prefer light shade and acid soil. The evergreen species tend to winter burn and must be protected during winter months: a burlap shade keeps the direct sun off plants and allows good aeration. Most plants described here have been tested only at the arboretum.

R. arborescens (Sweet Azalea). Trials in zones 4a, 4b, and 5a. The species is vegetatively fully hardy at the arboretum, but occasionally winter injury to the flower buds occurs. Arboretum plants are about 5 feet tall. This late-flowering shrub has fragrant, white blossoms that open in mid-June after the leaves are fully developed. For this reason, it is not as showy as the species that bloom before the leaves are fully developed.

Arboretum Hybrids. Hardy in zones 4a, 4b, and 5a. In arboretum trials plants have bloomed every year, even when the winter temperature has dropped to $-40°F$. The hybrids were developed by crossing *R.* x *kosterianum* with *R. prinophyllum*. They grow to 6 or more feet and bloom in May with large, showy, pink flowers that have a pleasant fragrance. The arboretum will introduce this hybrid group and announce its name in the spring of 1979.

R. atlanticum (Coast Azalea). Trial in zones 4a, 4b, and 5a. Low, spreading azalea, 4 feet tall, that has been surprisingly hardy. The large, white flowers are flushed with red in late May.

R. calendulaceum (Flame Azalea). Trial in zones 4a, 4b, and 5a. Has borderline hardiness. Arboretum plants are about 5 feet tall, and some years they produce plentiful bloom. The flowers are orange in late May.

R. canadense (Rhodora). Trial in zones 4a, 4b, and 5a. Low-growing, deciduous azalea. It is 3 feet tall and blooms in early May with small, lavender flowers. Prefers wet, boggy soil.

R. carolinianum (Carolina Rhododendron). Trial in zones 4a, 4b, and 5a. The flower buds are injured at temperatures below $-20°F$.

Some years arboretum plants have ample, pink bloom in late May, but more often, the bloom is sparse. The species is evergreen and grows to about 3 feet.

R. catawbiense (Catawba Rhododendron). Trial in zones 4a, 4b, and 5a. One of the better evergreen rhododendrons for this area, because the flower buds are hardy to about −25°F. Arboretum plants are 4 feet tall. The flowers on the species are magenta in early June, and there is a white-flowered variety, 'Alba', that is equally hardy. A number of cultivars have been named of hybrids between *R. catawbiense* and other species.

R. japonicum (Japanese Azalea). Trial in zones 4a, 4b, and 5a. The flower buds are hardy to about −20°F. This large-flowered, deciduous azalea from Japan grows to 6 feet. The flower color varies from orange to salmon red. The odor of the flowers is not very pleasant, especially when cut for interior decorations.

R. x kosterianum (Mollis Hybrid Azaleas). Trial in zones 4a, 4b, and 5a. The mollis hybrids are vegetatively hardy, growing to a height of 7 feet, but the flower buds are injured if the temperature drops much below −20°F. The hybrids were developed by crossing *R. japonicum* with *R. molle*, a species from China. They are largely seed propagated and after a number of generations they resemble *R. japonicum*. The plants bloom in late May, with flower color varying from yellow to red. The flowers have the same objectionable odor as *R. japonicum* flowers.

R. maximum (Rosebay Rhododendron). Trial in zones 4a, 4b, and 5a. The tallest of the evergreen rhododendrons that can be grown in our climate. In its native habitat it grows to a height of 20 or more feet, but because it must be protected against winter sun, it seldom becomes more than 5 or 6 feet tall in this region. The flowers are a light rose color in late June. This has not been as satisfactory as *R. catawbiense*.

R. mucronulatum (Korean Rhododendron). Hardy in zones 4a, 4b, and 5a. A hardy, deciduous rhododendron. Arboretum plants are about 4 feet tall. The species blooms in early May with lavender to rosy-purple flowers. The cultivar 'Cornell Pink' is planted more often than the species.

R. periclymenoides (Pinxterbloom). Trial in zones 4a, 4b, and 5a. In arboretum trials this shrub has not been as hardy as *R. prinophyllum*. It is native from Massachusetts to North Carolina and west to Tennessee, and where it is native it is often called wild honeysuckle. The shrub grows to a height of 4 or 5 feet and has light pink, nonfragrant flowers in late May.

PJM Hybrids. Hardy in zones 4a, 4b, and 5a. Introduced by Weston Nurseries in Massachusetts. These hybrids resulted from a cross between *R. mucronulatum* and *R. carolinianum*. They grow 3 feet tall and bloom with lavender-pink flowers in early May. The evergreen leaves are resistant to winter burn, but they look better if given some winter shade.

R. prinophyllum (Rose-shell Azalea). Hardy in zones 4a, 4b, and 5a. In arboretum trials the flower buds have been very hardy: abundant bloom has been obtained after a temperature of −40°F. However, plants have lacked vegetative vigor and have seldom exceeded a height of 2 feet. The pale pink flowers open in late May. This azalea is similar to *R. periclymenoides* but is considered a distinct species because its flowers are very fragrant and its flower buds are hardy.

R. schlippenbachii (Royal Azalea). Plant only in sheltered locations in zones 4a, 4b, and 5a. This azalea appears to have vegetative hardiness but lacks flower bud hardiness. It is 3 feet tall, and its light pink, bell-shaped flowers are large and showy but are seldom produced in abundance and often only below the snowline.

R. vaseyi (Pinkshell Azalea). Trial in zones 4a, 4b, and 5a. Some injury to the flower buds can be expected most winters, so the bloom is not spectacular. This native North American species grows to about 5 feet, and its light rose flowers open in mid-May.

R. viscosum (Swamp Azalea). Trial in zones 4a, 4b, and 5a. Similar to *R. arborescens* (sweet azalea). Arboretum plants are about 3 feet tall and rather mound shaped. The fragrant, white flowers open in June after the leaves are fully open.

R. yedoense var. *poukhanense* (Yodogawa Azalea). Trial in zones 4a, 4b, and 5a. Low, mound-shaped shrub from Korea. It grows 2 feet tall and flowers in mid-May with purplish, bell-shaped blossoms. A dependable bloomer.

RHUS (Sumac). Several species of *Rhus* are grown for their landscape effect. Because plants sucker, they make excellent bank covers. Most species turn brilliant red in the fall.

R. aromatica (Fragrant Sumac). Hardy in all zones. Low, mound shaped, and attractive as a mass planting. The mature height is only 3 feet. The leaves are trifoliate, green in summer, and an attractive yellow to red color in the fall.

R. glabra (Smooth Sumac). Hardy in all zones. A common, native species often planted on highway slopes to reduce erosion. The height varies with soil fertility; on good soils the plants can easily reach 12 or more feet. The leaves are pinnately compound and turn brilliant red in the fall. The cut-leaved cultivar 'Laciniata' is attractive in early spring but is often attacked by powdery mildew disease, which causes the foliage to turn gray. This plant is not to be confused with *R. typhina* 'Laciniata' (the cut-leaved staghorn sumac).

R. trilobata (Skunkbush Sumac). Hardy in all zones. Similar to *R. aromatica* (fragrant sumac) but a little taller, growing to a height of 4 to 5 feet. The crushed foliage is ill scented, giving the plant its common name. A dense, compact form has been selected and is growing at the arboretum.

R. typhina (Staghorn Sumac). Hardy in all zones. The tallest of the sumacs, often growing 15 to 20 feet tall. The stems are covered with a velvety growth of hairs, giving the stem tips the appearance of a stag's horn. The leaves are pinnately compound and turn bright red in the fall. The upright clusters of red fruits are very showy on female plants. The cultivar 'Laciniata', commonly called cut-leaved sumac, has deeply cut leaves and is widely planted. It colors later in the season than the species, turning a pleasing shade of orange-red.

RIBES (Currant, Gooseberry). Grown for their edible fruits and for landscape use. Most currants and gooseberries are alternate hosts for the white pine blister rust, which causes a leaf spot on currants and gooseberries and stem cankers on all 5-needled white pines. The disease slightly injures the various species of *Ribes* but can kill the more valuable white pine. The law prohibits planting currants and gooseberries in countries where white pine is important commercially.

R. alpinum (Alpine Currant). Hardy in all zones. The most widely planted currant for landscape use, often used in foundation plantings and as a clipped hedge. A mature plant is 4 to 5 feet tall. The sexes are separate on this species, and male plants are usually cultivated because they are reported to be resistant to the white pine blister rust. Another leaf spot disease that causes premature defoliation sometimes develops in the fall.

R. odoratum (Clove Currant). Hardy in all zones. An upright shrub growing to 5 feet. In early May the plants are covered with fragrant, yellow flowers. In the fall the leaves turn red.

ROSA (Rose). There are many rose species and cultivars to choose from. The garden roses, including the Floribundas, Hybrid Teas, and Grandifloras are discussed in Chapter 18. Old-fashioned roses (introduced 100 or more years ago) such as the Albas, Centifolias, Damaska, Gallicas, Hybrid Perpetuals, and Moss Roses are of interest primarily to the rose specialist. For this reason, these roses are not included. A few of the species and hardy shrub roses are planted in the general landscape, and some of these are included.

R. foetida (Austrian Brier). Hardy in zones 4a, 4b, and 5a. This shrub grows about 6 feet tall. In early June the plants are covered with deep yellow, single flowers about 2 to 3 inches in diameter. The fall fruits are red. Two cultivars, 'Bicolor' (Austrian Copper) and 'Persiana' (Persian Yellow), are often planted. 'Bicolor' has single, coppery-red flowers; 'Persiana' double, yellow flowers.

R. gallica 'Alika'. Hardy in zones 4a, 4b, and 5a. Vigorous, hardy shrub rose that grows to a height of about 6 feet. In June the plants are covered with single, red flowers that are large and showy. A striking plant when in bloom.

R. x *harisonii* (Harison's Yellow Rose). Hardy in zones 4a, 4b, and 5a. A favorite rose that is a cross between *R. foetida* and *R.*

spinosissima. It reaches a height of about 5 feet, and its double, yellow blossoms are produced in late May or early in June.

R. hugonis (Father Hugo Rose). Hardy in zones 4a, 4b, and 5a. A hardy shrub rose, growing to 6 feet. The single flowers are light canary yellow and produced in late May and early June. The foliage is fine textured.

R. 'Lilian Gibson'. Hardy in all zones. A spreading rose developed in South Dakota. It is 7 feet tall, and its double, pink flowers are very showy in early June.

R. multiflora (Japanese Rose). Trial in zones 4a, 4b, and 5a. Considerable winter dieback occurs. This rose is mentioned only because of the publicity it has received. It has been widely planted in fence rows as a game cover in the East, where it grows 8 feet tall. It is also used as an understock when propagating garden roses. The flowers, when the plant does bloom, are small, white, and single. They are produced in clusters, so the overall effect is pleasing. The small, red fruits are also attractive in late fall.

R. 'Prairie Dawn'. Hardy in all zones. This 6-foot-tall shrub rose with repeat bloom was developed at Morden, Manitoba. The double, pink blossoms resemble a hybrid tea rose. Bloom peaks in June, but some flowers can be found on the shrubs throughout the summer and fall.

R. primula (Primrose Rose). Hardy in all zones. Arboretum plants reach a height of 6 feet. This is the earliest-flowering shrub rose; the small, light yellow, single blooms are produced in profusion on arching stems in mid- to late May.

R. rubrifolia (Redleaf Rose). Hardy in all zones. Planted mainly for its reddish-colored foliage. The mature height is 5 to 6 feet. The flowers are small, single, and deep red; the fruits bright red and showy in the fall.

R. rugosa (Rugosa Rose). Hardy in all zones. An extremely hardy species with dark green, crinkled foliage on 4-foot-tall plants. The flowers are pink to white and single. The fruits are brick red and large. Numerous cultivars of the rugosa rose and its hybrids are planted; 'Grootendorst Supreme' and 'Pink Grootendorst' are popular. Many cultivars have repeat bloom, and their flower colors include yellow, pink, red, and white.

R. spinosissima (Scotch Rose). Hardy in zones 4a, 4b, and 5a. Very hardy shrub rose with prickly stems. Plants are compact and grow to about 4 feet. The single flowers are white, pink, or yellow, and the fruits are usually black. There are a number of cultivars and some of these have double flowers. This species has been used in the breeding of many cultivars.

R. villosa (Apple Rose). Hardy in all zones. The shrub grows to about 6 feet and is planted primarily for its large, red, pear-shaped fruits that may be as much as 1½ inches in diameter. The single, pink flowers are about 2 inches across.

Rubus deliciosus (Boulder Raspberry). Hardy in zones 4a, 4b, and 5a. A 6-foot-tall shrub with large, solitary, white flowers. It is a graceful plant with arching branches. The fruits are dark purple. A double-flowered form 'Plena' is also available.

Rubus odoratus (Flowering Raspberry). Hardy in zones 4a, 4b, and 5a. Another 6-foot-tall shrub. The large, maple-shaped leaves measure up to 6 inches across. The flowers are purple, fragrant, and 2 inches in diameter. Does best on moist soil and in partial shade.

SALIX (Willow). Described in Chapter 11. Several of the shrub species are useful ornamentals.

S. alba 'Chermesina' (Redstem Willow). Hardy in all zones. This is a tall tree, but it can be grown as a large shrub (to 9 feet) when cut back to the ground early each spring. This technique promotes the development of numerous stems that are a brilliant orange to red color in late winter.

S. caprea (Goat Willow). Hardy in zones 4a, 4b, and 5a. Commonly grown for its pussy willows, which are the largest and showiest of the willows. By cutting the plant back to the ground occasionally, it can be kept under 10 feet and produces better catkins.

S. purpurea (Purple Osier Willow). Hardy in all zones. This willow is often used as a snow fence in shelterbelts, where it reaches a height of 7 feet. The dwarf form 'Nana' is often planted as a formal hedge. It is listed as 'Blueleaf Hedge' in some catalogs.

SAMBUCUS (Elder). A genus of large, coarse shrubs with pinnately compound leaves. Flowers are cream colored and produced in upright panicles or in flat-topped clusters. Stem borers are a problem and often kill entire plants.

S. canadensis (American Elder). Hardy in all zones. A common, native shrub. It is 10 feet tall and produces small, creamy-white flowers in large, flat-topped clusters in late June. The fruits are blue to black berries which are often harvested for pies and elderberry wine. A number of cultivars have been selected for their fruits.

S. pubens (Scarlet Elder). Hardy in all zones. This 10-foot-tall native shrub is shade tolerant and one of the earlier shrubs to leaf in the spring. The small, creamy-white flowers are produced in erect, pyramidal clusters, and the bright red fruits are readily eaten by birds.

S. racemosa (European Red Elder). Hardy in all zones. Similar to *S. pubens* (scarlet elder) in height and appearance. A cultivar with dissected leaves, 'Redman', is often planted. 'Sutherland Golden', developed in Saskatoon, Saskatchewan, has attractive yellow foliage.

Shepherdia argentea (Buffaloberry). Hardy in all zones. A very large shrub, 15 feet tall, that is native along streams in the drier states of the West. The foliage is silvery and offers a pleasing contrast when used in a shrub border. There are separate male and female plants, so to get the colorful red fruits one must grow several plants. This shrub needs plenty of space.

Sorbaria sorbifolia (Ural False Spirea). Hardy in all zones. The smallest and most popular of the false spireas, growing to a height of about 5 feet. The small, white flowers are produced in upright panicles. These flowers are attractive when they are fresh but soon turn brown. The species is shade tolerant and produces suckers. Do not plant where suckering would be a problem.

SPIRAEA (Spirea). A large genus containing many shrub species. Size varies from less than 1 foot to 6 or more feet. Spireas are grown primarily for their white to red flowers. Most species bloom early in the spring on old wood; a few bloom in summer on new wood.

S. albiflora (Japanese White Spirea). Hardy in all zones. A low shrub, 1½ feet high, that blooms on new wood. It is best to remove the old fruit clusters in the spring by cutting the stems down to within a few inches above the ground. White flowers are then produced in rounded to flat clusters at the tips of new growth in July.

S. x *arguta* (Garland Spirea). Hardy in all zones. A 5-foot-tall hybrid species resulting from a cross between *S. thunbergii* and *S. multiflora*. This is the showiest of the early-flowering spireas. Flat clusters of white flowers are produced on arching stems in mid-May. 'Compacta' is lower and more compact than the species, reaching a height of 4 feet.

S. x *billiardii* (Billiard Spirea). Hardy in all zones. This hybrid species is a cross between *S. douglasii* and *S. salicifolia*. It grows 5 feet tall and produces rose-pink flowers in pyramidal spikes during late June and early July. The flowers soon fade to a brown color.

S. x *bumalda* (Bumalda Spirea). Hardy in all zones. This 2-foot-tall hybrid, a cross between *S. japonica* and *S. albiflora*, has given rise to several cultivars. 'Anthony Waterer' is the most popular variety, with bright pink flowers in flat-topped clusters. 'Froebel' and 'Crispa' are also popular cultivars. The culture is the same as for *S. albiflora* (Japanese white spirea).

S. x *multiflora* (Snow Garland Spirea). Hardy in zones 4a, 4b, and 5a. This cross between *S. crenata* and *S. hypericifolia* has done well in arboretum trials and grows to a height of about 5 feet. Small clusters of little, white flowers are produced in late May.

S. nipponica var. *rotundifolia* (Big Nippon Spirea). Hardy in zones 4a, 4b, and 5a. A medium-sized shrub growing approximately 6 feet tall. The branches are rather stiff and the color of the foliage is bluish green. White flowers are produced in small, flat-topped clusters in late May.

S. prunifolia (Bridalwreath Spirea). Trial in zone 4a; hardy in zones 4b and 5a. Some dieback can occur after a severe winter. Plants grow to a height of 4 feet. The only spirea that produces double white flowers and one of the few spireas with an attractive orange fall coloration.

S. thunbergii (Thunberg Spirea). Trial in zone 4a; hardy in zones 4b and 5a. Tip kill in the spring is not uncommon. This popular, 4-foot-tall species has fine-textured foliage and small, white flowers in early May before the leaves open.

S. x *vanhouttei* (Vanhoutte Spirea). Hardy in all zones. A cross between *S. cantoniensis* and *S. trilobata*, growing to a height of 6 feet. The long, arching branches covered with clusters of white flowers in early June make this a popular shrub. The most widely planted spirea.

Stephanandra incisa (Cutleaf Stephanandra). Trial in zones 4a, 4b, and 5a. Winter hardiness is borderline, and some years rather heavy pruning is required to remove dead wood. This is a graceful, 4-foot-tall shrub with finely dissected leaves. It is grown primarily for its foliage effect since the flowers and fruits are inconspicuous. The dwarf form 'Crispa' is better than the species where space is limited.

SYMPHORICARPOS (Coralberry, Snowberry). A small genus of shrubs grown primarily for their fruits which persist into winter.

S. albus (Snowberry). Hardy in all zones. This native shrub grows to a height of 4 feet and produces small, pink blossoms in mid-June and conspicuous white fruits in late fall which persist into winter. When loaded with fruits, the branches often bend to the ground. The shrub tolerates some shade and does best on moisture-retentive soil.

S. x *chenaultii* (Chenault Coralberry). Trial in zones 4b and 5a. Has not been reliably hardy; severe dieback can be expected most winters. This hybrid is a cross between *S. microphyllus* and *S. orbiculatus* and grows to a height of 2 feet.

S. orbiculatus (Coralberry). Hardy in all zones. A 3-foot-tall, native shrub grown for its colorful, purplish-red fruits which persist into winter. The flowers are small and inconspicuous. This shrub is frequently planted on highway slopes as a bank cover.

SYRINGA (Lilac). A large genus containing many ornamental species grown for their fragrant flowers. Size can vary from 5 feet to 20 feet, the height of a small tree.

S. x *chinensis* (Chinese Lilac). Hardy in all zones. This cross between *S. laciniata* and *S. persica* is widely planted as a screen or informal hedge. The plant grows more than 8 feet tall. It blooms in late May with small clusters of lilac flowers. It does not sucker, an advantage over *S. vulgaris* (common lilac).

S. meyeri (Meyer's Lilac). Hardy in all zones. One of the smaller lilacs, with little, crinkled leaves. It grows to 5 feet and is suitable in the foundation planting and in the foreground of the shrub border. The lilac flowers are produced in small, upright panicles in late May. Although this lilac was introduced by Dr. Meyer in 1908, it became very popular only recently when it was sold in the nursery trade under the name *S. palabiniana*.

S. microphylla (Littleleaf Lilac). Trial in zone 4a; hardy in zones 4b and 5a. This small, spreading lilac has not been as hardy as *S. meyeri* (Meyer's lilac). The height is 6 feet, the leaves are small, and flowers are pale lilac in late May. The cultivar 'Superba' is preferred to the species.

S. oblata var. *dilatata* (Korean Early Lilac). Hardy in all zones. Mature plants are about 10 feet tall. This is the earliest-blooming lilac, with pale pink flowers opening in early May. It is one of the few lilacs to develop a fall coloration: the leaves turn a rich wine-red color in October.

S. patula 'Miss Kim'. Hardy in all zones. Cultivar introduced by the University of New Hampshire; it was a chance seedling grown from seed obtained in the Pouk Han Mountains of Korea. Plants grow about 6 feet tall and are covered with fragrant, lavender flowers in early June. This lilac develops a burgundy-red color in the fall. One of the better of the newer lilacs.

S. x *persica* (Persian Lilac). Hardy in all zones. Often confused with *S.* x *chinensis* (Chinese lilac), the true Persian lilac is a hybrid resulting from a cross between *S. afghanica* and *S. laciniata*. Mature plants are about 6 feet tall. Small clusters of pale lilac-colored flowers are produced in late May.

S. x *prestoniae* (Preston Lilac). Hardy in all zones. This cross between *S. villosa* and *S. reflexa* has given rise to a number of fine cultivars that are late flowering in early to mid-June. Most are non-suckering and grow about 8 feet tall. 'Coral', 'Donald Wyman', 'Isabella', and 'James MacFarland' have done well in trials at the arboretum.

S. villosa (Late Lilac). Hardy in all zones. Of greatest value for the hybrids it has produced. The species is a large (12 feet), rather coarse shrub with flowers ranging from white to rosy lilac in early to mid-June. It is often planted where a dense screen is desired.

S. vulgaris (Common Lilac). Hardy in all zones. The commonest lilac and widely planted. It is a very large, suckering shrub, growing to 20 feet. The fragrant flowers are typically lilac colored and open from mid- to late May. There are hundreds of named cultivars of the common lilac. These have been selected for their flower size and coloring. Some have double flowers. Most cultivars produce fewer suckers than the species. Because of the large number of cultivars, it is best to visit a public garden featuring lilacs when they are in bloom to select cultivars that appeal to you. About 60 cultivars are in the arboretum planting.

Tamarix ramosissima (Five-stamen Tamarix). Hardy in all zones. This is the hardiest of the *Tamarix* species, growing to 10 feet. The small, pink flowers are produced in fluffy panicles in mid-July and intermittently throughout the summer. The leaves are minute, giving a feathery appearance to the plant. 'Cheyenne Red' and 'Summer Glow' are named cultivars that are similar to each other. Tamarix likes well-drained soil and is drought resistant.

VIBURNUM (Highbush Cranberry, Arrowwood, Nannyberry, Witherod). A large genus containing many species grown for their flowers and fruits. Most species have attractive fall colors.

V. carlesii (Korean Spice Viburnum). Trial in zones 4a, 4b, and 5a. Has borderline hardiness. The shrub grows to a height of about 4 feet. An early-flowering, fragrant viburnum, it produces small clusters of pinkish-white flowers in mid-May. Plant only in a sheltered location.

V. cassinoides (Witherod). Hardy in all zones. A small to medium shrub growing to about 5 feet. The small, creamy-white flowers are produced in flat-topped clusters in early June. The fruits undergo an interesting color change in the fall, from green to red to black. The green leaves turn brilliant red in late September and early October.

V. dentatum (Arrowwood). Hardy in all zones. A large shrub growing to a height of 10 or more feet. The small, creamy-white flowers are produced in flat-topped clusters in early June. The fleshy, berrylike fruits are dark blue to black in August and are eaten by birds as soon as they are ripe. Useful as a background shrub or for an informal or formal hedge.

V. lantana (Wayfaring Bush). Hardy in all zones. This large shrub, which grows to 10 feet, has thick, velvety-green leaves and creamy-white flowers in late May. The color of the fruits changes from green to red to black in early fall. Birds love the fruits and readily eat them as soon as they ripen.

V. lentago (Nannyberry). Hardy in all zones. One of the larger native viburnums, often reaching a height of 15 feet. The creamy-white flowers open in late May. The glossy green leaves turn purplish red in the fall. The black fruits are flattened and dry on the plants. After a frost the fruits are sweet and chewy. Birds love the fruits and feed on the plants in late fall and early winter. This shrub can also be grown as a small tree.

V. opulus (European Highbush Cranberry). Hardy in all zones. The most widely grown highbush cranberry, reaching a height of 10 or more feet. The flat-topped flower clusters open in early June. The marginal flowers in each cluster are white, sterile, and showy. The center flowers are small and creamy white. These are followed by clusters of bright red, inedible fruits in the fall. Aphids can be a problem on the maple-shaped leaves. The cultivar 'Roseum' is the old-fashioned Snowball. 'Compactum' is a dense form growing about 5 feet tall. 'Nana' is very dwarf, seldom exceeding 2 feet, and is nonflowering.

V. sargentii (Sargent Highbush Cranberry). Hardy in all zones. Large shrub, 10 or more feet tall, with attractive flowers and fruits similar to those of *V. opulus* (European highbush cranberry). The marginal flowers in each cluster are large and showy. Leaf scorch can be a problem in a dry year. The cultivar 'Flavum' has golden-yellow fruits.

V. trilobum (American Highbush Cranberry). Hardy in all zones. This native shrub is similar to *V. opulus*. It differs primarily in having edible fruits that can be used in making preserves. Two compact forms are available in the trade. 'Compactum' is an introduction from the eastern part of the United States. The J. V. Bailey Nursery of Newport, Minnesota is selling a compact form that develops a much better fall color than 'Compactum'; otherwise it is very similar.

Weigela florida (Old-fashioned Weigela). Trial in zones 4a and 4b; hardy in zone 5a. This species and the variety *mandshurica* are the hardiest weigelas. Plants grow about 6 feet tall. The flower color, a magenta pink, is not as showy as that of the many hybrids. The variety *mandshurica* has been used in breeding at the arboretum, and a number of selections have been made with improved form and flower color. The cultivar 'Variegata' has attractive foliage with pale yellow leaf edges. This cultivar is not as hardy as the species, and some tip kill can be expected.

Weigela Hybrids. Trial in zones 4a, 4b, and 5a. Most of the numerous cultivars on the market lack winter hardiness. Although some bloom can be expected each year, the tips of the stems usually die back and considerable pruning is required. Plants grow about 6 feet tall. 'Vanicek', also sold as 'Newport Red', is the most widely sold weigela cultivar in this area.

General Shrub Lists

LARGE SHRUBS
(over 8 feet)

Acer ginnala
Acer spicatum
Acer tataricum
Caragana arborescens
Cephalanthus occidentalis
Chionanthus virginicus
Cornus mas
Cornus racemosa
Cornus sericea
Cotinus obovatus
Euonymus alata
Euonymus europaea
Hamamelis virginiana
Hippophae rhamnoides
Hydrangea paniculata 'Grandi-
    flora'
Lonicera maackii
Lonicera tatarica
Philadelphus x virginalis
Prunus triloba
Prunus virginiana

Rhamnus cathartica
Rhamnus frangula
Rhus glabra
Rhus typhina
Salix alba 'Chermesina'
Salix caprea
Sambucus canadensis
Sambucus pubens
Sambucus racemosa
Shepherdia argentea
Syringa x chinensis
Syringa oblata var. dilatata
Syringa villosa
Syringa vulgaris
Tamarix ramosissima
Viburnum dentatum
Viburnum lantana
Viburnum lentago
Viburnum opulus
Viburnum sargentii
Viburnum trilobum

MEDIUM SHRUBS
(5 to 8 feet)

Acanthopanax sieboldianus
Aesculus parviflora
Amelanchier alnifolia
Amelanchier stolonifera
Aronia arbutifolia
Berberis koreana
Caragana microphylla 'Tidy'
Cornus alba
Cornus sericea 'Isanti'
Cotinus coggygria
Cotoneaster lucidus
Cotoneaster multiflorus
Deutzia x lemoinei
Dirca palustris
Elaeagnus commutata

Forsythia x intermedia
Forsythia ovata
Ilex verticillata
Kolkwitzia amabilis
Lespedeza bicolor
Ligustrum amurense
Ligustrum vulgare
Lonicera morrowii
Magnolia stellata
Philadelphus coronarius 'Aureus'
Physocarpus opulifolius
Prinsepia sinensis
Prunus x cistena
Prunus tomentosa
Rhododendron japonicum

Rhododendron x *kosterianum*
Rhododendron maximum
Rosa foetida
Rosa gallica 'Alika'
Rosa x *harisonii*
Rosa hugonis
Rosa multiflora
Rosa primula
Rosa rubrifolia
Rosa villosa

Rubus deliciosus
Rubus odoratus
Salix purpurea
Spiraea nipponica var. *rotundi-folia*
Spiraea x *vanhouttei*
Syringa microphylla
Syringa patula 'Miss Kim'
Syringa x *persica*
Weigela florida

SMALL SHRUBS
(under 5 feet)

Abeliophyllum distichum
Aronia melanocarpa
Aronia prunifolia
Berberis thunbergii
Buxus microphylla var. *koreana*
Caragana frutex
Caragana pygmaea
Caryopteris x *clandonensis*
Ceanothus americanus
Chaenomeles speciosa
Cotoneaster apiculatus
Cytisus hirsutus
Diervilla lonicera
Euonymus fortunei
Genista multibracteata
Hydrangea arborescens
Hypericum kalmianum
Hypericum prolificum
Kalmia poliifolia
Ledum groenlandicum
Ligustrum obtusifolium var. *rege-lianum*
Lonicera x *xylosteoides* 'Clavey's Dwarf'
Lonicera xylosteum 'Emerald Mound'
Myrica pensylvanica
Paeonia suffruticosa
Potentilla fruticosa
Prunus glandulosa

Prunus japonica
Prunus tenella
Rhododendron arborescens
Rhododendron atlanticum
Rhododendron calendulaceum
Rhododendron canadense
Rhododendron carolinianum
Rhododendron catawbiense
Rhododendron mucronulatum
Rhododendron periclymenoides
Rhododendron prinophyllum
Rhododendron schlippenbachii
Rhododendron viscosum
Rhododendron yedoense var. *poukhanense*
Rhus aromatica
Rhus trilobata
Ribes alpinum
Ribes odoratum
Rosa rugosa
Rosa spinosissima
Sorbaria sorbifolia
Spiraea albiflora
Spiraea x *arguta*
Spiraea x *billiardii*
Spiraea x *bumalda*
Spiraea x *multiflora*
Spiraea prunifolia
Spiraea thunbergii
Stephanandra incisa

Symphoricarpos albus
Symphoricarpos x *chenaultii*
Symphoricarpos orbiculatus

Syringa meyeri
Viburnum carlesii
Viburnum cassinoides

Special Shrub Lists

SHRUBS WITH SHOWY FLOWERS

Abeliophyllum distichum
Amelanchier species
Aronia species
Berberis species
Caragana species
Caryopteris x *clandonensis*
Ceanothus americanus
Chaenomeles speciosa
Cornus species
Cotoneaster multiflorus
Cytisus hirsutus
Deutzia x *lemoinei*
Diervilla species
Dirca palustris
Forsythia species
Genista multibracteata
Hydrangea species
Hypericum species
Kalmia poliifolia
Kolkwitzia amabilis

Ledum groenlandicum
Lespedeza bicolor
Lonicera species
Magnolia stellata
Paeonia suffruticosa
Philadelphus species
Physocarpus opulifolius
Potentilla fruticosa
Prunus species
Rhododendron species
Ribes odoratum
Rosa species
Rubus species
Sambucus species
Spiraea species
Syringa species
Tamarix ramosissima
Viburnum species
Weigela species

SHRUBS WITH COLORED FRUITS
(planted to attract birds)

Acer ginnala
Acer tataricum
Amelanchier species
Aronia species
Berberis species
Cornus species
Cotoneaster species
Euonymus species
Hippophae rhamnoides
Ilex verticillata

Lonicera species
Prinsepia sinensis
Prunus species
Rhamnus species
Rhus species
Rosa species
Sambucus species
Shepherdia argentea
Symphoricarpos species
Viburnum species

SHRUBS WITH COLORED OR VARIEGATED FOLIAGE

Berberis thunbergii 'Atropurpu-
     rea'
Berberis thunbergii 'Crimson
     Pygmy'
Cornus alba 'Argenteo-marginata'
Cornus alba 'Gouchaultii'
Cornus alba 'Spaethii'
Cotinus coggygria 'Royal Purple'
Elaeagnus commutata

Philadelphus coronarius 'Aureus'
Physocarpus opulifolius 'Luteus'
Prunus x *cistena*
Prunus virginiana 'Shubert'
Sambucus racemosa 'Sutherland
     Golden'
Shepherdia argentea
Weigela florida 'Variegata'

SHRUBS WITH BRILLIANT FALL COLOR

Acer species
Aronia species
Chionanthus virginicus
Cornus species

Cotinus obovatus
Euonymus species
Rhus species
Viburnum species

SHRUBS FOR INFORMAL HEDGES

Acer ginnala
Aronia melanocarpa
Berberis thunbergii
Caragana arborescens
Caragana pygmaea
Cornus sericea 'Isanti'
Cotoneaster lucidus
Lonicera x *xylosteoides* 'Clavey's
     Dwarf'
Lonicera xylosteum 'Emerald
     Mound'

Physocarpus opulifolius 'Nanus'
Potentilla fruticosa 'Jackmannii'
Prunus virginiana 'Shubert'
Rhamnus frangula 'Tallhedge'
Ribes alpinum
Spiraea x *vanhouttei*
Syringa x *chinensis*
Syringa meyeri
Viburnum dentatum
Viburnum opulus 'Compactum'
Viburnum trilobum 'Compactum'

SHRUBS FOR FORMAL HEDGES

Acer ginnala
Aronia melanocarpa
Berberis thunbergii
Buxus microphylla var. *koreana*
Caragana frutex 'Globosa'
Cotoneaster lucidus
Euonymus alata
Lonicera morrowii
Lonicera tatarica 'Zabellii'

Lonicera x *xylosteoides* 'Clavey's
     Dwarf'
Physocarpus opulifolius 'Nanus'
Ribes alpinum
Syringa meyeri
Viburnum dentatum
Viburnum opulus 'Compactum'
Viburnum trilobum 'Compactum'

Chapter 13

Selection and Care of Evergreens

This chapter includes only the conifers and not the broad-leaved evergreens. (These broad-leaved evergreens are covered in Chapters 12 and 15.) Several deciduous conifers are also included since their summer effect in the landscape is the same as that of the other needle evergreens.

Because our winter season is long, evergreens are especially welcome in the landscape. It is best to use them in border plantings where they will be visible from inside the house during the winter months. Certain creeping evergreens make attractive ground covers.

Some evergreens like arborvitaes, yews, and certain junipers are subject to winter burn. Shading the plants from the winter sun either by planting them where they will receive no direct winter sun or by using a burlap shade reduces this type of injury. Drive about 5 stakes into the ground around the susceptible plant. Fasten burlap around the stakes to a height that will shade the plant. This should be done in the fall while the weather is still pleasant. Certain cultivars are more resistant to winter burn and these should be planted.

Abies balsamea (Balsam Fir). Hardy in all zones. This native fir, which grows 30 feet tall, is often used for Christmas trees. It develops an attractive pyramidal form and is dark green. It does best on moisture-retentive soils.

Abies concolor (White Fir). Hardy in zones 4a, 4b, and 5a. A truly beautiful tree for specimen planting, reaching a height of 30 feet. Plants tend to be irregular when young, but once established, they develop into very symmetrical, upright trees. The needles are long and silvery blue.

Chamaecyparis pisifera (Sawara False Cypress). Trial in zones 4a, 4b, and 5a. This is the only species of *Chamaecyparis* that has done well in arboretum trials. The 30-foot-tall species is an upright tree resembling *Thuja occidentalis* (the native arborvitae). 'Filifera' is a compact cultivar with irregular form and narrow branches. A specimen in the dwarf conifer area at the arboretum is now 10 years old and is growing very well.

JUNIPERUS (Juniper). A large genus with scalelike leaves produced in whorls of 3. The seeds are produced in cones that resemble berries. Most species are drought resistant. *J. virginiana* and *J. scopulorum* are alternate hosts for cedar-apple rust, a serious disease of apples. On these susceptible junipers, the rust forms small, brown galls which shed their spores after the first warm rains in the spring. At the time of spore discharge the galls send out long, orange, gelatinous horns that are very noticeable. These species should not be planted within ¼ mile of a commercial apple orchard.

J. chinensis (Chinese Juniper). Hardy in zones 4a, 4b, and 5a. A highly variable species, ranging in size from low spreading shrubs (1 foot tall) to large trees (40 or more feet). The species is seldom planted but the following cultivars are commonly grown: 'Ames' is broadly pyramidal and 8 feet tall. 'Blaauw', a vase-shaped shrub, grows about 3 feet tall with bluish-green foliage. 'Hetzii' is a spreading shrub approximately 5 feet tall and has bluish-green foliage. 'Maney', introduced from Ames, Iowa, is an upright, spreading juniper that reaches a height of about 5 feet. The foliage is bluish green. The stems are brittle and breakage by snow is not uncommon. This selection is very hardy. A recent introduction called

'Mint Julep' is low, vase-shaped, and bright green. 'Mountbatten' is a narrow, upright tree to 10 feet, with bluish-gray foliage. 'Pfitzeri-ana' (Pfitzer's juniper) is widely planted. It is spreading and irregular, and its color is gray-green. Three sports of 'Pfitzeriana' are 'Pfitzeriana Aurea', which has a golden cast; 'Pfitzeriana Compacta', which is smaller and more compact; and 'Pfitzeriana Glauca', which has silvery-blue foliage. 'Plumosa' is a low (to 3 feet), spreading shrub with plumelike branches, and 'San Jose' is a fast-growing, creeping juniper less than 1 foot tall with bluish-green needles.

J. communis (Common Juniper). Hardy in all zones. This variable species is seldom planted. The following varieties and cultivars are frequently used: *J. communis* var. *depressa* (Ground Juniper) is vase-shaped and native, with awl-shaped leaves and a green summer color. The needles take on a purplish color in the fall. *J. communis* var. *saxatile* (Mountain Juniper) is a dwarf, mountain form that forms dense, 2-foot-tall mats. The cultivar 'Aurea' is similar to *J. communis* var. *depressa* but has a yellowish cast which is colorful in early summer. The plant grows to a height of 2 feet. 'Effusa', a dwarf, spreading form, is about 1 foot tall with small needles. 'Repanda' is a compact, spreading shrub about 3 feet tall.

J. horizontalis (Creeping Juniper). Hardy in all zones. A low, creeping shrub, usually less than 1 foot tall, with short, scalelike needles. It is highly variable and many cultivars are on the market. The following are a few of the more common ones: 'Bar Harbor' has trailing, bluish-green branches that hug the ground. 'Blue Chips' is a compact creeper with bluish-green foliage. 'Douglasii' (Waukegan juniper) is a spreading shrub 12 to 15 inches tall. Its steel-blue foliage takes on a purplish cast in the fall. 'Hughes' is another silvery-blue, low, spreading juniper that is very popular. 'Plumosa' (Andorra juniper) is widely planted but has not done well in arboretum trials. Its foliage is grayish green and takes on a purplish cast in the fall. Arboretum plants usually show considerable winter browning. 'Webberi' is a rather new introduction and grows low, forms a mat, and is bluish green. 'Wiltonii', sometimes sold as 'Wilton Carpet', has an intense, silvery-blue color and makes a fine ground cover.

J. procumbens (Japanese Garden Juniper). Hardy in zones 4a, 4b, and 5a. This may be only a variety of *J. chinensis* and is so considered by some authorities. It forms a dense mat with awl-shaped needles. A single plant spreads about 6 feet and is 6 inches tall. Some winter burn, caused by the sun, may be seen in an open winter with insufficient snow to cover the plants. 'Nana' is a slower-growing cultivar that is sometimes planted.

J. sabina (Savins Juniper). Trial in zone 3b; hardy in zones 4a, 4b, and 5a. A variable species with a fine, soft texture. The foliage emits a disagreeable odor when bruised and has a bitter taste. This characteristic helps distinguish the species from *J. horizontalis*. The cultivars of this species are planted more commonly than the species: 'Arcadia' is a very hardy selection from Morden, Manitoba. It grows to a height of about 1½ feet and has green foliage. 'Blue Danube' is a low, spreading shrub, 1½ feet tall, with bluish-green foliage; 'Broadmoor' a dwarf, spreading plant, 1½ feet tall, with a green color. 'Skandia', another very hardy introduction from Morden, Manitoba, is 1-foot-tall, spreading, and dark green.

J. scopulorum (Rocky Mountain Juniper). Hardy in all zones. This small, upright tree grows to a height of 20 feet and is native from the Badlands of North and South Dakota westward into the mountain states. The trees are characteristically upright and range from green to blue green. The species differs from *J. virginiana* in the length of time it takes for the berries to ripen: two years is required for *J. scopulorum*, one year for *J. virginiana*. Numerous cultivars are on the market. These are widely used, mostly for foundation plantings or screens. They are dense plants that grow about 15 feet tall, except as noted. 'Blue Heaven' is a narrow, upright tree with an intense, blue color. 'Cologreen' grows upright and has a bright green color. 'Lakewood Globe' forms a natural globe that is 8 feet tall with bluish-green foliage. 'Medora' is a very narrow, upright selection from Medora, North Dakota, but difficulty in propagation has limited its use. 'Moffetii' is dense, pyramidal, and bluish-green. 'Steel Blue' is an upright, steel-blue tree. 'Sutherland' is compact, upright, with green foliage; 'Tabletop' low (6 feet), mound-shaped, with a bluish-green color; and 'Welchii' dense, conical, with silvery-green foliage.

J. virginiana (Eastern Red Cedar). Hardy in all zones. The largest juniper, often growing 30 or more feet tall. A mature tree usually has an open, spreading appearance. Although native, this species is not used to any great extent in landscape plantings. The following cultivars are available: The dark green 'Canaertii' is a narrow, upright tree to 15 feet, with stout, spreading branches. 'Kosteri', a low, spreading form, is 3 feet tall, grayish-blue, and turns purple in the fall. It is similar in appearance to 'Pfitzeriana' (Pfitzer's juniper). 'Hillii' is a compact, pyramidal tree, 15 feet tall, with green foliage that turns purplish in the fall.

LARIX (Larch). A genus of deciduous conifers. The needles are produced in clusters at the end of short branches. The fall color is golden yellow.

L. decidua (European Larch). Hardy in zones 4a, 4b, and 5a. A large tree, 40 feet tall, with a single trunk and wide-spreading branches. The green color of the new leaves in the spring and the golden-yellow fall color are most attractive. Many cultivars exist but few are planted in this area. The cultivar 'Pendula' has drooping branches and is an interesting novelty.

L. kaempferi (Japanese Larch). Hardy in zones 4a, 4b, and 5a. May also be listed as *L. leptolepis*. This 30-foot-tall tree is smaller than *L. decidua* (European larch) but otherwise quite similar.

L. laricina (American Larch or Tamarack). Hardy in all zones. Native to northern swamps, this tree is similar in general appearance to *L. decidua*. It is drought tolerant and does well on upland soils.

Metasequoia glyptostroboides (Dawn Redwood). Trial in sheltered locations in zones 4a, 4b, and 5a. Considerable winter injury to the buds occurs. A deciduous conifer, the dawn redwood was introduced into this country from China in 1946. In milder climates it grows rapidly and forms a symmetrical, upright tree, but in our climate the growth is irregular and more shrubby than treelike, with plants reaching a height of about 15 feet.

PICEA (Spruce). A large genus of forest and landscape trees. The angular, pointed needles are spirally arranged on the branches. When the needles drop, a jagged leaf base remains on the twigs.

P. abies (Norway Spruce). Hardy in zones 4a, 4b, and 5a. One of the taller spruces, reaching a height of 50 feet. The large 4- to 6-inch cones and the drooping branchlets on the horizontal branches distinguish this species. Many dwarf cultivars are on the market. The following do well: 'Acrocona' is a slow-growing selection, 15 feet tall, whose cones develop at the tips of lateral branches; it is an interesting novelty. 'Clanbrassiliana', a compact, rounded shrub, is broader than tall and seldom exceeds 3 to 4 feet. 'Nidiformis' (Nest Spruce) grows very slowly: a mature specimen may be 5 or 6 feet across and only a few feet tall. 'Pumila' is dwarf sized and globe shaped, growing to a height of 3 feet.

P. glauca (White Spruce). Hardy in all zones. The common spruce native across the northern United States and Canada. It grows 40 feet tall. The foliage is typically green, but trees with a bluish cast are not uncommon. This species is widely planted in windbreaks and for screen or background plantings. The variety *densata*, native to the Black Hills of South Dakota, is denser than the species and widely planted. The cultivar 'Conica' is commonly called the dwarf Alberta spruce. It has a very slow growth rate and forms a dense, conical tree. This cultivar is subject to winter sunscald and must be shaded in the winter.

P. mariana (Black Spruce). Hardy in all zones. Native to swamps. It is narrow, dark green, and grows 30 feet tall. The needles are usually shorter than those on *P. glauca* (white spruce). It grows well under cultivation and could be used more in landscape plantings.

P. pungens (Colorado Spruce). Hardy in all zones. Reaching 40 feet at maturity, this popular ornamental is widely planted for windbreaks and in landscape plantings. Foliage color varies from green to blue. The blue forms are usually grouped under the variety *glauca*. A few selections of these blue forms are given cultivar names. These trees grow to 40 feet, except as noted, and include: 'Hoopsii', a dense, pyramidal form that is especially blue; 'Koster', a world famous blue form that is narrow and upright; 'Moerheimii', a narrow, upright form with irregularly whorled branches; 'Montgomery', a very slow-growing dwarf form that is 3 feet tall; and 'Thomsen', a symmetrical, silver-blue tree with very thick needles.

PINUS (Pine). A large genus of trees grown for lumber and for landscape uses. The long needles are produced in clusters of 2 to 5 needles. The 5-needle pines are subject to white pine blister rust disease, a disease which can kill the trees.

P. aristata (Bristlecone Pine). Trial in zones 4a, 4b, and 5a. A very slow-growing species from the mountains of southwestern United States. It is long-lived and specimens of native trees are known to be over 3,000 years old. The height seldom exceeds 6 feet under cultivation. Winter burn can be a serious problem on this dwarf evergreen.

P. banksiana (Jack Pine). Hardy in all zones. Grows 40 feet tall. This native pine has two rather short needles in each cluster. The leaves are bright green in summer but may turn brownish green in autumn. This species deserves to be used more as an ornamental. A dwarf, globe-shaped form not exceeding 5 feet has been grown from seeds collected on witches brooms (a dense cluster of small branches). It is an attractive dwarf suitable for rock garden plantings. 'Uncle Fogey' is the cultivar name given to a weeping form of the Jack pine. This tree is an interesting novelty.

P. cembra (Swiss Stone Pine). Hardy in zones 4a, 4b, and 5a. A slow-growing tree, reaching 30 feet, that is narrow and upright. It produces 5 rather stiff needles in a cluster. A number of cultivars are on the market but few are sold in this area.

P. densiflora (Japanese Red Pine). Trial in zones 4a, 4b, and 5a. Most strains have not proved hardy. Trees grown from seed collected from a planting made by the Forestry College in Cloquet, Minnesota have grown well in the arboretum, reaching a height of 30 feet, and these should be a source for a hardy strain of this fine ornamental tree. 'Umbraculifera' is a dwarf form, 8 feet tall, with an umbrella-shaped crown. Winter burn has been a problem on this cultivar.

P. mugo var. *mugo* (Mugho Pine or Mugho Swiss Mountain Pine). Hardy in all zones. A mountain form widely used in landscaping, reaching a height of 15 feet. It is a common practice to shear this plant in the nursery to a uniform, rounded form. If allowed to grow naturally, the variety becomes a beautiful, informal, large shrub or small tree.

P. nigra (Austrian Pine). Hardy in zones 4a, 4b, and 5a. Reaches 40 feet at maturity. This 2-needle pine has long, dark green needles. The species is highly resistant to winter burn and makes a fine specimen tree.

P. ponderosa var. *scopulorum* (Rocky Mountain Ponderosa Pine). Hardy in all zones. Growing 40 feet tall, this variety is smaller than the species but much hardier and better adapted for landscape planting in this area. It is distinguished by long needles borne in clusters of 2 or 3 needles. Widely planted in shelterbelts.

P. resinosa (Red Pine or Norway Pine). Hardy in all zones. A 60-foot-tall tree. The needles of this native pine are long and in clusters of 2. The tree grows best on sandy loam soils. Winter burn can be a problem on young trees grown in exposed areas.

P. strobus (Eastern White Pine). Hardy in all zones. Native, 5-needle pine growing to a height of 60 feet. Young trees must be protected from the winter sun to avoid winter burn. Dwarf forms can be grown from seeds collected on witches brooms. 'Fastigiata' is a narrow, columnar form that grows 40 feet tall.

P. sylvestris (Scotch Pine). Hardy in zones 4a, 4b, and 5a. This 50-foot-tall pine is often grown for Christmas trees. Hardy seed sources should be used in growing this species. The scotch pine has a reddish bark and mature trees are very picturesque. 'Fastigiata' is a columnar form that is sometimes planted.

Pseudotsuga menziesii var. *glauca* (Blue Douglas Fir). Hardy in zones 4a, 4b, and 5a. Grows 40 feet tall. This is the Rocky Mountain form of Douglas fir and the only one hardy in our area. The dark green foliage, the pointed buds, and the 3-lobed bracts between the cone scales help identify the Douglas fir. An excellent specimen tree.

Taxodium distichum (Bald Cypress). Trial in zones 4a, 4b, and 5a. Reaching 30 feet at maturity, this southern species grows as far north as southern Illinois. Seedlings from the northern limit of its range are doing well in the arboretum. Like the larches, this tree is deciduous.

TAXUS (Yew). Characterized by dark green needles and red, berry-like fruits. Most species and cultivars are subject to winter burn and must be planted where they will receive winter shade or snow cover.

T. canadensis (American Yew). Hardy in all zones. A low-growing, spreading shrub that is native. It is 4 feet tall and its green needles take on a purplish cast in the fall.

T. cuspidata (Japanese Yew). Hardy in zones 4a, 4b, and 5a. A variable species that may grow either spreading or upright. Spreading forms grow 4 feet tall, upright forms 15 feet tall. 'Nana' is a compact, spreading form that has done well. 'Capitata' is an upright form that flourishes on north exposures. A few selections that resist winter burn have been made, but these have not been given cultivar names.

T. x *media* (Anglo-Jap Yew). Hardy in zones 4a, 4b, and 5a. A hybrid between *T. cuspidata* and *T. baccata*. Its appearance is variable and both upright and spreading forms are common. 'Taunton' is one of the most dependable cultivars, growing 3 feet tall. A selection that shows promise has also been made at the arboretum. It is 3 feet tall.

Thuja occidentalis (American Arborvitae). Hardy in all zones. A highly variable species with many named cultivars of various forms and sizes. The typical species is a broad, pyramidal tree that is 40 feet tall and common in northern swamps. This arborvitae makes a fine screen planting. Winter burn can be a problem on the south side of buildings. 'Aurea' has golden foliage, especially in the spring when new growth starts, and a broad, pyramidal form. 'Dark Green', a fine selection, is 30 feet tall and resistant to winter burn. 'Fastigiata' is a narrow, upright tree, 30 feet tall, that is subject to winter burn in exposed sites. 'Hetz Midget' is small and globe shaped, seldom growing taller than about 1½ feet. It is good for edging or in rock garden plantings. 'Pyramidalis' resembles 'Fastigiata' and is 30 feet tall. 'Techny' is a broad, pyramidal tree,

25 feet tall, with a dark green color. 'Wareana', often called Siberian arborvitae, is very hardy and grows into a broad, pyramidal tree 20 feet tall. 'Woodwardii' is a true globe growing to about 6 feet. It is subject to winter burn and should be planted only where it will have winter shade.

Tsuga canadensis (Canada Hemlock). Hardy in all zones. A 50-foot-tall tree grown for its graceful, fine-textured branches. It is often planted as a clipped hedge in eastern states. Winter burn is a serious problem in our area. Nursery-grown trees that are shipped into this area are likely to show winter burn, especially when young. Yet seedlings grown from native trees near Mille Lacs lake have shown no winter burn. The weeping form 'Pendula' can be used in sheltered locations that receive winter shade. It is slow growing and seldom becomes more than 6 feet tall.

Chapter 14

Selection and Care of Vines

Vines may be used in the landscape for covering fences or walls. They may also be grown on specially constructed trellises and pergolas. Vines differ in their method of climbing. Some vines, like the grape, climb by tendrils which attach the vines to the support. These tendrils may be modified stems or leaves. Other vines climb by twining or by wrapping themselves around the support. Some climb clockwise and others climb counterclockwise. Bittersweet, wisteria, and moonseed are examples of twining vines. A few vines, such as Boston ivy, attach themselves to their support by sucker-like disks, or haustoria. Some plants must be tied to their supports. Climbing roses are actually not natural climbers. Their stems are too weak to support the weight of their leaves and flowers, so they sprawl over the ground. Their stems must be tied to a support if the flowers are to be displayed at eye level. The following vines are suitable for planting in this area:

Actinidia arguta (Bower Actinidia). Hardy in zones 4a, 4b, and 5a. A vigorous, twining vine sometimes used for screening. The flowers and the fruits are inconspicuous, but the glossy, green leaves produced on red petioles are attractive.

171

Aristolochia durior (Dutchman's Pipe). Trial in zones 4a, 4b, and 5a. An interesting, twining vine with big, kidney-shaped leaves and large green to purple flowers shaped like a Meerschaum pipe. The foliage stays green until killed by frost.

Campsis radicans (Trumpet Vine). Trial in zones 4a and 4b; hardy in zone 5a. Appears to be vegetatively hardy, but flower buds can be injured in winter. This is a rapid-growing vine that clings to walls by small, rootlike holdfasts. It can also twine around its support. Plant this vine in a sheltered location where it will receive full sunlight.

Celastrus rosthornianus (Chinese Bittersweet). Hardy in zones 4a, 4b, and 5a. Produces an abundant crop of fruits on the female plants. The outer husk is yellow at maturity and opens to expose the red inner aril (seed covering). The outer shell often drops from the fruits after they are harvested. This vigorous, twining vine requires a sturdy support. Cultivate several plants to be sure of getting both male and female plants.

Celastrus scandens (American Bittersweet). Hardy in all zones. This native vine is very popular and is often planted for its colorful fruits which are excellent for winter decoration. The fruits have an outer orange husk that opens to expose the red aril. These outer husks remain attached to the base of the fruits. As with *C. rosthornianus* (Chinese bittersweet), both male and female forms must be planted.

CLEMATIS (Clematis). When given winter protection, hardy in all zones. Clematis species and cultivars are among the most popular vines. They climb by twisting their leaf stalks around their support. For this reason a wire mesh support like chicken wire or an aluminum mesh trellis is used. At the arboretum we use chicken wire supported on a wooden lattice trellis. In the fall we simply remove the chicken wire with the vines attached and lay the vine flat on the ground. When cold weather comes, we cover the vines with straw much as one would cover strawberries. In the spring the chicken wire is reattached to the trellis, and when new growth develops, the vines are pruned back to the first strong shoots from the base.

The old vines are then pulled loose from the chicken wire screen.

When planting clematis, dig a deep hole and plant the vine so that the crown of the plant is about 2 inches below the soil surface. Clematis do best on cool soil. Mulching about the first of July with compost helps keep the soil cool and moist. Some gardeners plant a ground cover to protect the roots from the hot sun.

Iron chlorosis can be a problem when clematis are planted too close to the house foundation. Lime leaching out in the soil from the foundation wall can tie up the available iron. Contrary to all that has been written about clematis, adding lime is seldom necessary in this region, since our soils have sufficient amounts of lime.

Most of the clematis planted are large, flowered cultivars of hybrid origin. 'Appleblossom', 'Duchess of Albany', 'Duchess of Edinburgh', 'Etoile Violet', 'Huldine', 'Jackman', 'Lady Veda Stewart', 'Mme. Baron Veillard', 'Mme Chalmondeley', 'Mme. Edward Andre', 'President', 'Red Jackman', 'Victoria', and 'Ville de Lyon' have done well in arboretum plantings.

Species that have flourished are *C. crispa*, with dark purple, bell-shaped flowers, *C. orientalis*, with yellow, bell-shaped flowers; *C. paniculata*, with small, white flowers in the fall; and *C. texensis*, with bright red flowers shaped like rosebuds.

LONICERA (Honeysuckle). Described in Chapter 12. Several species are vines.

L. x *brownii* 'Dropmore Scarlet'. Hardy in all zones. This hybrid honeysuckle is a vigorous, twining vine developed at Dropmore, Manitoba by the late Frank Skinner. It is a cross between *L. sempervirens* and *L. hirsuta*. It produces red, trumpet-shaped flowers all summer until they are killed by frost. A sturdy support is required because of the weight of the vine.

L. heckrottii (Everblooming Honeysuckle). Trial in zones 4a, 4b, and 5a. Has borderline hardiness and often kills back nearly to the ground. This is often sold under the name gold flame. It blooms on new wood and usually gives a satisfactory display by the latter part of summer. The flowers are large and showy, with yellow on the inside and purple on the outside of each petal.

L. sempervirens (Trumpet Honeysuckle). Trial in zones 4a, 4b, and

5a. Commonly grown honeysuckle with long, orange to scarlet, trumpet-shaped flowers from June until August. It is not as hardy or as floriferous as *L. x brownii* 'Dropmore Scarlet'.

L. x tellmanniana (Tellmann Honeysuckle). Trial in zones 4a, 4b, and 5a. Vines at the arboretum have been fast growing but not very long-lived. They may do well for several years and then fail to start growing one spring. This hybrid of *L. tragophylla* and *L. sempervirens* has large, deep yellow, trumpet-shaped flowers. Blooms only in June.

Parthenocissus quinquefolia (Virginia Creeper). Hardy in all zones. A native vine common at the edge of a woods. The leaves are palmately compound with 5 leaflets. These leaflets turn brilliant red in the fall. The species clings to its support by tendrils or by suckerlike disks. Two cultivars, 'Engelmannii' and 'Saint-Paulii', are often planted. They have smaller leaflets than the species. 'Saint-Paulii' is best for a brick or stone wall because its suckerlike disks are better developed.

Parthenocissus tricuspidata (Boston Ivy). Trial in zone 4a; hardy in zones 4b and 5a. Dieback sometimes occurs after a severe winter, but new growth from the base soon covers the wall. Indeed, this is the best vine for clinging to stone or brick walls: the green leaves cover the wall in summer, and the branching pattern against the wall is attractive in winter. The leaves turn vivid scarlet in the fall. 'Lowii' has smaller leaves than the species.

Polygonum aubertii (Silver Fleecevine). Trial in zones 4a, 4b, and 5a. This vine is not very hardy and winter dieback is common. It is a fast-growing vine with dense, bright green foliage and fluffy, white flower clusters in the fall.

ROSA (Climbing Roses). A number of species have gone into the breeding of modern climbing roses, but few of the climbing roses are winter hardy without protection. They are considered in Chapter 18, which deals with the various garden roses.

Vitis riparia (Riverbank Grape). Hardy in all zones. Native to this area. It grows up into trees and can become very large, with stems that are 2 or more inches in diameter. All grapes attach themselves to their support by twining and by tendrils. This wild grape can be grown on a fence or it can cover a pergola. The fruits are small but can be used for making jelly.

Wisteria floribunda (Japanese Wisteria). Trial in zones 4a, 4b, and 5a. The hardiest wisteria. It is vegetatively hardy but seldom blooms profusely in this region. It climbs by twining and requires a sturdy support. Pant in a sheltered location. Summer pruning may help set the flower buds. The many named cultivars of this species have not been tested at the arboretum.

Chapter 15

Selection and Care of Ground Covers

Interest in and knowledge of ground covers has increased greatly in recent years. A ground cover is any plant that is fairly dense and that protects the soil from erosion. Most ground covers used in the home landscape are low, but when selecting a cover for a steep slope, where erosion is a problem, the soil-binding ability rather than the height should be the main consideration.

Ground covers are usually planted where one does not wish to have a lawn. Some ground covers can be grown where it is too shady for a lawn, others in small spaces or on slopes where mowing is not practical.

When selecting a ground cover, one should consider soil, degree of shade, winter snow cover, and desired plant height. Turf grasses are the best possible ground covers where their use is practical. Using other plants as ground covers adds interest and variety to the landscape.

One should not plant ground covers with the expectation that they will require little or no maintenance. At the arboretum, the ground cover area costs more to maintain than any comparable area with the possible exception of that devoted to garden roses. Be sure the area to be planted is weed free. Spring is the best time to plant ground covers, although potted plants can be set in the ground later. Spacing should be such that the plants fill in and completely cover the ground in a single growing season.

The following species and cultivars offer promise as ground covers. No hardiness ratings are given because most of the ground covers listed are fully hardy. Exceptions are noted in the text.

Adiantum pedatum (Maidenhair Fern). Plants grow from 1 to 1½ feet tall and their fine-textured leaves add beauty to any woodland setting. An excellent ground cover on rich, woodsy soil in shade.

Aegopodium podograria 'Variegatum' (Variegated Goutweed). A handsome, shade-tolerant plant grown under trees, where grass fails. It is 1 foot tall, and its variegated leaves with white margins are attractive. Small, white flowers are produced in flat-topped umbels. This is an aggressive ground cover and often encroaches on the lawn. Do not plant near a flower border.

Ajuga reptans (Bugle Weed). The best of the *Ajugas*. Plants spread by underground stems and grow to 6 inches. The large leaves form a rosette of basal leaves, and the white to purple flowers are produced in erect spikes. Two cultivars, 'Burgundy Glow' and 'Bronze Beauty', have done well in arboretum trials. *Ajugas* may winter kill in an open winter; some winter cover like clean straw or marsh hay should be used in exposed sites.

Andromeda polifolia (Bog Rosemary). Native plant growing in sphagnum bogs where the soil is acid. Mature plants are about 1½ feet tall. The evergreen leaves are white on the undersurface, giving the plant a bluish-green appearance. The small, urn-shaped flowers in early June are at first pink, fading to white. Not suitable for planting except on acid soils.

Arctostaphylos uva-ursi (Bearberry). This evergreen ground cover is 6 inches tall and forms dense carpets in northern Minnesota. The leaves often turn purplish in the fall. Red berries persist into winter. This ground cover does poorly on neutral or slightly alkaline soil, so unless your soil is naturally acid, you will need to acidify it to grow bearberry.

Arenaria montana (Mountain Sandwort). Low, dense ground cover growing to 6 inches. It produces large, white flowers in late spring and has a mosslike texture.

Artemisia schmidtiana 'Nana' (Silver Mound Artemisia). A dwarf, mound-shaped ground cover, 1 foot tall, with silvery foliage of fine texture. Plants spaced 1 foot apart would fill in solid. This ground cover needs good drainage and dependable snow cover.

Asarum canadense (Wild Ginger). Native plant producing large, heart-shaped leaves on 6-inch plants. It does well in shade and often forms an extensive carpet. The red flowers are produced under the leaves in early spring. The leaves are killed by frost.

Asarum europaeum (European Wild Ginger). This native of Europe has small, evergreen leaves and is only 4 inches tall. It makes a delightful ground cover on moist soil that is high in organic matter. It grows best in shade. *A. caudatum* and *A. shuttleworthii* are also evergreen but have not been thoroughly tested in this area.

Athyrium goeringianum 'Pictum' (Japanese Painted Fern). One of the more beautiful ground covers for a shady area. Plants are about 6 inches tall at maturity and have variegated leaves mottled with gray, green, and wine. The cultivar does best on soil that is high in organic matter.

Aurinia saxatile (Gold Dust). A sprawling, 1-foot-tall ground cover with yellow flowers in early spring. It requires well-drained soil. The cultivar 'Compactum' is doing well in the arboretum ground cover area.

Bergenia cordifolia (Bergenia). A bold perennial, 1½ feet tall, with large leaves that stand erect at varying angles. Pink flowers are produced on upright spikes in early May. This perennial prefers moist soil and can be grown in full sun or partial shade.

Campanula carpatica (Carpathian Bellflower). A small plant growing 1 foot tall. Since this bellflower does not sucker, it is best to space the plants rather close together. The small leaves and the bell-shaped flowers that range from white to violet make this a most attractive ground cover.

Campanula poscharskyana (Poscharsky Bellflower). A low, mat-forming plant that is a true creeper, not more than 6 inches tall. The bell-shaped flowers are bluish purple and continue to bloom throughout the summer and fall. Plant in full sun on rich, fertile soil. The best bellflower for ground cover purposes.

Cerastium tomentosum (Snow-in-summer). A fast-growing ground cover that forms a dense, 6-inch-high mat. The leaves are woolly, thus giving a grayish appearance to the plants. The small, white flowers cover the plants in June. Can become a lawn weed.

Comptonia peregrina (Sweet Fern). Reaching a height of 2 or more feet, this native species is often planted on highway slopes, where it is excellent for controlling erosion. The fernlike leaves have sweet fragrance—hence the common name. Established plants are difficult to transplant. Grows well on soils that are dry, acid, and sandy.

Convallaria majalis (Lily-of-the-Valley). Familiar, shade-tolerant plant often grown on the north side of buildings. The small, bell-shaped flowers are borne on erect, 6-inch stems and are very fragrant. Flowers are either white or pale pink. The leaves tend to turn brown and die in late summer.

Cornus canadensis (Bunchberry). The smallest dogwood, growing only 6 inches tall. The small, yellow flowers are produced in a dense head surrounded by 4 showy, white bracts in late May or June. Clusters of bright red berries are striking in late summer and fall. The leaves are evergreen and produced in whorls. This plant requires moist, acid soil. It can grow in fairly dense shade. Under the right growing conditions, this plant is a delight; a mass planting is a thing of beauty in the spring and again in the fall.

Coronilla varia (Crown Vetch). Brought over from Europe and soon naturalized through the East. In recent years it has been widely planted on highway slopes and wherever a rapid-growing bank cover is needed. This spreading vine makes a thick ground cover and grows 1½ feet tall. Pink, pealike flowers are produced in dense clusters from June to September. A gold-leaved form was introduced by the arboretum and named 'Gold Leaf'. It is not as vigorous as the species.

Dianthus caryophyllus 'Aqua'. A hardy carnation with bluish-green foliage and white carnation flowers on 1-foot-tall stems. Faded flowers should be removed. This makes a fairly dense ground cover.

Dianthus deltoides (Maiden Pink). Forms a dense, green carpet with narrow, grasslike leaves. In late May and June the 6-inch-tall plants are covered with small, red to pink flowers. This ground cover cannot compete with aggressive weeds like quack grass.

Duchesnea indica (Mock Strawberry). This trailing plant, which resembles a strawberry, is 6 inches tall and forms a dense mat. The flowers are yellow. The fruits are red and shaped like a small strawberry.

Epimedium alpinum (Alpine Epimedium). A low plant that grows 1 foot tall. The leaves are compound with small leaflets. When they first open in the spring they have a reddish cast but soon turn green. In May and early June the plants are covered with loose panicles of small, reddish-yellow flowers. This is an excellent ground cover around evergreens and in a woodland garden.

Euonymus fortunei (Wintercreeper). A variable species with evergreen leaves. Only the creeping forms, those less than 1 foot tall, that are planted where there will be dependable snow cover are suitable in this climate. 'Coloratus' has large leaves that turn purple in the fall, 'Gracilis' smaller leaves that have white variegation, and 'Kewensis' tiny leaves. Plant only in a sheltered location with dependable snow cover; branches that project above the snow will be killed.

Euonymus obovata (Running Euonymus). This trailing plant with deciduous leaves grows 1 foot tall and turns brilliant red in the fall. It is more vigorous than the evergreen *E. fortunei*, and the plants can be spaced farther apart.

Festuca ovina 'Glauca'. This sheep fescue forms dense, 1-foot-tall bunches that have a bluish-green cast. For best results, plants should be spaced about 1 foot apart.

Forsythia 'Arnold Dwarf'. A 3-foot-tall shrub of hybrid origin, resulting from a cross between *F.* x *intermedia* and *F. japonica* var. *saxatile*. It produces few flowers. Stems root readily where they touch the ground. An excellent low shrub for covering banks.

Galium verum (Yellow Bedstraw). This low bedstraw grows 1½ feet tall and has small, whorled leaves and tiny, yellow flowers in summer. It can invade a lawn and become a weed. Grows well in full sun and on poor soil.

Gaultheria hispidula (Creeping Snowberry). Low, creeping, evergreen plant growing to a height of 1 foot. The white berries add interest in the fall. Plant only on acid, peaty soil. A good terrarium plant.

Gaultheria procumbens (Wintergreen). Native plant forming dense, 6-inch-tall carpets in its natural habitat, which includes this region. It is known for its young leaves that have a wintergreen flavor and for its red fruits that persist among the evergreen leaves all winter. In the early spring it is a treat to eat these tasty, red fruits with a wintergreen flavor. This plant demands acid soil and partial shade.

Gypsophila repens var. *rosea* (Rosy Creeping Baby's Breath). A 1-foot-high, spreading plant that blooms in midsummer. When in full bloom it is a beautiful ground cover. Grows best in full sun and on limestone soil.

Hedera helix (English Ivy). This trailing plant, which grows 6 inches tall, is widely used in the home as a house plant. It is generally not considered hardy in this climate. The Bulgarian strain and the cultivar 'Ogallala' have shown a surprising degree of hardiness. Plants started on the north side of our house in 1970 are still thriving. Each year they climb onto the concrete blocks but are killed back to the snow line each winter. These selections are also doing well at the arboretum in protected sites. Plant only where there will be good snow cover.

Hemerocallis fulva (Tawny Daylily). Almost any daylily can be used as a ground cover. The tawny daylily spreads to form large, 2-foot-tall patches requiring little or no care. Plants do well in full sun or partial shade. 'Kwanso' has double flowers.

HOSTA (Plantain Lily). Most species and cultivars of *Hosta* can be planted as ground covers in shady areas. Size varies from 6 inches to 3 feet. The large leaves shade the ground and crowd out most weeds. Grown more for their foliage effects than for their bloom.

Iris cristata (Crested Iris). The only iris that qualifies as a ground cover. It grows 6 inches tall. The swordlike leaves are attractive, and when the plants are in bloom in May a mass planting produces a dramatic effect.

Juniperus horizontalis (Creeping Juniper). The most widely planted *Juniperus* species for ground cover purposes. The low, spreading branches form a dense carpet. Leaf texture and color are highly variable. Height also varies but most cultivars are less than 1 foot tall. Numerous cultivars are on the market and each has certain qualities that one may be looking for. 'Bar Harbor', 'Blue Horizon', 'Blue Rug', 'Blue Vase', 'Douglasii', 'Hughes', 'Prince of Wales', and 'Wiltonii' are a few of the cultivars being tested at the arboretum. 'Plumosa' is often planted, but considerable winter burn on this cultivar has been observed at the arboretum. Before buying a particular cultivar, it would be advisable to visit a nursery to compare the various cultivars.

Juniperus procumbens (Japanese Garden Juniper). A creeping, 6-inch-tall juniper with a coarser texture than *J. horizontalis* (creeping juniper). The color is bluish green. The dwarf form 'Nana' is better than the species where space is limited.

Juniperus sabina (Savins Juniper). A variable species from Europe. Some of its cultivars are better than the species for ground cover purposes. 'Skandia' is perhaps the lowest-growing and the best of these cultivars. Its height is 1½ feet.

Lamium maculatum (Spotted Dead Nettle). This rather coarse ground cover is 1¼ feet tall. The leaves have a whitish blotch along the midribs, and the purple flowers form in axillary and terminal whorls. This plant prefers well-drained soil and partial shade. Some winter protection is needed in an open winter with little snow.

Linnaea borealis (Twinflower). A delightful, native creeper. Dense, 6-inch-tall carpets sometimes form with small leaves and pairs of bell-shaped, pinkish-white flowers. Plant on acid, peaty soil in partial shade.

Lotus corniculatus (Bird's-foot Trefoil). A common roadside plant that has escaped cultivation. It grows to 1½ feet and makes an attractive ground cover with its small, cloverlike foliage and yellow, pealike flowers. It sometimes winter kills but usually reseeds itself.

Lysimachia nummularia (Moneywort). The creeping stems grow rather flat on the ground and are 6 inches tall. The small, opposite leaves are rounded, and the yellow, single flowers are produced in the leaf axils. The plant prefers a moist site and does better in partial shade than in full sun. A light winter mulch or a good snow cover is necessary to ensure winter survival.

Mahonia repens (Dwarf Holly-grape). Growing 1¼ feet tall, this is the lowest growing of the holly-grapes native to Colorado and the Black Hills of South Dakota. Arboretum plants came from the mountains near Boulder, Colorado and have proved hardy where they have adequate snow cover. Being a broad-leaved evergreen, the species shows winter burn if the leaves are exposed above the snow. If growing conditions are right, this makes a fine ground cover. The yellow spikes of flowers in May are followed by clusters of bluish-black fruits in the fall.

Maianthemum canadense (Wild Lily-of-the-Valley). This native wild flower spreads by underground rhizomes. The few leaves are on 6-inch-tall stems. The short, erect racemes of white flowers resemble those of the cultivated lily-of-the-valley. Shade is required.

Menispermum canadense (Moonseed). A twining vine that normally creeps along the ground but sometimes climbs into surrounding shrubbery. It grows to 6 feet. The leaves are triangular and shaped like English ivy leaves. The fruits are black berries with flattened, moon-shaped seeds. The plants kill back in winter but grow from the base in the spring. A shaded spot is needed.

Mentha requienii (Creeping Mint). The lowest of all ground covers, forming a dense mat less than 1 inch thick. The tiny leaves have a mintlike fragrance when crushed. This plant is not fully hardy and requires a winter mulch.

Mitchella repens (Partridgeberry). Where growing conditions are favorable, this makes a dainty, creeping ground cover that is only 4 to 6 inches tall. The funnel-shaped flowers are white with a tinge of purple and borne in pairs in May. These are followed by bright red berries in late fall. Requires acid, peaty soil and shade.

Myosotis scorpioides (Forget-Me-Not). A colorful, creeping ground cover. It is 6 inches tall and has small, blue flowers which are attractive in miniature flower arrangements. Under the right growing conditions, it spreads rapidly and may need to be controlled. Forget-me-not dies to the ground in the fall and usually comes up in the spring from the old crowns. It also self-sows and seedlings soon fill in the space during the spring. Does best on moist soil.

Pachysandra terminalis (Japanese Spurge). This evergreen ground cover grows 8 inches tall. The small, white flowers are produced in May, the white berries in the fall. Plants require shade and good snow cover. Excellent on the north side of the home or as a woodland ground cover.

Paxistima canbyi (Canby Pachistima). Low ground cover, 1 foot high, that is grown primarily for its evergreen foliage resembling tiny holly leaves. It grows on a wide variety of soils and in full sun or partial shade. Snow cover is important to prevent winter burn.

Petunia parviflora. A tender perennial killed by frost and grown as an annual. The species *parviflora* is very low (4 inches) and dense, with tiny flowers. It makes an excellent ground cover and usually reseeds itself. Like other annuals, it leaves the ground bare during the winter and early spring.

Phalaris arundinacea 'Picta' (Ribbon Grass). This 2- to 4-foot-tall cultivar of the reed canary grass has striped leaves with alternating bands of white or yellow and green. Occasionally a plant reverts to all green leaves typical of the species. Such a plant should be removed as soon as it is observed.

Phlox borealis (Arctic Phlox). This species of creeping phlox is 6 inches tall, dark green, and narrow leaved. The general effect resembles *Juniperus horizontalis* (creeping juniper). In mid-May the plants are covered with magenta-colored flowers. The plants remain green until snowfall. One of the better phlox species for ground cover purposes.

Phlox subulata (Moss-pink). A common rock garden plant, 6 inches tall, with pink, purple, or white flowers in early May. It is not as dense as *P. borealis* (Arctic phlox) and weeds can be more of a problem.

Polygonum affine (Himalayan Fleece-flower). Low, mat-forming ground cover with spikes of reddish flowers about 6 inches tall. The leaves are approximately 4 inches long and most of them are basal. This makes an interesting ground cover for small areas.

Polygonum cuspidatum var. *compactum* (Dwarf Japanese Fleece-flower). Dense ground cover growing to a height of 2 feet. It can be very invasive. The flowers are small and inconspicuous in late summer. The fruits are red and add a touch of color in early fall. This variety is probably the plant being sold as *P. reynoutria.*

Potentilla tridentata (Wineleaf Cinquefoil). The best species of *Potentilla* for ground cover use. It is native to the North Shore of Lake Superior and grows 10 inches tall. The small, white, roselike flowers open in May and June, and the dark green, strawberrylike leaves turn wine-red in the fall. The species is not fussy about soil type or pH but does require good drainage.

Rhus aromatica (Fragrant Sumac). The lowest-growing sumac.

Plants spaced 3 feet apart soon fill in to form a dense mat about 3 feet tall. The trifoliate leaves resemble poison ivy leaves. The flowers are small and yellow in early May, the fruits red and berrylike in midsummer. In the fall the leaves turn yellow and scarlet.

Rhus trilobata (Skunkbush Sumac). Closely related to *R. aromatica* but somewhat taller.

Rubus parvifolius (Japanese Raspberry). Not well known. In arboretum trials it has formed a dense, 1-foot-high mat. This species has greatest value as a bank cover.

Saponaria ocymoides (Rock Soapwort). This low, spreading alpine from the mountains of Europe grows 10 inches tall and forms an attractive ground cover. The flowers are pink in late May or June and last about a month. To maintain a neat appearance the plants should be mowed with a rotary mower after they have bloomed. The plants develop taproots, so they are difficult to transplant when mature. However, volunteer seedlings can easily be transplanted.

SEDUM (Stonecrop). There are many species and cultivars of *Sedum* on the market. Most are low and mat forming, but a few are upright and suitable in the perennial border. In the arboretum ground cover area we have about 25 different kinds ranging in size from the tiny *S. mentha* 'Requieni' which is less than 1 inch tall to *S. spectabile* which may be as tall as 1½ to 2 feet. Flowers add interest but some with inconspicuous flowers may make better ground covers than those with showy flowers. A visit to the arboretum would be useful in deciding which sedum to grow. All species and cultivars prefer a sunny location and well-drained soil.

Spiraea japonica 'Alpina' (Alpine Mikado Spirea). Less than 1 foot tall. If planted 1 foot apart, the plants soon fill in and form a very dense cover which is practically impervious to weeds. The small, pink flowers add interest.

Stachys byzantina (Lamb's-ears). This 1¼-foot-tall plant has interesting leaves covered with white to silvery, woollike hairs. The flowers are small, purple, and produced in erect spikes. This is a rather coarse ground cover and needs winter protection.

Taxus canadensis (Canadian Yew). Native conifer that spreads in a vase-shaped manner. It grows 4 feet tall and its needles usually take on a purplish coloration in late fall. Suitable only in shade and requires dependable snow cover.

Taxus cuspidata (Japanese Yew). An excellent ground cover where winter shade is present, for example, on the north side of a building. Spreading forms rather than upright forms should be planted. 'Taunton' and 'Cross Spreading' are most resistant to winter burn and grow 3 feet tall.

Thymus serpyllum (Mother-of-thyme). The best thyme species that can be grown. It forms a low, dense mat that is 6 inches tall. The small, purple flowers add summer interest. The varieties lemon thyme and golden thyme are also excellent ground covers.

Tiarella cordifolia (Foamflower). This woodland plant is 8 inches tall and produces small, white, star-shaped flowers borne on erect spikes in late spring. It requires shade and does best on acid soil high in organic matter.

Vaccinium vitis-idaea (Cowberry). Low (8 inches), mound shaped, and evergreen. The tiny, pink, bell-shaped flowers are produced in small, nodding racemes in late May. The fruits are bright red and add fall interest. Like other members of the heath family, the cowberry requires acid soil.

Veronica chamaedrys (Germander Speedwell). Low, creeping perennial, 6 inches tall, with small, bue flowers in axillary racemes in early June. The leaves are nearly evergreen, and this makes it a good ground cover throughout the year. Prefers sun and grows well on most soils.

Viburnum opulus 'Nana' (Dwarf European Highbush Cranberry). Low, mound-shaped shrub usually under 2 feet tall. It rarely forms flowers or fruits. When planted 1½ feet apart it fills in and makes a good ground cover. Thrives in partial shade and makes a good bank cover for a north-facing slope.

Vinca herbacea (Herbaceous Periwinkle). Creeping, 6-inch-high ground cover that kills back to the ground each winter. In the spring it sends out creeping stems with blue flowers about 1 inch across. A good substitute for *V. minor* (the evergreen periwinkle) where winter kill may be a problem.

Vinca minor (Periwinkle). Low, creeping evergreen forming a 6-inch-tall carpet. The species produces single, 5-petaled, blue flowers. White- and purple-flowered varieties are also on the market. Periwinkle is grown most successfully in shaded areas that have dependable snow cover. In exposed sites it might help to mulch in late fall with a light covering of clean straw.

VIOLA (Violet). Many species and varieties of violets make excellent ground covers when planted in a woodland setting. They grow 10 inches tall and are especially appreciated in the spring when in bloom. Plants do best in light shade.

Waldsteinia fragarioides (Barren Strawberry). This relative of the strawberry spreads by creeping stems and forms a dense, 6-inch-high mat where conditions are favorable. It has yellow flowers and small, inedible fruits.

Chapter 16

Perennial Plants for the Sunny Flower Border

Very little is published on perennials for upper midwestern gardens. In this chapter only perennials, exclusive of spring-flowering bulbs, that prefer full sun are considered. Many perennials bloom earlier in the spring than annuals and should be used in the flower border. If annuals alone are used, it is necessary to replant the entire border each spring. A well-planned flower border can bloom continuously from early spring until late fall, but to achieve this result both perennials and annuals must be used.

When planning the flower border, it is necessary to learn as much as you can about the plants to be used. A few accent plants that stand out because of their form or color should be planted toward the back of the border. It is best to plant in drifts of several plants of a kind. Taller plants should be used toward the back of the border and lower ones in front. Try to avoid a formal effect by varying the height of the background plants. Among the lists of perennials beginning on p. 215 are recommended foreground and background plantings. An edging of a low, compact annual should be used to separate the lawn from the rest of the border. Consider time of bloom and flower color. White is a peacemaker and should be used between plants whose colors might clash.

Perennials die to the ground in the fall, so winter survival is dependent upon protecting the parts of the plant below the soil surface. This can be done by planting where snow cover is dependable or by using a winter mulch. Because almost all perennials are hardy, no hardiness ratings are given in this chapter and Chapter 17.

The following are some of the better perennials to be used:

ACHILLEA (Yarrow, Sneezewort). A large genus of aromatic, perennial herbs belonging to the composite, or sunflower, family. Leaves are simple and toothed or pinnately dissected. Flower heads are usually in flat-topped corymbs and are rarely solitary.

A. filipendulina (Fern-leaf Yarrow). Grows 3 to 4 feet tall. The grayish-green leaves are finely dissected, and the small, yellow flowers are produced in flat-topped clusters during July and August. The cultivars 'Gold Plate' and 'Coronation Gold' are preferable to the species.

A. millefolium (Common Yarrow). A common pasture weed, 1½ to 2 feet tall, with fernlike foliage and flat-topped clusters of off-white flowers. Several cultivars have been selected; their flowers range from deep pink to rosy red. 'Crimson Beauty', 'Fire King', and 'Red Beauty' are frequently planted and bloom in July and August.

A. ptarmica (Sneezewort). From 1 to 1½ feet tall. Several cultivars with double, white flowers in July and August are on the market. These are: 'Angel's Breath', 'Perry's Giant', and 'The Pearl'. The species can be invasive, and division every few years is required.

Aconitum napellus (Aconite Monkshood). One of the better of the several monkshood species used in the garden. It grows 3 to 4 feet tall and has finely divided leaves. Blue, hooded flowers are produced in late August and September when there are few other blue flowers. The variety *bicolor* with its two-toned flowers of white and purple and the cultivar 'Sparks' with its deep violet-blue flowers are preferred to the species. The monkshoods are poisonous to livestock. They are usually planted individually or in small clumps.

Alcea rosea (Hollyhock). Often listed under the genus *Althaea*. Short-lived perennial or biennial growing 5 to 8 feet tall and blooming in July and August. A few plants bloom the first year, but most do not bloom until the second year from seed. The species is single flowered, but many double-flowered forms in a variety of flower colors are on the market. This flower was at one time more popular than it is today. Shorter plants that bloom the first year, like the 'Powderpuff' hybrids, are helping to improve the popularity of this species. Hollyhocks are perpetuated by self-seeding. A rust disease is common on the leaves, and unless it is controlled it can mar the beauty of the plants.

Amsonia tabernaemontana (Willow Amsonia or Bluestar). A 2- to 3-foot-tall plant native to the southeastern United States and Texas. The narrow, willowlike leaves and the small, steel-blue flowers in late May and June make this an attractive plant. It is fully hardy and seems to have few insect and disease problems.

Anaphalis margaritacea (Pearly Everlasting). This native grows 1½ to 2 feet tall and is suitable for the perennial border but seldom planted. The pearly-white, buttonlike flowers in late summer can be cut and dried for winter arrangements.

Anchusa azurea (Italian Alkanet). Short-lived perennial, 4 to 6 feet tall. The small, blue flowers in May and June are most attractive, but the coarse foliage offers little interest during the rest of the season. The plant is propagated by self-seeding, and this can be a problem in a small garden.

Anemone pulsatilla (Pasque Flower). Often listed under the genus *Pulsatilla*. This European species grows 6 inches to 1 foot tall and is one of the earlier-blooming flowers, often blooming by mid-April. The flowers resemble the crocus and range from light blue to almost purple. *A. pulsatilla* is similar to the American species *A. patens*, the state flower of South Dakota. Indeed, some botanists consider the American species a variety of *A. pulsatilla*. These species demand well-drained soil and full sunlight. They are better in a rock garden than in a mixed flower border.

Anemone sylvestris (Snowdrop Windflower). One-foot-tall, European species that appears to be fully hardy. The flowers are white, about 2 inches across, and in full bloom during May. The double-flowered 'Flore Pleno' is on the market. It is best to divide this species every few years.

AQUILEGIA (Columbine). There are numerous species and many garden hybrids of *Aquilegia*. Their height varies from 1½ to 2 feet. They are beautiful when in bloom during June and July and well worth the space in the garden, but they require well-drained soil and are usually short-lived. A leaf miner also takes its toll and mars the beauty of the foliage. The 'McKanna Giant' hybrids and 'Mrs. Scott Elliot' hybrids are available in a range of colors and are generally more desirable than the species. The yellow-flowered *A. chrysantha*, the light blue *A. caerulea*, and the red *A. canadensis* are also worth trying.

Armeria maritima (Sea-Pink or Common Thrift). A rock garden plant useful toward the front of a perennial border. The leaves are narrow and the plants form a dense mound 1½ feet across and 1 foot high. *A. maritima* blooms in late May and June, producing tight clusters of rose-pink flowers on elongate stems.

ARTEMISIA (Artemisia, Sage, Wormwood). Of the many species of *Artemisia*, most are woody but a few are herbaceous and suitable for planting in the flower border. The artemisias like full sun and well-drained soil.

A. ludoviciana (Western Sage). Formerly listed as a variety of *A. albula*. The plant has silvery foliage and grows to a height of 2 to 3 feet. The cultivars 'Silver King' and 'Silver Queen', selected for their silvery-white foliage, are planted more often than the species.

A. schmidtiana 'Nana' (Silver Mound Sage). A dwarf, mound-shaped plant 1 foot high and 1½ feet across. The leaves are finely lobed and silvery-white.

ASCLEPIAS (Milkweed). There are many species of milkweed, and some become troublesome weeds. Milkweeds have a taproot and are difficult to transplant, so use small seedlings or plant seeds directly in the garden. Only two species of milkweed should be considered as garden flowers:

A. incarnata (Swamp Milkweed). Grows 2 to 3 feet tall. The large, flat flower clusters are pink to purple and fragrant in July. Although this milkweed is native to swamps and wet soils, it flourishes on well-drained soils if watered during dry periods. An excellent cut flower.

A. tuberosa (Butterfly Weed). Grows to 1½ feet and is one of the showier native flowers. The orange flowers appear in July and August. It requires well-drained soil and prefers sand.

ASTER (Aster). Many species of aster are roadside weeds. *A. novaangliae* (New England aster), *A. novi-belgii* (New York aster), *A. ericoides* (heath aster), and a few other species have been used by hybridizers to develop the modern aster cultivars. These hybrids vary greatly in height and flower color. Some are under 1 foot tall and others may be as tall as 3 feet. Flower color ranges from white to red to purple. Most of these asters are sold under cultivar names and bloom in late fall, often after annuals are killed by frost.

Astilbe x *arendsii* (Astilbe or Perennial Spirea). Most garden cultivars of astilbe are hybrids of *A. chinensis* var. *davidii* and other species. They range from 1½ to 2 feet. The small, spirealike flowers, which bloom in June and July, are clustered in showy, upright panicles. The flower color ranges from white to nearly purple. Astilbes prefer rich soil and ample moisture, and they tolerate some shade.

Aurinia saxatile (Basket of Gold). Also listed as *Alyssum saxatile*. This sprawling plant is 1 foot tall and produces erect flower clusters in early May. The small, yellow, 4-petaled flowers are quite showy. Plant in well-drained soil. Excellent for rock gardens.

Baptisia australis (False Indigo). Tall (3 to 4 feet) perennial belonging to the pea family. The indigo-blue flowers are borne in terminal racemes during June. These are followed by inflated pods which are useful in dried arrangements. *B. australis* grows on most soils and has few insect and disease problems.

Belamcanda chinensis (Blackberry Lily). Grows 2 to 3 feet tall. This is not a lily but a member of the iris family. The foliage resembles a giant iris. The flowers open in August when few perennials are in bloom. They are star shaped, 2 inches across, and orange with red spots. When the seed pods burst, the black seeds, clustered like a blackberry fruit, are exposed. Plant in well-drained soil. Unwanted seedlings that may volunteer are easily removed.

Bergenia cordifolia (Heartleaf Bergenia). This 1½-foot-tall plant has cabbagelike leaves that are heart shaped and evergreen. The leaves develop a reddish tint in the fall and may die back in an open winter. Erect panicles of red to pink flowers form in early May. Belongs to the saxifrage family.

Bergenia crassifolia (Bergenia). A similar species to *B. cordifolia* but the leaves are a little more elongated.

Brunnera macrophylla (Siberian Bugloss). From 1 to 1½ feet tall. Another plant with a basal rosette of large, heart-shaped leaves. In May the plant is covered with upright racemes of clear blue, starlike flowers. The foliage is attractive after the flowers fade. May be short-lived.

Callirhoe involucrata (Poppy Mallow). This sprawling, 1-foot-tall plant is useful in a rock garden or in the foreground of a flower border. The flowers open in June and are mallowlike, up to 2½ inches across, and range from rose to crimson-purple. It is best to seed where plants are desired.

CAMPANULA (Bellflower). A large genus of useful garden plants with bell-shaped flowers ranging from white to purple. A few species, such as *C. rapunculoides*, become noxious weeds and should never be planted.

C. carpatica (Carpathian Bellflower). This low bellflower, 6 to 8 inches tall, is a favorite in rock gardens but is equally useful in the flower border The white or blue flowers cover the plants in June and July. May be short-lived.

C. glomerota var. *dahurica* (Dahurian Bellflower). Grows to 1½ feet. The deep blue flowers are clustered in the axils of the upper leaves in June. Under favorable growing conditions this variety can spread rapidly, but it can be confined without difficulty.

C. medium (Canterbury Bell). A 1½-foot-tall biennial requiring winter protection. The beautiful, large flowers range from white to violet-blue. The cultivar 'Calycanthema' is called the cup-and-saucer canterbury bell; its showy calyx forms the cup. Plants must be grown in a cold frame the first year and transplanted to the garden in the early spring of the second year.

C. persicifolia (Peach-leaved Bellflower). Reaches a height of 2 to 3 feet. This is one of the better bellflowers for the flower border. The erect stems bear an abundance of white to blue flowers, which are excellent for cutting. Plants must be divided every 3 to 4 years to maintain their vigor. A number of named cultivars are on the market.

C. rotundifolia (Common Harebell). This 1-foot-tall native plant is rather small for the perennial border but is excellent in the rock garden. Most leaves are basal and the blue flowers are produced on slender stems.

Cassia marilandica (Wild Senna). This native plant grows 3 to 4 feet tall. The bright yellow flowers are produced in 3-inch clusters in August. The compound leaves are finely divided and attractive throughout the growing season.

Centaurea macrocephala (Globe Centaurea). Grows 3 to 4 feet tall. The large, stiff leaves give a coarse texture to this perennial, and the 3-inch, thistlelike flower heads are golden-yellow and showy in June and July.

Centaurea montana (Perennial Bachelor's-Button). The most popular species of *Centaurea*, reaching a height of 1½ to 2 feet. The blue-violet flowers are 2 to 3 inches across in July and August. 'Alba' has white flowers and 'Coerulea' has blue flowers. This perennial should be divided every other year. It also self-sows.

Chelone glabra (White Turtlehead). This native grows in wet soils to a height of 2 to 3 feet. The turtle-shaped flowers are white in August and September. Keep the soil moist.

Chelone obliqua (Rose Turtlehead). Similar to *C. glabra* except for the flower color.

CHRYSANTHEMUM (Daisy, Garden Chrysanthemum). A large genus belonging to the composite, or sunflower, family. The genus contains *C.* x *morifolium* (the popular garden and florist chrysanthemum) in addition to numerous species of daisies.

C. arcticum (Arctic Daisy). Hardy perennial producing large flowers on erect stems that are 1¼ to 1½ feet tall. The centers are yellow, with white ray flowers. This plant blooms late in the fall and some years it may not complete its bloom before the temperature drops below the freezing point.

C. coccineum (Painted Daisy). Growing 1½ to 2 feet tall, this perennial has fernlike foliage and produces showy flowers in June and July. It has yellow disk flowers and white to dark red ray flowers. This plant is not long-lived, and winter protection is advised. Excellent for cut flowers. Pyrethrum of commerce, a familiar insecticide, is made from the dried flower heads.

C. leucanthemum (Ox-eye Daisy). This roadside weed with its white ray flowers is most attractive but scarcely a plant to be used in the perennial border because of its tendency to spread by underground rhizomes.

C. x *morifolium* (Garden, or Florist, Chrysanthemum). Reaches a height of 1 to 5 feet. The garden chrysanthemum has been cultivated for centuries in the Orient. Several species have gone into the breeding of the modern chrysanthemum. Early bloom was introduced in the late 1930s by the University of Minnesota's Department of Horticultural Science, which has conducted an active breeding project on garden chrysanthemums for over 40 years. Nebraska and the Morden Experiment Station have also been active in developing early-blooming varieties for northern gardens, and private breeders have contributed a number of fine cultivars. Until breeding work started at the university, no varieties would bloom early enough to escape our fall frosts. Today we have the choice of many fine varieties that reach their peak of bloom in September.

Chrysanthemums range from low, mound-shaped plants to the tall, florists' varieties that are trained to a single stalk and bloom.

Most garden varieties are 2 feet tall or less, and flowers vary from very small, button-shaped blossoms to giant blooms 6 inches or more across. They may be single, semi-double, or fully double and white, yellow, pink, red, or purple. Blue is virtually the only color not present in chrysanthemum flowers.

This popular fall flower requires well-drained soil and blooms best in full sunlight. It should be divided each spring, or new plants should be started from rooted cuttings. Pinch back the new growth at planting time and again a few weeks later to produce a compact plant with an abundance of blooms. No pinching should be done after July 1. If garden space is limited, flowering-size plants can be purchased in the fall and set in the garden where you wish the plants to bloom.

C. x *superbum* (Shasta Daisy). Often listed under *C. maximum,* one of the parents of the Shasta daisy. Grows 1½ to 2 feet tall. The hardiness of the Shasta daisy is borderline in this area. If protected over the winter, the plant is beautiful for landscape effect and for cutting. Flowers may be either single or double, with white ray flowers in June and July. Numerous cultivars are on the market.

Cimicifuga racemosa (Black Snakeroot). Tall plants (5 to 6 feet) and a good accent toward the back of the border. The erect racemes of white flowers in June and July give a spirelike effect. For best results, provide moist soil high in organic matter.

CLEMATIS (Clematis). Most species of *Clematis* are climbing vines (see Chapter 14), but a few are compact enough to be used in the perennial border.

C. heracleifolia var. *davidiana* (Blue Tube Clematis). Grows 2 to 3 feet tall, is mound shaped, and has coarse foliage with deep blue, tubular flowers in August and September.

C. integrifolia (Solitary Clematis). Grows to a height of 2 feet and produces blue, bell-shaped flowers in July and August. It requires staking because the stems are weak.

C. recta (Ground Clematis). Reaches 4 to 5 feet and requires staking. The small, white, tubular flowers are produced in June and

July. The variety *mandshurica* is taller and produces larger flowers.

Coreopsis lanceolata (Perennial Coreopsis). Grows 2 feet tall with bright yellow, daisylike flowers that are about 2 inches across in July and August. This low-maintenance perennial requires good drainage and full sun.

DELPHINIUM (Delphinium). A large genus with many species. The large-flowered hybrid delphiniums have evolved mainly from *D. elatum*. In England there are many named cultivars that are propagated by vegetative division. In this country most delphiniums are grown from seed. The 'Pacific Hybrids' and 'Blackmore and Langdon Hybrids' are popular. The tall plants, 6 or more feet, have stately panicles of showy, white to purple flowers, which are prized for bold flower arrangements. Plant in a wind-protected area. Staking also helps prevent wind damage. Insects and diseases like aphids and mildew can be a problem and must be controlled; red spiders may also be troublesome. These hybrid delphiniums are usually short-lived, and new plants should be started each year.

Dianthus barbatus (Sweet William). Strains of this popular biennial range from 6 inches to 2 feet and have single or double flowers in a variety of colors. Sweet William self-sows and, once established, maintains itself in the garden.

Dianthus caryophyllus (Carnation). Grows 1 to 2 feet tall. Most carnations are tender and grown in greenhouses, but a few are sufficiently hardy to winter outdoors in protected sites. 'Aqua' has white, double flowers in July and silvery foliage. It was introduced by the North Platte Experiment Station in Nebraska.

Dicentra eximia (Fringed Bleeding Heart). Reaching a height of 1 foot, this native of the eastern mountains of the United States has become a popular garden flower. Its fernlike foliage and repeat bloom make it a desirable plant. The flowers are red and more elongated than the flowers of *D. spectabilis* (the common bleeding heart). The plant does well in sun or light shade. Individual plants may be short-lived, but volunteer seedlings can be transplanted easily.

Dicentra spectabilis (Bleeding Heart). This bleeding heart deserves its popularity. It comes up early in the spring and forms a spreading, 2-foot-tall plant with soft, fernlike foliage. It blooms in May with showy, heart-shaped, pinkish-red flowers. After producing fruits and seeds, the plant dies to the ground by midsummer. Annuals can be planted to fill in the space for summer and fall bloom. Requires well-drained soil to be long-lived.

Dictamnus albus (Gasplant). Hardy perennial reaching a height of 2 to 2½ feet. It blooms in late May or June, but the attractive foliage makes the plant good looking even when it is not in bloom. The species has upright racemes of white flowers; the cultivar 'Rubra' produces rose-colored flowers. The gasplant develops a taproot and is difficult to transplant except in the seedling state. The dried fruits are often used in winter bouquets.

Digitalis grandiflora (Yellow Foxglove). Sometimes listed as *D. ambigua*. Grows 2 to 3 feet tall. The erect racemes of pale yellow flowers are blotched with brown in early July. Although the species is a perennial it is best treated as a biennial.

Digitalis purpurea (Common Foxglove). This biennial is 3 to 4 feet tall and of borderline hardiness. First-year plants must be protected the initial winter in our climate. If you winter the plants successfully, the tall spikes with tubular flowers of various colors open in June. After flowering, the second year, the plants should be removed since the seed stalks become unsightly. 'Foxy' is a new strain that blooms the first year from seed if started indoors in March.

Doronicum cordatum (Leopard's Bane). Reaches a height of 1 to 1½ feet. The yellow, daisylike flowers are about 2 inches across and open in May. Doronicums like soil that is high in humus and grow equally well in full sun or partial shade. The plants die down in midsummer so it is best not to grow them in large masses.

Echinacea purpurea (Purple Coneflower). Sometimes listed under the genus *Rudbeckia*. Grows 2 to 3 feet tall. The coarse leaves of this perennial are covered with bristles. The flowers terminate upright stems in midsummer. The disk flowers are brownish and form a rounded cone; the hanging ray flowers are purplish.

Echinops ritro (Small Globe Thistle). A 2-foot-tall plant. The white, spiny leaves and the steel-blue, thistlelike flowers in August add interest to this hardy perennial. The plant thrives on poor soils and in full sun.

Echinops sphaerocephalus (Great, or Common, Globe Thistle). Reaches a height of 4 to 5 feet. The flowers are silvery-gray in August; the leaves somewhat spiny and covered with silvery-white hairs.

EPIMEDIUM (Epimedium). The epimediums are grown more for their foliage than for their flowers, although the delicate blooms ranging from white to red are attractive in May when viewed at close range. The heart-shaped leaves are semi-evergreen (they stay green for part of the winter) and leathery in texture. Plants prefer shade but grow in full sun if the soil is kept moist. Cut the old plants down to the ground in the spring to display the new leaves and flowers.

E. alpinum (Alpine Epimedium). Low plant, 1 foot tall, with white flowers that may have a pinkish tinge.

E. grandiflorum. No common name is given for this species. Plants are 1 foot tall with pink to crimson flowers.

E. pinnatum (Persian Epimedium). A low plant, 1¼ feet tall, with yellow flowers.

Eremurus stenophyllus (Desert-candle). Grows to 3 feet. The basal leaves are narrow and stiff. The erect flower stalk develops in June and July. The yellow flowers open from the base upward, forming a candle that may be over 1 foot long. After flowering, the foliage dies down, so it is best to plant the species next to spreading plants that will occupy the space in late summer and fall.

ERYNGIUM (Sea Holly). The white to steel-blue, thistlelike flowers bloom for a long time in July and August and are excellent dried for winter bouquets. The foliage is bluish. All species develop a taproot so transplanting mature plants is difficult.

E. alpinum (Bluetop Sea Holly). Compact plant, 1½ feet tall. The foliage and stems are blue. The white to blue flowers are the largest of the sea hollies, 1¼ inches across, and surrounded by a prickly, blue calyx.

E. amethystinum (Amethyst Sea Holly). Plants grow 2 feet tall. Leaves are spiny and flowers are blue and small.

E. yuccifolium (Rattlesnake-master). Upright plants, 3 feet tall, with blue-gray, yuccalike leaves that have spiny margins. Small, white flower heads at the top of the stems are attractive.

Eupatorium coelestinum (Mist Flower). Resembles the ageratum and is often referred to as the hardy ageratum. It is about 2 feet tall and has blue to lavender flowers in late summer.

Eupatorium purpureum (Joe-Pye Weed). This 4-foot-tall native of moist sites is suitable only for planting in a wild flower garden. The late bloom in August and September is attractive.

EUPHORBIA (Spurge). Of the numerous species of *Euphorbia*, many are weeds but a few are worth growing. All prefer full sunlight and well-drained soil.

E. corollata (Flowering Spurge). Produces small, white flowers on 2-foot stems from June to September. Flowers resemble *Gypsophila* (baby's breath).

E. cyparissias (Cypress Spurge). A low plant, 1 foot tall, with yellow floral bracts that turn purple as they mature. Flowers are showy in May and June.

E. epithymoides (Cushion Spurge). A mound-shaped plant up to 1½ feet high. The chartreuse-yellow floral bracts are colorful in late April and May.

Filipendula rubra (Queen-of-the-Prairie). Excellent for the back of the flower border, growing 4 to 5 feet tall. The small, pink, spirealike flowers are produced during June and July in large terminal panicles that rise above the foliage. This vigorous plant prefers moist soil and should be divided after 3 to 4 years.

Filipendula ulmaria (Queen-of-the-Meadow). Similar to *F. rubra* but it is shorter (3 to 4 feet) and the flowers are white.

Gaillardia x *grandiflora* (Blanket Flower). Although there are several native species of *Gaillardia*, the hybrid *G.* x *grandiflora*, a cross between *G. aristata* and *G. pulchella*, has provided most of the cultivars that are grown. 'Baby Cole', a low (1 foot), compact form, has been most attractive during July and August in arboretum trials. The disk flowers give a pincushion effect and the ray flowers are usually a shade of yellow or red. The blanket flower tends to have weak stems and to be rather short-lived. Plants prefer well-drained soil. Named varieties can be propagated from root cuttings.

Gentiana andrewsii (Bottle, or Closed, Gentian). Grows to 1½ feet. Many species of gentian are suitable for rock gardens, but the bottle gentian is virtually the only species grown in the perennial border. The only opening in the blue, tubular flower is a tiny pore at the tip. This is a late-flowering gentian with blooms in August and September. It prefers a moist site.

GERANIUM (Cranesbill). There are numerous species of *Geranium* ranging in height from 6 inches to 1½ feet. Many are suitable only for rock gardens but a few are attractive in the front of a perennial border. These plants are not to be confused with the species of *Pelargonium*, commonly called geraniums, that are grown so commonly in greenhouses, in homes, and as mass plantings in public parks.

G. maculatum (Spotted Cranesbill). Native to eastern North America including Minnesota. Grows to 1½ feet, with rose-purple flowers in June.

G. sanguineum (Bloodred Cranesbill). Introduced from Eurasia. Grows 1½ feet tall and produces reddish-purple flowers in late June and July.

Geum quellyon (Chile Avens). Also listed as *G. chiloense*. A native of South America. The large, basal leaves have a broad terminal lobe, and the flowers are red on erect, 1½-foot stems in June. 'Mrs. Bradshaw' has semi-double, red flowers and grows best on moist soil.

Geum triflorum (Old Man's Whiskers or Purple Avens). This 1-foot-tall native of the northern prairies has fernlike, basal leaves and nodding flowers that never open fully. The flowers are produced in late May and early June and have pinkish-purple petals. The first common name is derived from the tufts of feathery achenes that are produced after the plant flowers. Best used in the wild flower garden, this plant requires well-drained soil and good light.

Gypsophila paniculata (Baby's Breath). Most commonly grown species of *Gypsophila*, reaching a height of 3 feet. The single, white flowers are produced in large panicles from July to September. The small flowers are used in flower arrangements and are readily dried for winter bouquets. The cultivar 'Bristol Fairy' has double, white flowers.

Gypsophila repens (Creeping Baby's Breath). Low (1 to 1½ feet) and spreading, with single, white flowers from July to September. 'Rosea' has pink flowers. The plants require good drainage.

Helenium autumnale (Sneezeweed). This tall (3 to 5 feet), autumn-flowering perennial adds color to the border. The daisylike flowers, which are produced in August, are in shades of yellow and red. 'Butterpat', 'Brilliant', and 'Moorheim Beauty' are named cultivars. Plants must be divided every few years to maintain vigor and quality of bloom.

Heliopsis helianthoides (Sunflower Heliopsis). A tall perennial of the Eastern United States, growing to a height of 4 to 5 feet. The flowers, which resemble *Helianthus* (Sunflower), are produced in August. The heads are 2½ inches across. The ray flowers are light yellow, the disk flowers yellowish-brown. The following cultivars are frequently planted: 'Golden Plume', 'Gold Greenheart', and 'Summer Sun'. The subspecies *scabra* has orange-yellow flowers.

HEMEROCALLIS (Daylily). There are many species and cultivars of *Hemerocallis*, ranging from 2 to 4 feet tall. Species, like *H. flava* (lemon daylily) and *H. fulva* (orange daylily), are seldom planted except in collections and for bank covers. Named cultivars of mixed parentage are appearing at a rapid rate. Colors and substance (firmness) of flowers have been vastly improved. Individual flowers survive only a day but the plant produces a succession of bloom lasting several weeks. By choosing varieties with different blooming dates, continuous bloom can be obtained for several months. Daylilies are useful in a mixed flower border and tolerate some shade. With hundreds of cultivars to choose from, it is difficult to know what to plant. Visit a garden featuring daylilies and select those you like.

Hesperis matronalis (Dames Rocket). Garden flower belonging to the mustard family. It grows 2 to 3 feet tall. Flowers range from white to shade of purple and are produced in late May and June. Individual plants do not live more than a few years but new plants grow readily from seed. Naturalized plantings from volunteer seedlings are common.

Heuchera sanguinea (Coral Bells). Grows 1½ to 2 feet tall. This perennial produces a basal rosette of heart-shaped leaves. Flower stalks are branched, with numerous small, pink to red, bell-shaped flowers. Bloom peaks in June and July, and repeat bloom is often produced by removing faded flowers. The species is not too hardy, so plants may be short-lived. Hybrids with other species like *H. richardsonii* have been developed by Mr. Robert Simonet of Edmonton, Alberta, and these are very hardy and colorful. Numerous cultivars are on the market. Experiment to find the cultivars best suited to your garden.

Hibiscus moscheutos (Rose Mallow). A tall perennial to 8 feet, producing large, white, pink, or rose flowers 4 inches across in August and September. The subspecies *palustris* (marsh rose mallow) was crossed with the species *H. coccineus* and *H. militaris* to produce larger-flowered hybrids. One of these is 'Southern Bell', which received an All-America Award a few years ago. Its flowers measure 7 inches across and are in a variety of bright colors.

IRIS (Iris). Literally thousands of iris species and cultivars are on the market. These range from dwarf plants a few inches tall to the giant, bearded iris that may be 3 to 4 feet tall. The iris flower has 6 perianth segments (sepals and petals). The 3 outer segments are reflexed and hanging. These are called the "falls." The 3 inner ones are upright and called the "standards." Prominent hairs, or a "beard," may also be present at the base of the "falls." Irises are classified as bearded or beardless, depending on the presence or absence of these hairs. Man has hybridized irises since they began to be cultivated as garden plants. Many modern cultivars scarcely resemble their original species parents. The following species and their hybrids are the ones most commonly grown:

I. cristata (Crested Iris). A dwarf iris 6 inches tall, commonly planted as a ground cover. Flowers are light violet to purple in early May.

I. x *germanica* (Bearded Iris). The exact origin of the bearded iris is not known. A number of species were probably involved in the development of this important group of garden irises. The bearded irises are classified according to size into dwarf (3 inches to 1 foot), intermediate (1 to 1½ feet), and tall (1½ to 3½ feet) groups. There are over 1,000 named cultivars and new ones are produced every year. The best way to select cultivars for your garden is to attend one of the flower shows staged each spring by the Minnesota Iris Society or to visit a public garden such as the one at the arboretum. You will be surprised that there are so many beautiful irises to choose from.

I. kaempferi (Japanese Iris). One of the more beautiful irises, blooming in July with broad, flat-topped flowers 6 inches across. Flower colors include white, lavender, deep purple, blue, lavender-pink, and all shades in between. Numerous cultivars have been developed by Japanese hybridizers. These Japanese irises are not widely grown because their soil requirements are exacting: they need acid soil that is high in organic matter, moist in summer, and well drained during the winter.

I. pseudacorus (Yellow Flag). A large, European species, 4 feet tall, that thrives on wet soils. The yellow, beardless flowers are attractive in late May and early June.

I. sibirica (Siberian Iris). Grows in dense clumps with grasslike foliage. Plants are 1½ to 2 feet tall. The flowers are beardless and produced at the end of slender stems in early June. Numerous cultivars are on the market. Their flower colors range from white to purple, with intermediate shades of blue. Visit a public garden or

a commercial grower when the Siberian irises are in bloom to select cultivars for planting.

I. spuria (Spuria Iris). These irises are similar to *I. sibirica* but
bloom later and with larger flowers. The leaves are also broader.
Flower colors range from white to deep purple. A few cultivars
have yellow flowers. You can see the spuria iris in bloom at the
arboretum during mid-June.

LIATRIS (Blazing Star or Kansas Gayfeather). This common roadside plant can be attractive when grown in the perennial border. It
is 2 to 3 feet tall and blooms in late summer and fall. Produced in
dense, terminal spikes, the flowers are typically purple, although
white forms are known. Plants require well-drained soil and full
sun. *L. punctata* (dotted gayfeather), *L. pyncnostachya* (Kansas
gayfeather), *L. scariosa* (tall gayfeather), and *L. spicata* (spike
gayfeather) are the species most commonly grown.

LILIUM (Lily). There are more than 80 species of *Lilium* in the
north temperate zones of the world. A few species are planted in
the garden, including *L. canadense* (Canada Lily), *L. candidum*
(madonna lily), *L. concolor* (star lily), *L. lancifolia* (tiger lily), *L.
martagon* (martagon lily), *L. regale* (regal lily), and *L. speciosum*
(showy lily). However, most species grow in a particular type of
soil in a limited geographic area, and unless the garden can provide
these conditions of soil, temperature, and moisture, they gradually
die. The hybrid lilies are more popular than the species because
through selection they combine the best characteristics of the several species that went into their breeding and they are capable of
growing and thriving on a variety of soils and in different climatic
regions. These hybrids are sold as named cultivars like 'Enchantment'. The North Star Lily Society has done much to popularize
the lily in this area. It also sponsors the lily collection in the arboretum and puts on a lily show each July.

Lilies can be grown in rows for cut flowers or combined with
other perennials in the perennial flower border. By selecting species and cultivars with different flowering dates, continuous bloom
can be obtained from early June until mid-September. When planning the border find out the height of the species and cultivars to

be planted, since the height of lilies varies from 1 foot to 5 or more feet. This information can be obtained from the grower you purchase your bulbs from or the catalog descriptions provided by mail-order companies and garden centers.

Most lilies require well-drained soil and bloom best in full sunlight. The bulbs are usually planted in early October so that roots can form before the ground freezes. A mulch applied before the ground freezes lengthens the time when rooting can occur. Plant the bulbs about 6 inches deep. Botrytis blight, a fungus disease which can be controlled by spraying, and mosaic, a virus disease for which there is no cure, are the important diseases.

Flower form fits one of three types. In the trumpet lilies, like the Easter lily, the petals and sepals form a flaring tube, or trumpet. In the turkscap lilies the petals and sepals are reflexed and flowers assume a nodding position. In the cupshaped lilies the petals and sepals are cupped and are either upward facing or outward facing.

Lilies are also classified according to the country of origin and the dominant species used in hybridizing. The following classes are recognized by the North American Lily Society:

Martagon Hybrids. These are early, June-flowering hybrids resulting from crosses between *L. martagon* and *L. hansonii*. They are tall lilies, up to 3 feet. Flowers are of the turkscap type, with yellow, pink, lavender, light orange, and red the common colors.

Asiatic Hybrids. Several Asiatic species were used in the breeding of this class. Plants range from 1½ to 3 feet. Flowers are shaped like a cup or a Turk's cap and are bright red, yellow, and orange. These lilies bloom in June and July.

Trumpet and Aurelian Hybrids. The true trumpets have long, flaring flower tubes, which are shorter in the Aurelian hybrids. *L. henryi* and *L. regale* are the dominant parents. Plants are from 2 to 5 feet tall. Flower colors range from white through yellow to purple. Most cultivars bloom in July.

Oriental Hybrids. These are the ultimate in lily breeding. *L. auratum* and *L. speciosum* are the major parents for this class. Plants are from 1 to 3 feet tall. Flowers are saucer shaped, white to red, with stripes and dots of other colors. These are the latest-flowering lilies, blooming in August and sometimes into early September.

Linum perenne (Perennial Flax). Of the many species of flax, the perennial flax is the one most commonly planted. It is 2 feet tall and has flowers produced on slender stems throughout the summer. The plants bloom the first year from seed.

Lithospermum canescens (Puccoon). This native prairie plant, 1 to 1½ feet tall, produces clusters of orange-yellow flowers in May and June. It grows best in full sun on sandy or well-drained soil. Mature puccoons are difficult to transplant.

Lobelia cardinalis (Cardinal Flower). Grows to 3 feet. This beautiful, native plant produces tall spikes of cardinal-red flowers in late summer. It is found along streams on wet soils and prefers a moist spot in the garden. Although the plant is short-lived, where growing conditions are favorable it self-sows and a planting can last many years.

Lobelia siphilitica (Great Blue Lobelia). Grows 2 to 3 feet tall and has showy, blue flowers borne in the axils of the upper leaves. Like *L. cardinalis* (cardinal flower), this lobelia prefers moist soil.

Lupinus perennis (Wild Lupine). Native to sandy soils, this plant reaches a height of 1½ feet. The palmately compound leaves and the blue, pealike flowers in June make this an attractive plant. It does best on acid soils, and seeds should be sown where you want plants to grow. The Russell hybrids are of uncertain origin. Where growing conditions are favorable, they provide a bold display with their flowers of various colors.

Lychnis chalcedonica (Maltese Cross). Grows to 3 feet. The bright, scarlet flowers in June and July are formed in dense clusters at the top of the plant. This species requires well-drained soil and full sunlight.

Lychnis viscaria (German Catchfly). A 1¼-foot-tall plant. It is shorter than *L. chalcedonica* and has reddish-purple flowers. Several named cultivars like 'Alba', 'Splendens', and 'Splendens Flore-Pleno' are on the market.

Lycoris squamigera (Magic Lily, Hardy Amaryllis). One of the few plants belonging to the amaryllis family that can be grown outdoors in this area, reaching 1½ feet. The bulbs are planted in the fall, the leaves come up in the spring, and in July the plant dies to the ground. In late August or early September the flower stalks appear and soon develop several large lilac to purple, lilylike flowers lasting several weeks. Requires well drained soil.

Lysimachia clethroides (Gooseneck Loosestrife). Grows to 3 feet. The common name comes from the white flower spikes that bend over at the tips, producing the curious "gooseneck" appearance. The flowers open in July and August, and the leaves turn bronzy-yellow in September. This plant likes moist soil and requires frequent division.

Lysimachia punctata (Garden Loosestrife). Grows 2 to 3 feet tall. The leaves of this perennial are whorled, and yellow flowers develop in the axils of the leaves. Partial shade and a moist site are preferred.

Lysimachia vulgaris (Golden Loosestrife). Similar to *L. punctata*. Plants are 2 feet tall.

Lythrum virgatum (Lythrum). This 3-foot-tall European species is similar to *L. salicaria*, which has naturalized on many wet soils in the area. 'Dropmore Purple', 'Morden Gleam', 'Morden Pink', and 'Morden Rose' are cultivars of this species. These lythrums form erect clumps, with spires of rose-pink to purple flowers in July and August. Old plants are difficult to move. Young plants are grown from cuttings.

Macleaya cordata (Plume Poppy). This tall (5 feet) perennial should be planted near the back of the border and only if space permits. The large, heart-shaped leaves and the numerous, creamy-white flowers in terminal panicles are showy. Tends to self-sow.

Monarda didyma (Garden Bee Balm). Grows 2 to 2½ feet tall and spreads rapidly. The species is very showy when in bloom, usually from June to August. The flowers are bright scarlet and produced in terminal heads. The many named cultivars offer a wide range of flower colors from white to purple. Plants are subject to mildew, and division is required every few years to maintain vigor.

Oenothera fruticosa (Sundrops). This low (1¼ feet), mat-forming perennial is most attractive when in full bloom during June and July. The lemon-yellow, cup-shaped flowers are 1½ inches across. The perennial requires ample soil moisture.

PAEONIA (Peony). One of the more popular garden plants, growing to a height of 2½ feet. Early-flowering species of peonies start blooming in late May; garden hybrids reach their peak of bloom in mid-June. Peonies are long-lived perennials that grow best in full sunlight on clay loam soil of high fertility. The soil should be prepared to a depth of 1½ feet. A fertilizer high in phosphorus should be worked into the soil at planting time. September is the best time to plant peonies. A division containing from 3 to 5 buds, or "eyes," is used. Plant so that the buds will be 2 inches below the soil surface; deeper planting results in poor bloom. Keep the soil cultivated around the plants to reduce competition. Remove faded flowers but do not cut back the foliage until the tops are killed by frost.

P. anomala (Ural Peony). One of the earlier peonies to bloom, with crimson-red flowers. The leaflets are finely dissected into narrow lobes.

P. tenuifolia (Fernleaf Peony). This peony is grown as much for its fernlike foliage as for its bloom, which usually occurs by Memorial Day. The petals are deep crimson, the stamens yellow, and the leaflets finely dissected.

Hybrid Peonies. The popular garden peonies are hybrids derived from the species *P. lactiflora* and *P. officinalis*. These hybrids are classified according to their flower structure. The single peonies have one row of petals surrounding a center of petaloid (petallike) stamens that are narrow and short and either yellow or the same color as the petals. These are considered the most beautiful of all peonies. In the double peonies all the stamens are petaloid and similar in color to the outer petals. The single peonies start flowering in early June. These are followed by the Japanese type of singles. The doubles are the latest to bloom and usually last through June. Flower color ranges from white to red. Hundreds of cultivars of the hybrid peonies have been introduced.

Papaver nudicaule (Iceland Poppy). This handsome poppy is 1½ feet tall and has a wide range of flower colors. It blooms for a long period in midsummer. The flower stalks are long and slender. The plant is short-lived and best treated as an annual or biennial.

Papaver orientale (Oriental Poppy). The most popular of the poppies, growing 2 to 2½ feet tall. Over 60 named cultivars offer a wide range of flower colors. 'Barr's White' is white with purple blotches, 'Curtis Giant Flame' has large, blazing-red flowers; and 'Curtis Salmon Glow' has double flowers of salmon-orange color. The diameter of individual flowers can be as much as 6 to 8 inches. Bloom peaks in June, and the plants die down in late summer, when they should be divided. Poppies make excellent cut flowers if the ends of the cut stems are seared with a flame before placing in water.

PENSTEMON (Beard Tongue). A large genus of 250 species native to the western United States. These are beautiful plants when in full bloom under natural conditions. Under cultivation most species are short-lived. If several species are grown, hybridization occurs and the resulting seedlings will be unlike their parents. The size of plants can vary from a few inches to 3 feet. Well-drained soil is required. The following species are sometimes planted:

P. barbatus (Beardlip Beard Tongue). Tallest of the beard tongues, growing to 3 feet. It has bright red, 2-lipped flowers borne in axillary clusters throughout the summer.

P. grandiflorus (Showy Beard Tongue). Short-lived perennial, 2½ feet tall, native to the prairie states. The tall spikes of large, 6-inch flowers are lilac colored in late May and early June.

Phlox paniculata (Garden Phlox). Grows 2 to 2½ feet tall. This popular perennial does much better in climates with cool summers than in our area, where its performance is often disappointing. The foliage tends to be affected by leaf diseases, and by the time the flowers start to open in June and July, the leaves are gone. Powdery mildew is the most common leaf disease, but other species of fungi are also involved. There are hundreds of named cultivars in a wide range of colors, and some of these plants are truly beautiful. A visit to a grower of garden phlox should help you select cultivars for your garden. Certain cultivars seem more resistant to disease than others, so it is advisable to plant a number of cultivars and select those that grow best for you. Keeping the plants watered during dry spells and spraying with a good fungicide also help. Remove the faded flowers to prevent seed formation, for volunteer seedlings usually revert to an unattractive magenta color typical of the species. Let us hope that disease-resistant strains will be produced some day.

Physostegia virginiana (False Dragonhead). The 3-foot-tall species produces purplish-red, bilobed flowers on erect terminal spikes. The flowers have a fancied resemblance to a dragon's head. A number of cultivars are on the market, with flower colors ranging from white to crimson. 'Alba' has white flowers, 'Grandiflora' bright pink, and 'Rubra' red. This perennial is somewhat invasive and should be divided every few years to prevent it from taking over the border.

Platycodon grandiflorus (Balloon Flower). This close relative to the bellflowers is 2 feet tall. In bud the flowers are shaped like a balloon; open flowers are blue, cup shaped, and 2 inches across. The balloon flower likes well-drained soil, and under proper growing conditions an established clump lives for years. White and pink cultivars like 'Albus' and 'Roseus' are on the market.

Pulmonaria angustifolia (Blue Lungwort). Low (1 foot), mound-shaped plant with green, straplike leaves. The small, blue flowers cover the plant in early May. Prefers moist soil and light shade.

Pulmonaria saccharata (Bethlehem Sage). Similar to *P. angustifolia* but its leaves are spotted with white.

Ranunculus acris 'Flore-Pleno' (Double Buttercup). Grows 2 to 3 feet tall. Of the hundreds of species of buttercup, only one is commonly planted and this only in the double-flowered form. This is because most species self-sow and can become weeds. The small, yellow, buttonlike flowers are produced in open panicles during May. Does best on moist sites.

Rudbeckia hirta (Black-eyed Susan). Corase perennial, growing 2 feet tall, with dark-colored disk flowers and yellow to orange ray flowers. The gloriosa daisies are tetraploid forms of this species and are grown for their mass of blooms that covers the plants all summer. The gloriosa daisies are short-lived and best grown as annuals; they self-sow.

Rudbeckia laciniata 'Hortensia' (Golden Glow). This tall (6 feet) perennial is a favorite. The large, fully double, yellow flowers are produced at the tips of lateral branches. Use toward the back of the border. Plants must be staked in windy locations.

Salvia x *superba* 'Purple Spires'. Grows to 1½ feet. This sterile hybrid produces a mass of blue flowers on erect spikes in June. If faded flowers are removed, repeat bloom occurs throughout the summer. A most satisfactory perennial.

Scabiosa caucasica (Perennial Pincushion). A 2-foot-tall perennial with large, compound flowers resembling a pincushion. The blue flower clusters are 3 inches across. Hybrids with this species like the 'Isaac House Hybrids' include white, amethyst-blue, and lavender-blue forms. The flowering period is from June to September. Plants may need to be divided after a few years.

Sedum spectabile (Showy Stonecrop). Most of the many species of *Sedum* are low and spreading and suitable only in rock gardens or for ground covers. *S. spectabile* is an excellent border perennial. It forms a 1½-foot-tall, mound-shaped plant covered with clusters of rose-pink flowers in August and September. Numerous cultivars are on the market, with flower colors ranging from white to wine-red. 'Album' (white), 'Rubrum' (red), and 'Purpurea' (purple) are popular cultivars.

Sedum telephium (Live-forever). Similar to *S. spectabile* but with copper or Indian-red flowers.

SOLIDAGO (Goldenrods). The numerous species of goldenrod are conspicuous in our native landscape. In England and in Europe they are truly appreciated and numerous garden hybrids have been developed. In this country we associate them with hay fever, a reputation they do not deserve. Actually, the pollen of the goldenrod is sticky and transmitted only by insects. The goldenrod may carry the foreign pollen of *Ambrosia artemisifolia* (the common ragweed) which has settled on its fluffy, yellow flowers. The goldenrod deserves to be planted in the flower border for its long period of fall bloom.

Stokesia laevis (Stokes Aster). Grows to 1½ feet. The large, showy, asterlike blooms in August and September are striking. Numerous cultivars such as 'Alba', 'Caerulia', and 'Rosea' are on the market, in colors ranging from white to deep blue. This short-lived perennial requires well-drained soil.

Tanacetum vulgare (Tansy). This 3-foot-tall plant can be terribly invasive and its use should be limited to out-of-the-way parts of the garden. The yellow flower clusters are used for dried flower arrangements.

Thalictrum aquilegifolium (Columbine Meadowrue). Grows to 3 feet. There are many species of meadowrue native to this area, but this is the one most commonly planted. Numerous small, purplish flowers are produced in open panicles above the divided, columbinelike foliage in late May and early June.

Thermopsis caroliniana (Carolina Lupine). Growing 4 feet tall, this member of the pea family has trifoliate leaves and erect, yellow flower spikes in July. It resembles a yellow lupine—hence its common name. In windy locations it may be desirable to stake the plants.

Tradescantia x *andersoniana* (Spiderwort). A complex garden hybrid produced by crossing *T. ohiensis*, *T. subaspera*, and *T. virginiana*. This plant with grasslike foliage and white to violet, 3-petaled flowers can be attractive in the border. It grows 1½ feet tall, and its stems are likely to fall over unless they are staked. The greatest bloom occurs in June and July. A number of named cultivars are on the market, for example, 'Alba', 'Rosea', and 'Violacea'.

Trollius europaeus (Globeflower). Grows 2 feet tall. Numerous cultivars of this species, including 'Giganteus', 'Grandiflorus', and 'Superbus', are on the market. Their large, yellow to orange, double flowers resemble the buttercup and are produced in June. Plants do best on moist soil.

Valeriana officinalis (Common Valerian). A 4-foot-tall perennial. The small, light lavender flowers are borne in flat-topped clusters during July and are heavily fragrant. Staking may be required in windy locations. Grows on most soils.

Verbascum phoeniceum (Purple Mullein). Grows 2 to 3 feet tall. This short-lived perennial tends to behave like a biennial. A rosette of straplike leaves forms the first year and erect flower stems form the second year. The flowers range from white to purple and are produced on loosely branched spikes. Many hybrids and named cultivars are on the market. These include 'Pink Domino', 'Bridal Bouquet', and 'Gainsborough'. Cultivars can be propagated from root cuttings.

Yucca glauca (Soapweed). A native of the northern prairies, reaching a height of 3 feet. It grows well but has been slow to bloom. The flowers are greenish-white and not as showy as *Y. smalliana* flowers. Same culture as *Y. smalliana*.

Yucca smalliana (Adam's Needle). Virtually the only species of *Yucca* planted in northern gardens. It is often sold as *Y. filamentosa*. The plant is 5 feet tall and its evergreen leaves may turn yellow in an open (with little or no snow) winter. Tall spikes of white, lilylike flowers open in July. The yuccas like well-drained soil and full sunlight. The arboretum has had best results where snow drifts in and protects the crowns of the plants.

Lists of Perennials for Sunny Borders

LOW PLANTS FOR FOREGROUND PLANTINGS
(2½ feet and under)

Aquilegia hybrids
Asclepias tuberosa
Aster nova-angliae

Astilbe x *arendsii*
Aurinia saxatile
Campanula carpatica

Campanula glomerata var. *dahurica*
Chrysanthemum coccineum
Chrysanthemum x morifolium
Dianthus barbatus
Dictamnus albus
Gaillardia x grandiflora
Gypsophila repens
Hemerocallis hybrids
Heuchera sanguinea
Iris x germanica
Lilium hybrids
Lycoris squamigera

Monarda didyma
Oenothera fruticosa
Paeonia hybrids
Papaver orientale
Phlox paniculata
Platycodon grandiflorus
Pulmonaria angustifolia
Rudbeckia hirta
Salvia x superba 'Purple Spires'
Sedum spectabile
Tradescantia virginiana
Trollius europaeus

TALL PLANTS FOR BACKGROUND PLANTINGS
(over 2½ feet)

Achillea filipendulina
Aconitum napellus
Alcea rosea
Baptisia australis
Cassia marilandica
Centaurea macrocephala
Chrysanthemum x morifolium
Cimicifuga racemosa
Delphinium hybrids
Echinops sphaerocephalus
Eremurus stenophyllus
Filipendula rubra
Helenium autumnale

Hemerocallis hybrids
Hibiscus moscheutos
Iris x germanica
Iris pseudacorus
Lilium hybrids
Lobelia cardinalis
Lychnis chalcedonica
Lythrum virgatum
Macleya cordata
Rudbeckia laciniata 'Hortensia'
Thermopsis caroliniana
Valeriana officinalis

PERENNIALS FOR CUT FLOWERS

Achillea filipendulina
Aquilegia hybrids
Asclepias incarnata
Centaurea montana
Chrysanthemum coccineum
Chrysanthemum x morifolium
Delphinium hybrids
Echinops sphaerocephalus
Gaillardia x grandiflora
Gypsophila paniculata

Hemerocallis hybrids
Hibiscus moscheutos
Iris hybrids
Lilium hybrids
Lupinus perennis
Lythrum virgatum
Paeonia hybrids
Papaver orientale
Platycodon grandiflorus
Rudbeckia hirta

FRAGRANT PERENNIALS

Aquilegia chrysantha
Astilbe x *arendsii*
Dianthus caryophyllus
Dictamnus albus
Iris x *germanica* (most blue irises)

Monarda didyma
Paeonia hybrids
Phlox paniculata
Valeriana officinalis

Chapter 17

Perennial Plants for Shady Gardens

Many homes are built in the woods or in yards with many trees. Plants that like full sunlight do poorly under such conditions. Few flowering plants thrive in deep shade, but some native woodland wild flowers and ferns should be considered for shady gardens. (Ferns are listed separately at the end of this chapter.) Certain annuals and tender perennials like *Begonia* x *semperflorens* and *Impatiens wallerana* can also be used. (See Chapter 20.) Besides shade, root competition from trees can be a problem. Additional watering and fertilizing may be required for best results.

Actaea pachypoda (White Baneberry). A 2-foot-tall plant that is found in deep to moderate shade in hardwood forests. The leaves are compound and the leaflets toothed. Small, white flowers are produced in upright racemes during late May and early June, followed by China-white, poisonous berries with prominent black eyes on stout pedicels. Red-fruited forms are occasionally found. Plants can be grown by direct seeding as soon as the seeds are ripe. They usually bloom the third year. Old clumps can be divided in early spring. Plant in partial shade on soil that is high in organic matter.

218

Actaea rubra (Red Baneberry). Grows 1½ to 2 feet tall. The species is similar to *A. pachypoda* (white baneberry), but its fruits are red, produced on slender pedicels, and lack the prominent "eyes." White-fruited forms of this species are also found.

Anemone quinquefolia (Wood Anemone). This 6-inch-tall species often forms a carpet on the forest floor. The leaves are compound, with 3 to 5 lobes, or divisions; the single, white flowers are produced on erect stems. Plants can be grown from seeds or old clumps divided. Plants may also be available from nurseries specializing in wild flowers.

Anemonella thalictroides (Rue Anemone). Resembles *A. quinquefolia* (wood anemone) in general appearance and height. However, the flowers are produced in clusters instead of singly and are usually tinged with pink. The species is not as attractive as the double-flowered cultivar 'Schoaf's Double Pink', which was found in southern Minnesota and is now being propagated and sold throughout the United States. The flowers of the double form are fully double and last a long time. The plant reproduces from fleshy corms that develop underground. Provide good drainage and plenty of leaf mold or humus.

Aralia nudicaulis (Wild Sarsaparilla). This 1-foot-tall plant has a single stem with 3 compound leaves, each of which has 5 leaflets. The flower stalk bears 3 clusters of small, greenish flowers, followed by green berries that turn black. The species spreads underground by fleshy rhizomes. Divide plants in early fall; rhizomes should be horizontal and barely covered with soil. Grow in light shade on well-drained soil.

Aralia racemosa (Spikenard). Grows 2 to 5 feet tall. The plant blooms in late June and early July, producing clusters of tiny, white flowers on erect stems that project above the compound leaves. The purple-red berries ripen in the fall. This species is ordinarily found in open shade and plants are usually scattered. Plant in dispersed clumps along a woodland trail in the fall or in early spring when the plant is dormant.

Arisaema triphyllum (Jack-in-the-Pulpit). A 1½-foot-tall plant. The peculiar flower stalk, enclosed in a spathe (sheath), forms in late May, and clusters of red berries ripen in August. The jack-in-the-pulpit grows on any rich, forest soil; it prefers shade and does best on moist soil. Plants can be grown from seed, planted as soon as ripe, or by transplanting the fleshy corms in the fall. The cooked corms were a source of starch for the Indians. The raw corms contain crystals of calcium oxalate, which can render a person speechless if the raw corms are eaten. Fruits should not be eaten.

Asarum canadense (Wild Ginger). A fine ground cover in a woodland garden, wild ginger is 6 inches tall and spreads by creeping rhizomes that produce heart-shaped leaves. The rhizomes have a spicy, gingerlike fragrance when dug. Small, reddish-brown flowers form under the leaves in May. Propagation is by seeds and by divisions of the rhizomes. Plant in fall or early spring in soil high in organic matter.

Chimaphila maculata (Spotted Pipsissewa). Similar to *C. umbellata* var. *cisatlantica* except the leaves are spotted.

Chimaphila umbellata var. *cisatlantica* (Pipsissewa). This 6-inch-high evergreen plant creeps along the ground from an underground rhizome. The leaves are narrowly wedge shaped and about 4 inches long. The flowers are cup shaped, white to pink, and borne in small clusters during June and July. This species requires acid soil and is usually found near pine trees. If growing conditions are right, this is a very nice plant. Propagate by rooting cuttings in a mixture of sand and acid peat.

Claytonia virginica (Spring Beauty). This tiny, May-flowering plant can form dense carpets 4 to 6 inches high. The leaves are narrow and opposite. The small, white flowers have pink- to rose-colored veins that are distinctive. Spring beauties die down soon after flowering, so it is best to plant them among ferns for a nice summer effect. Plant in the fall using the small, tuberlike growths that develop underground. Rich soil and light shade are needed.

Clintonia borealis (Bluebead Lily). Grows to 8 inches and has broad, strap-shaped leaves forming a basal rosette. Clusters of small, greenish-yellow, bell-shaped flowers are produced on an erect stem in early June, and steel-blue fruits ripen in August. Plants require moist, acid soil high in organic matter.

Convallaria majalis (Lily-of-the-Valley). This 8-inch-tall plant is an excellent ground cover in a shaded garden. The nodding, bell-shaped, white flowers are fragrant and often picked for small flower arrangements. 'Rosea', a pink cultivar, and 'Prolificans', with double, white flowers, are available. Overcrowded plants should be divided in the fall and moved to a new location.

Cornus canadensis (Bunchberry). This miniature (6 inch) dogwood has a whorl of leaves below the inconspicuous flower cluster that opens in June and July. Four white bracts resembling petals surround the cluster. A cluster of bright red berries develops in the fall. This delightful plant requires moist, acid soil. Propagation is by division.

Cypripedium acaule (Moccasin Flower). Grows to 8 inches. Each plant has 2 basal leaves and a single flower on a leafless stalk. The species is very difficult to transplant and is best enjoyed in its natural habitat: on hummocks in tamarack swamps and in open, Jack pine woods. Plants require acid soil.

Cypripedium calceolus (Yellow Lady's-Slipper). Reaches a height of 1½ feet and has yellow, slipperlike flowers that open in late May. Small-flowered forms belong to the variety *parviflorum*, large-flowered forms to the variety *pubescens*. This species is the easiest-grown lady's-slipper. Almost any woods soil high in organic matter is satisfactory. Grow in light shade and do not let other plants compete for light and nutrients.

Cypripedium reginae (Showy Lady's-Slipper). The showiest lady's-slipper, with broad stem leaves and large, white flowers striped with rose or purple. With the right culture the plant grows 2 feet tall and multiplies. In nature it is usually found on hummocks in sphagnum bogs. In the garden it grows well on specially prepared soil high in organic matter. Acid peat is excellent for modifying the soil. The site should be moist and partly shaded. Avoid companion plants that might compete. Dormant plants can be purchased from licensed nurseries. All lady's-slippers are on the protected list.

Dentaria laciniata (Cut-leaved Toothwort). Grows to 10 inches. This member of the mustard family produces a loose cluster of white flowers above the palmately lobed leaves in late May and early June. It should be planted in rich, somewhat moist forest soil. Propagate from seeds or by division in fall or early spring.

DICENTRA (Bleeding Heart, Dutchman's-Breeches, Squirrel Corn). A genus of about 20 species native to North America and Asia. The foliage is finely divided and fernlike. The flowers are usually heart-shaped and white, red, or purple.

D. canadensis (Squirrel Corn). This 6-inch-tall plant comes up early in the spring with fernlike foliage and loose clusters of heart-shaped flowers on erect stems. The white flowers often have a pink to pale lavender tint. After the plant flowers in early May, its foliage begins to die down and by late June the plant disappears. Plant with ferns in an open woodland where the spring sun can filter through the leafless trees.

D. cucullaria (Dutchman's-Breeches). Very similar to *D. canadensis* (squirrel corn) except for the white flowers, which resemble pantaloons hung on an arching stem. Like *D. canadensis*, the foliage dies down after the seeds mature in June. New plants are started by transplanting the fleshy corms or nodules that develop in the soil.

D. eximia (Wild Bleeding Heart). Grows 1 foot tall. This native of the eastern states produces pink to lavender, heart-shaped flowers that hang from arching stems. The foliage resembles a fern, but unlike the foliage of *D. cucullaria* (Dutchman's-breeches), it stays green all season. Bloom peaks in May, but repeat bloom can be expected until frost. Individual plants may be short-lived, however, volunteer seedlings come up near the original plants.

D. spectabilis (Bleeding Heart). This 2-foot-tall plant, described in Chapter 16, can also be used in the woodland garden if the shade is light.

Epigaea repens (Trailing Arbutus). Grows to 6 inches and is evergreen and semi-woody. The leathery leaves and trailing stems often form extensive mats on acid soils and in the shade of pine and oaks. The fragrant, white to pink flowers in May are delightful, but because they were widely used in corsages, this wild flower was almost eliminated from our northern woods early in this century. Trailing arbutus must have acid, well-drained soil and light shade. New plantings should be started from seed or rooted cuttings. Do not attempt to move mature plants. On the protected list.

Erythronium albidum (White Trout Lily). This 6-inch-tall wild flower has mottled, basal leaves and produces nodding, white, lilylike flowers in May. After flowering, the plant dies down to the ground. It grows on most woodland soils but prefers slightly acid soil. It takes five years or longer to produce plants of flowering size from seeds. White trout lily can also be started by planting the small bulbs in the fall.

Erythronium americanum (Yellow Trout Lily). Very similar to *E. albidum* except for the color of the flowers.

Eupatorium rugosum (White Snakeroot). A common woodland flower in midsummer and early fall. The small, white, buttonlike flowers are produced in flattish clusters at the top of the 2-foot-tall stem. Moist soil is essential for obtaining good bloom. This plant does well in the perennial border.

Gaultheria procumbens (Wintergreen). Creeping, evergreen plant that is semi-woody and 4 inches tall. The small, white, bell-shaped flowers are often tinged with pink and are produced from late June to August. The flowers are seldom showy because they are hidden by the glossy, green leaves. The red berries mature in the fall and often remain on the plants all winter under the snow. Both the young leaves and the fruits have a wintergreen flavor. Requires well-drained, acid soil.

Geranium maculatum (Wild Geranium). Grows to 1½ feet. This native, woodland plant is usually scattered in moist, shady areas. The flowers rise above the leafy stems and are produced in loose clusters. The single flowers are magenta-pink and about 1 inch across in late May and June. The seeds are produced in elongated fruits resembling a crane's bill. New plants can be produced by division or from seed. Divisions should bloom the first year, but it takes several years to produce flowering plants from seed.

Gillenia trifoliata (Bowman's Root). Grows 2 feet tall. The small, white to pale pink, star-shaped flowers are produced in little clusters above the trifoliate leaves. This wild flower grows best in high shade at the edge of a woods, and it prefers slightly acid soil. Grow from seed sown in the fall.

Habenaria psychodes (Small Purple Fringed Orchid). The commonest fringed orchid, often found in moist meadows in northern areas. It is 2 feet tall, and its erect spikes of fringed flowers are striking in June. The species grows well in a moist, woodland setting. Plants must be purchased from a licensed grower.

Helleborus niger (Christmas Rose). Easily cultured member of the buttercup family, growing 1 foot tall. The greenish-white to pinkish flowers open soon after the snow melts and last a long time. New plants can be grown from seed and need soil high in organic matter and light shade.

Hemerocallis (Daylilies). These popular garden flowers can also be grown in light shade. For details see Chapter 16.

Hepatica acutiloba (Sharplobe Hepatica). This attractive wild flower blooms soon after the snow melts and grows to 6 inches. The flowers arise from the crown and are borne at the tips of erect stems. Flower color varies from white to pink to blue. A basal rosette of leaves with pointed leaf lobes develops as the flowers fade. Old clumps can be divided and replanted in early spring. Common in deciduous woods where the soil is about neutral.

Hepatica americana (Roundlobe Hepatica). Very similar to *H. acutiloba* except its leaves have rounded lobes and it prefers acid soil. The plant is usually found in northern woods and is sometimes found growing with *H. acutiloba*.

Heracleum sphondylium subsp. *montanum* (American Cow Parsnip). Sometimes listed as *H. lanatum* or *H. maximum*. This plant is very tall, reaching 6 feet. Its big leaves are maplelike, and its white flowers are in large, terminal umbels. The first year from seed the plant develops a basal rosette of leaves; the flower stalk forms the second year. Requires moist soil, light shade, and should be treated like a biennial.

HOSTA (Plantain Lily). A large group excellent for the shade garden. Plants range from a few inches to several feet. Although plantain lilies are grown primarily for their foliage effects, many have attractive flowers in late summer. The taxonomy of the genus *Hosta* is confused. Hybridization between species makes species identification impractical with the numerous cultivars. Foliage variegation may be white or a shade of yellow. Variegated types sometimes revert to fully green leaves typical of the original species. The following species and their hybrids are most commonly planted: *H. decorata* (blunt plantain lily), *H. fortunei* (tall cluster plantain lily), *H. lancifolia* (narrow-leaved plantain lily), *H. plantaginea* (fragrant plantain lily), *H. sieboldiana* (short cluster plantain lily), *H. undulata* (wavy-leaved plantain lily), and *H. ventricosa* (blue plantain lily). Over 200 species and cultivars are growing in the arboretum.

Jeffersonia diphylla (Twinleaf). Grows to 10 inches. This wild flower is interesting because of its short-lived, hepaticalike flower borne at the tip of a long, slender stem and because of its 2-lobed leaves. The flowering occurs in late May. The twinleaf prefers slightly acid soil. New plants are obtained by division and by seeding where plants are to bloom.

Linnaea borealis (Twinflower). Low (4 inch), creeping plant with leafy branches that are terminated by 2 bell-shaped, white or pink flowers. The flowering period is from late June to August. The twinflower requires acid soil high in organic matter. Where growing conditions are favorable, it makes a delightful ground cover.

Maianthemum canadense (Wild Lily-of-the-Valley). Native plant common at the base of tree stumps in moist sites, usually on north-facing slopes. It is erect, 4 inches tall, and has 1 or 2 clasping leaves and a raceme of small, white flowers in late May and early June. This plant does well in soils high in organic matter. Usually started from seeds planted in peat pots. Field sods can also be transplanted in early spring.

Mertensia virginiana (Virginia Bluebell). Grows to 1½ feet. This plant is colorful in late May and early June when it is covered with clusters of nodding, bell-shaped, blue flowers. 'Alba', a white-flowered form, is sometimes grown. Soon after flowering the plant dies to the ground. It grows best in light shade and on moist soil, especially in the spring when it is actively growing. Propagation is from seed and by division. Tuberous rootstocks can be dug and transplanted in late summer.

Mitchella repens (Partridgeberry). Low (6 inch), creeping plant that produces small, pink to white flowers in June and July. Red berries form in the fall. Popular in terrariums, the plant must have acid, humus-rich soil and shade to be grown in the shady garden. Plants can be started from cuttings, or established plants can be divided.

Orchis spectabilis (Showy Orchis). Not uncommon in moist woods. The plant is 6 inches tall, with basal, dark green leaves. The upright stems bearing from 3 to 10 purple and white flowers open in late May and June. Unless growing conditions are favorable, the plant gradually disappears. To increase your planting, divide established plants in the fall when they are dormant. Showy orchis must be purchased from a licensed wild flower nursery.

Podophyllum peltatum (Mayapple). Reaches a height of 1¼ feet. In the spring, 2 umbrella-shaped leaves are formed on a short stem. These are interesting as they unfold. Underneath the leaves on short, lateral stems are large, white, saucer-shaped flowers, which are produced in late May or early June. These flowers are seldom seen unless one looks under the leaves. The fruits are yellow and resemble a small apple—hence the common name. This plant can be grown on most soils if the site is shaded. Propagate by root division in the fall or from seed.

Polemonium reptans (Jacob's-Ladder). Grows to 1½ feet, with pinnately compound leaves. In May and early June this mound-shaped plant is covered with china-blue, bell-shaped flowers. Propagation is by division in mid-August or early spring. The plant self-sows freely and the resulting seedlings are easily transplanted.

Polygala pauciflora (Fringed Polygala). Dainty, 4-inch-high plant with rose-purple, orchidlike flowers in June. It is found in rich soil under deciduous trees. Successfully grown only on acid soil.

Polygonatum biflorum (Small Solomon's Seal). The true Solomon's Seal. It has arching stems and grows 2 feet tall. Small, pale yellow to greenish, bell-shaped flowers hang in pairs from the axil of the alternate leaves in June and July. Dark blue berries mature in August. Plant on any humus-rich soil in partial shade. Propagate by division. Rhizomes should be planted horizontally at a 1- to 2-inch depth in the fall.

Polygonatum commutatum (Great Solomon's Seal). Similar to *P. biflorum* but much larger (5 feet) and requires moister soil to develop fully.

PRIMULA (Primrose). Of the many species of primrose, some are hardy and others are tender. All primroses develop a basal rosette of leaves and send up erect flower stems in late May or early June. Most hardy species have yellow to orange flowers; a few have pink flowers. Primroses like moist soil and light shade. The species primulas can be seed propagated, and mature plants can be divided. The following species have wintered and flowered at the arboretum: *bulleyana* (yellow), *elatier* (yellow), *florindae* (yellow), *frondosa* (rose-lilac), *japonica* (purplish-red), *pulverulenta* (red), and *vialii* (bluish-violet). No doubt many other species are equally hardy.

Pyrola elliptica (Shinleaf). Grows 6 to 8 inches tall. The shinleaf has a basal rosette of leathery, semi-evergreen leaves that stay green for part of the winter. In June the plants send up an erect flower stalk with small, fragrant, cup-shaped flowers that droop along the stem. The flowers range from white to pink. Acid soil and light shade are required, and transplanting can be done in the fall.

Sanguinaria canadensis (Bloodroot). Common spring flower that is 6 inches tall. The leaves are broad and characteristically lobed; the creeping rhizome is red, giving the plant its common name. The snowy-white, starlike flowers are borne above the leaves in late April and early May. Individual flowers last only a few days. The double-flowered form 'Multiplex' is also available and is much better than the species; the flowers are fully double and last a week or longer. Bloodroots are easily grown. Fall is the preferred time for dividing old clumps and starting new plantings. Plant rhizomes horizontally and about 1 inch deep. Light shade and soil high in organic matter are preferred.

Smilacina racemosa (False Solomon's Seal). This 2-foot-tall plant is similar to *Polygonatum biflorum* (the true Solomon's seal) except the flowers are produced in terminal, creamy-white, plumelike clusters in late May and June. The berries are straw colored and speckled in July and August. Propagate by division.

Smilacina stellata (Star-flowered False Solomon's Seal). Similar to *S. racemose* but much shorter (1 foot). The tiny, starlike flowers are in small, terminal clusters.

Streptopus roseus (Rose Twisted-Stalk). This 1½-foot-tall plant is similar to *Polygonatum biflorum* but the stem is zigzag and only 1 flower forms in the axil of each leaf. Flowers are drooping bells ranging from dull rose to pink. This species prefers slightly acid soil that is moist but not wet. Propagation is by division.

Tiarella cordifolia (Foamflower). Grows to 6 inches. The foamflower produces erect racemes of feathery, white flowers that rise above the maplelike, basal leaves. It requires acid soil and thrives on rich soil in moist woods. Propagate by dividing mature clumps or by starting plants from seed. When growing conditions are right, this makes a fine woodland ground cover.

Trientalis borealis (Starflower). Reaches a height of 6 inches. A whorl of 6 or more leaves is at the top of a stiff, wiry stem. Above the leaves are 1 or 2 star-shaped, white flowers on short, stiff stems. The flowers are produced in late May and are replaced by tiny, white seed balls in August. Starflowers prefer slightly acid soil and require shade. Propagation is by division in the fall. Plants can also be grown by starting seeds in flats.

TRILLIUM. A large genus of about 30 species native to woodlands of North America and Asia. Three leaves are produced in a whorl on erect stems, and 3-petaled flowers are white, green, yellow, pink, or purple.

T. cernuum (Nodding Trillium). Grows to 1½ feet. A nodding flower hides underneath the leaves that are at the top of the stem. The white flowers, produced in late May, are about 1 inch across. The nodding trillium prefers a moist, shaded location. Propagate from seeds or by planting bulbs in the fall.

T. erectum (Purple Trillium). In late May this 1-foot-tall trillium produces maroon-colored flowers on an erect, short stem that projects above the leaves. Occasionally, plants produce pale yellow or straw-colored flowers. The flowers give off an offensive odor. Culture is similar to that for *T. cernuum* (nodding trillium).

T. grandiflorum (Showy Trillium). The showiest trillium, growing to 1¼ feet. Large, 3-inch, white flowers are produced in late May and early June on a short stem that rises about the leaves. In the spring some of our local woods are literally white with this native wild flower. The flowers turn pink as they age. Under favorable growing conditions clumps increase in size and may require division after a few years.

T. nivale (Snow Trillium). The earliest-blooming trillium and the shortest (4 inches). The small, white flowers resemble a miniature *T. grandiflorum* (showy trillium). The snow trillium prefers slightly acid soil high in organic matter. Under ideal growing conditions it forms a carpet of bloom in late April.

T. sessile (Toad Trillium). Grows 8 inches tall, with sessile, maroon-red flowers that develop directly above the mottled whorl of leaves. Culture is similar to that for other trilliums.

T. undulatum (Painted Trillium). A 10-inch-tall plant, this is an attractive trillium and probably the most difficult to be grown. The petals are white with crimson streaks. This plant requires cool, moist, acid soil and shade.

T. viride (Wood Trillium). Similar to *T. sessile* (toad trillium). The petals are elongated and greenish. The variety *lutea* has greenish-yellow petals and is sometimes given a species rank.

Uvularia grandiflora (Merrybells or Bellwort). Grows 1 foot tall. The hanging, yellow, bell-shaped flowers are in loose clusters and produced in late May and early June. The stems are sometimes twisted and dichotomously branched. Clumps of this wild flower are quite beautiful and an asset to any shady garden. Plants can be divided in the fall or early spring, or they can be started from seeds.

VIOLA (Violet). There are many species of violet to choose from. Most bloom in late May and into June, and all but the garden hybrids have blue, yellow, or white flowers on 6-inch- to 1-foot-tall plants. *V. sororia* (common blue violet), *V. pubescens* (downy yellow violet), and the white-flowered *V. canadensis* (Canada violet) are good species for planting. Except for the birdsfoot violets, *V. pedata* and *V. pedatifida*, most violets prefer shady, woodland soil. Propagation is by division in early spring or by seeds.

Ferns

For the woodland garden, few plants are better than ferns in providing a long season of beauty. They add interest from the time the fronds (leaves) unfurl in the spring until the tops are killed by frost. Most ferns like shade and do best in soil high in organic matter.

Since the structure of ferns differs from flowering plants, a few terms used in the following descriptions should be defined. The stem of the fern is underground and is called a rhizome. The leaves arise from the rhizome and are called fronds. The fronds of most ferns are compound, with many divisions. The primary divisions, or outgrowths from the midrib (rachis) of the frond, are called the pinnae. The pinnules are divisions of the pinnae. Reproduction in ferns occurs by spores, which are produced in clusters of sporangia (spore cases). Each cluster is called a sorus, the covering on the sorus an indusium. These sori may be produced on the undersurface of a vegetative frond or on separate, spore-producing leaves called sporophylls. The spores are ejected from the sporangia and germinate in moist soil to form small, flat plants the size of a fingernail. Eggs and sperms are produced on the undersurface of these minute plants. The fertilized egg grows into a new fern plant.

The following ferns are easily grown:

Adiantum pedatum (Maidenhair Fern). One of the more graceful ferns, growing to 1½ feet. The pinnae are dichotomously branched and form a delicate, flattened fan. The frond is borne on an erect, black stalk. Spores are produced near the edge of the blade on the undersurface of the pinnae. The maidenhair fern requires rich, loose soil high in organic matter, and the soil must be kept moist.

Athyrium filix-femina (Lady Fern). This 2-foot-tall plant is one of the more common wood ferns. The frond consists of many feathery pinnae that are alternately arranged. The upper pinnae are tapered and point forward. The sori are crescent shaped and regularly spaced on the lower surface of each pinna. The plants multiply and spread under favorable growing conditions.

Athyrium goeringianum 'Pictum' (Japanese Painted Fern). Grows to 10 inches. The Japanese painted fern is very attractive, with gray-green fronds splashed with red along the veins. This introduced fern is surprisingly hardy and easily grown.

Botrychium virginianum (Rattlesnake Fern). A 1½-foot-tall fern. Each of its upright stalks bears a triangular cluster of finely divided pinnules about halfway up. The stalk terminates in a grapelike cluster of specialized sporophylls. Requires shade and rich, loose, moist woodland soil.

Camptosorus rhizophyllus (Walking Fern). Only 2 to 3 inches tall, this creeping fern has long, narrow fronds that taper to a slender tip. It can be found clinging to moss on limestone ledges and usually grows near streams on north-facing surfaces. It is difficult to grow the walking fern on sites without natural limestone rocks. Plant in rock crevices or in specially prepared soil between two limestone rocks and keep the plants moist. The tips of the leaves bend over and where they touch a moist surface, new plants form.

Cystopteris bulbifera (Bulblet Fern). Grows 1½ feet tall. The fronds of this fern are finely divided and taper to a narrow tip. Bulblike growths about the size of a pea develop on the undersurface of the fronds. They drop to the moist earth and a new plant develops from each "bulb." The plant also reproduces by spores. This fern does best on moist soil and is often found growing in the crevices of a limestone rock.

Dryopteris austriaca var. *spinulosa* (Spinulose Wood Fern). Common fern in the woods. The fronds are upright and often 2 feet tall. The lower pinnae along the rachis are asymmetrical, with the longest pinnule on the lower side nearest the rachis. The lobes of the pinnules are pointed. The sori are covered with kidney-shaped indusia. Fronds of the species are used by florists as fillers in flower arrangements. Grow in shade on moist soil high in organic matter.

Dryopteris cristata (Crested Wood Fern). Common in low, wet soils. This 2-foot-tall fern has a dark green, leathery frond that is semi-evergreen (it stays green for part of the winter). The lobes of the pinnules are pointed. Must be watered during dry periods.

Dryopteris goldiana (Goldie's Wood Fern). The tallest wood fern, growing to 4 feet. Although large, it is graceful and easily grown. For best development it should be planted in the shade where the soil is moist and high in organic matter.

Matteuccia pensylvanica (Ostrich Fern). A large native fern growing to a height of 4 feet. The large, sterile fronds are pinnately compound and taper to a narrow base. The sporophylls are brown and erect, growing to 1½ feet. Requires wet soil.

Onoclea sensibilis (Sensitive Fern). A common fern in swamps where it forms carpetlike stands. The fronds are 2 feet tall and pinnately compound with wavy-toothed pinnae. The sporophylls are brown and erect with grapelike sori at the top. The common name refers to the plant's sensitivity to frost. Requires a moist site.

OSMUNDA (Flowering Fern). The common name of this genus is misleading since no true flowers are produced. The spores in this genus are produced on sporophylls or on modified, fertile portions of sterile fronds. The sori are not protected by an indusium. Three native species are often planted:

O. cinnamomea (Cinnamon Fern). Reaches a height of 3 feet. Usually yellowish-green, this fern develops a brown sporophyll similar to that of *Onoclea sensibilis* (sensitive fern) and *Matteuccia pensylvanica* (ostrich fern) except it is less rigid and soon falls to the ground. The sterile fronds are elongated and taper upward. The lobes of the pinnules are rounded. An excellent fern where moisture conditions are favorable and the soil is slightly acid.

O. claytonia (Interrupted Fern). The vegetative fronds of this 4-foot-tall fern resemble those of *O. cinnamomea* (cinnamon fern), but the spore-producing portion of the frond is limited to a short section in the middle of the frond. The basal and terminal pinnae are normal, but the pinnae in the center are modified for spore production and resemble small, brown clusters of grapes. This characteristic gives the plant its common name. The fern prefers acid soils but grows on neutral soils if moisture and shade conditions are right. A most satisfactory fern.

O. regalis var. *spectabilis* (Royal Fern). Reaches 4 feet. A well-grown royal fern is a thing of beauty. The basal portion of the frond is vegetative but the terminal pinnae are modified for spore production. As in *O. claytonia* (interrupted fern), the spore-producing pinnae resemble clusters of grapes. Requires moist soil and prefers an acid site.

Polypodium virginianum (Common Polypody). Little (8 inch), evergreen fern found growing in the crevices of rocks and sometimes on rotten logs. The fronds are 6 to 8 inches long and about 2 inches wide. The blade is deeply lobed but continuous on either side of the rachis. This fern is best planted among rocks. The soil should be high in organic matter.

Polystichum acrostichoides (Christmas Fern). A 1-foot-tall evergreen fern with long fronds, 2 to 3 feet long, radiating from the crown. This fern likes cool, moist soil and prefers a north exposure. It is very attractive at the base of a stump. When the snow melts the old leaves are still green.

Thelypteris hexagonoptera (Broad Beech Fern). This little fern is 1 foot tall and spreads rapidly by underground rhizomes. The leaf blade is triangular. The pinnae and pinnules are deeply lobed, but the blade is continuous along the rachis. Plant in a sheltered location on rich, acid soil. Keep the plants watered during dry spells.

Thelypteris palustris (Marsh Fern). Common fern of wet places. It is 3 feet tall and its graceful fronds have very fine lobes that extend almost to the midrib on each of the pinnae. The pinnae are opposite along the rachis. This fern spreads rapidly and is best for naturalizing in wet soils.

Thelypteris phegopteris (Long Beech Fern). Grows to a height of 1 foot and resembles *T. hexagonoptera* (broad beech fern) except the fronds are longer and the lower pinnae point downward rather than form a triangle.

Woodsia ilvensis (Rusty Woodsia). This little fern grows to 6 inches and is usually found in the crevices of rocks. The fronds are covered with rusty hairs which are most pronounced during periods of prolonged drought. This fern is excellent in a rock garden. It likes neutral soil high in organic matter.

Chapter 18

Garden Roses

Garden roses are treated separately in this book because they are so popular and are virtually the only tender shrubs that are recommended for this region. Successful rose gardening depends on purchasing quality plants and on providing special care.

Purchasing Plants

Most nurseries that grow garden roses are located in Oregon, California, and Texas, where the winters are mild. The various cultivars are budded on special rootstocks, which are usually produced from seeds or rooted cuttings. In the nursery the rootstocks are generally cultivated for a full growing season. In the fall a bud of the desired cultivar is inserted near the ground line. The following spring the rootstock is cut back directly above the inserted bud. The bud then develops into the rose plant which is dug after one or two growing seasons. Plants are dug in the fall and graded (number one plants, those having 3 or more sturdy stems, are separated from the smaller, number two plants). After refrigerated storage they are distributed to the various wholesale and retail nursery outlets.

Dormant, bare root plants can be purchased in the early spring from local nurseries and garden centers or through mail-order companies. Packaged roses can also be purchased from many chain stores. A little later in the spring and into early summer, container-grown plants are available from most nurseries and garden centers.

The Rose Bed

It is best to grow garden roses in separate beds rather than in the shrub or flower border, because they require special methods of winter protection and a regular spray program to control pests. The rose bed can parallel the drive or the back of the lawn area. The size and shape of the bed varies with the location and the number of plants to be grown. The depth of the bed depends on whether the roses are to be viewed from one side or from all sides. All plants should be clearly visible without walking into the bed. Spacing of roses within the beds is important. Consider the mature size of the plants and space them so that each plant will not be crowded. It is better to grow a few plants well than to crowd too many plants into a limited space. The minimum spacing that is recommended varies from 2 to 3 feet, depending on the type of roses to be grown.

Preparing the Soil

Roses do best on well-drained, clay loam soil. Unless your soil is ideal, it is best to remove at least 1 foot of the surface soil and replace it with quality topsoil to which liberal quantities of organic matter have been added. If enough organic matter is added, it is possible to grow good-looking roses on sandy loam soil. Add about 2 pounds of an 0-10-10 fertilizer for every 100 square feet of surface and work it into the soil to get the phosphorus and potassium into the root zone of the rose plants. With poorly drained soils it may be necessary to install a tile drain at the bottom of the bed or to raise the bed to provide surface drainage.

Planting

Bare root roses should be planted early in the spring. Use number one plants and be sure that they are dormant. Soak the plants overnight before planting but do not leave them in water for more than about 12 hours. Make a fresh cut at the tips of the roots and remove any broken roots. Dig a hole large enough to accommodate the roots without crowding. Mold a cone-shaped pile of soil at the bottom of the hole. Set the plant on this cone so that the roots spread out naturally in the hole. The depth of the hole and the height of the cone of soil should be such that the graft union will be about even with the surface of the soil. Fill in with good soil around the roots and firm the soil. Leave a shallow depression at the top for watering. Add enough water to soak the soil thoroughly. Newly planted roses do not require much pruning since this was done at the nursery. As soon as the water soaks in, mound the soil around the base of the plant to cover the plant completely. (The soil protects the dormant buds from drying out.) Keep this mound of soil on the plant for 10 to 14 days, depending on the temperature. (Roots form sooner in warm soils.) Remove the mound of soil when the buds start to grow.

Container roses can be planted later, after the extent of winter injury can be ascertained. As with bare root roses, the depth of planting should be such that the graft union will be at or near the ground line. With container roses the graft union can usually be seen above the soil level.

Fertilizing

Roses are heavy feeders and must be fertilized at regular intervals. It is best to fertilize each month. Use a fertilizer relatively high in nitrogen, such as a 10-5-5. Use a 10 percent nitrogen fertilizer at the rate of about 1 pound for each 100 square feet of surface. Continuous use of a complete fertilizer can result in a buildup of phosphorus and potassium. If a soil test shows a surplus of these elements, use a straight nitrogen fertilizer like ammonium nitrate or urea to maintain healthy plants with a dark green color. Do not fertilize after early August to allow time for the plants to mature before winter.

Watering

Roses require liberal quantities of water. Soak the soil at each watering to the depth of the root system. On moisture-retentive soil the equivalent of 1 inch of rainfall per week is needed; on sandy soil, more water is required. It is best to water in the morning. A soaker watering device is preferred to overhead sprinklers. If you use a sprinkler, water early enough in the day so that the foliage will be dry by evening. Wet foliage at night may cause black spot and powdery mildew diseases to develop.

Mulching

A summer mulch is a tremendous aid in growing quality roses, for it helps control weeds and provides more uniform soil temperature. Less watering is required when a mulch is used. Almost any organic mulch material is acceptable, including partly decomposed tree leaves, grass clippings, chopped hay, and chopped straw. These are relatively inexpensive and give a neat appearance to the rose bed. Apply the mulch as soon as the soil warms up in the spring, usually about the middle of June. A winter mulch of tree leaves, clean straw, or marsh hay is also recommended; it is applied in late October or early November.

Pest Control

A pest control program is required for growing quality roses. Insect pests include aphids, leaf cutter bees, rose midge, thrips, stem borers, and leaf hoppers. Red spiders can also be a problem. Common diseases are black spot, powdery mildew, and rose rust. The best way to control these pests is with a regular, preventive spray program. Most successful rose growers spray or dust once a week throughout the growing season. The spray or dust should contain an effective fungicide, like Phaltan and Benlate, and one or more insecticides and miticides, depending on the insects or mites that may be present. Most garden centers sell mixed rose sprays and dusts that contain both insecticides and fungicides. These are very satisfactory for the beginner. After gaining experience, try some of the newer pesticides as additional problems arise. Pesticides change yearly; new ones appear and old ones are removed from the sales racks. Consult your county Agricultural Extension office for recommendations.

Always read pesticides instructions carefully. Do not leave opened pesticide containers around where there are small children. Handle the chemicals carefully and safely, and wash thoroughly after using spray chemicals. Wet the undersurfaces of the leaves as well as the upper. Covering the plants completely is as important as using the right chemicals. Remember that most rose diseases can be prevented but it is difficult to control them after they get a good start.

Winter Protection

All garden roses are injured when the temperature drops much below 20°F. One must give them the necessary winter protection before temperatures drop to the danger level in the fall. Even the so-called subzero roses require complete winter protection. Any time after October 20 and before November 1 is safe to cover roses. Many methods of covering roses have been tried, with varying results.

"MINNESOTA TIP"

Most successful rose growers agree that the best and safest method for protecting roses is complete soil cover. This method was developed in Minnesota and is called the "Minnesota Tip." Spray the plants with a dormant spray and tie the canes in a tight bundle, using a rot-resistant twine. Dig a trench that is the depth and width of a spade from the base of the plant. The trench must be as long as the plant is tall. With a spading fork, loosen the soil around the base of the plant. Gradually bend the canes into the trench and cover with the soil removed when digging it. Mark the base of the plant with a stake. It is best to tip all the plants in a bed in the same direction, for this makes it easier to lift the plants the following spring. After this phase of winter protection is complete, the soil is practically level. As cold weather arrives in November, apply a winter mulch. It should be at least 6 inches deep and should cover the entire bed. Boards or chicken wire should be put over the mulch to keep it from blowing away. Some growers use a chicken wire fence around the rose bed to contain the mulch. If mice are likely to be a problem, put down some moth balls or mouse bait before applying the mulch. In the spring remove the mulch about the first of April. As soon as the soil dries in mid-April, lift the roses, using a spading fork.

HILLING

Another method that is used to protect roses is hilling. A mound of soil is heaped around the base of each plant to a height of about 1 foot. This is done in late October. Mulch is added between and above the mounds of earth when weather turns cold in November. More mulch is required and far more winter injury usually occurs with this method than with the "Minnesota Tip" method. Rose cones are sometimes used, but results have generally not been too satisfactory.

Pruning

Regardless of the method of winter protection used, some pruning is required in the spring. It should be done in late April after new growth has started. Remove weak stems, stems that cross and rub against each other, and all dead wood. Cut back each stem to an outward-pointing bud unless you want the plant to grow upright. The height to prune your roses depends on the extent of winter injury and on where you desire the flowers to develop. The more you prune, the smaller the plant and the fewer the flowers. Treat all cuts with a wound dressing like Tree-Cote paint or fingernail polish to prevent the entry of the rose borer.

Cut Roses

Rose flowers should be enjoyed in the home as well as in the garden. The flowers last longer if they are cut in bud rather than when the flowers are fully open. Cut the stems to the length needed for the flower arrangement planned. Make the cut directly above a well-developed leaf and about ¼ inch above the bud in the leaf axil. Place the cut stems in water immediately, and remove faded flowers as soon as the petals start to drop.

Types of Roses

There are three major groups of garden roses: floribundas, hybrid teas, and grandifloras. Climbing, miniature, and tree roses belong to the above classes.

FLORIBUNDAS

Cluster roses developed by crossing thé small-flowered, cluster-type poliantha roses with hybrid teas. There are fewer flowers per cluster on the floribundas than on the polianthas, but the flowers are much larger, sometimes 3 to 4 inches across. The flowers may be single, semi-double, or fully double. The plants are smaller than the hybrid teas and grandifloras, usually not over 2 to 3 feet tall. Space plants 2 feet apart. 'Apricot Nectar' (apricot blend), 'Betty Prior' (medium pink), 'Circus' (yellow blend), 'Fashion' (pink blend), 'Gene Boerner' (medium pink), 'Ginger (orange-red), 'Ivory Fashion' (white), 'Little Darling' (yellow blend), 'Red Gold' (yellow blend), 'Spartan' (orange-red), and 'Vogue' (pink blend) are popular cultivars in this area.

HYBRID TEAS

A cross between the hybrid perpetual roses and the tender tea rose of China. The flowers are usually large, 3 to 5 inches across, and fully double except they may be single in cultivars like 'Dainty Bess'. There is generally 1 flower per stem. Hybrid tea roses grow 4 or 5 feet tall and are planted for cut flowers as well as for their landscape effect. Space plants 2½ to 3 feet apart. The following cultivars do well in this area: 'Avon' (dark red), 'Century Two' (medium pink), 'Charlotte Armstrong' (deep pink), 'Chrysler Imperial' (deep red), 'Dainty Bess' (light pink), 'First Prize' (pink blend), 'Helen Traubel' (pink blend), 'Miss All-American Beauty' (medium pink), 'Pascali' (white), 'Peace' (yellow blend), and 'Tiffany' (pink blend).

GRANDIFLORAS

Developed by crossing floribundas with hybrid teas. The flowers are usually clustered, but the clusters have fewer flowers than the floribundas. The size of the flowers is about the same as the flowers of the hybrid teas. Plants are more vigorous than the floribundas and often reach a height of 5 feet. Space plants 2½ to 3 feet apart. Recommended cultivars include: 'Aquarius' (pink blend), 'Capitan' (medium red), 'Carrousel' (dark red), 'John S. Armstrong' (dark red), 'Montezuma' (orange-red), 'Queen Elizabeth' (medium pink), and 'Starfire' (medium red).

CLIMBING AND PILLAR ROSES

Garden roses with vigorous, long stems, up to 10 or more feet long, that require support. They may be floribundas, hybrid teas, or grandifloras. The following are good cultivars for this area: 'Blaze' (medium red), 'Climbing Dainty Bess' (light pink), 'Climbing Mrs. Sam McGredy' (orange blend), 'Climbing Tropicana' (orange blend), 'Dr. W. Van Fleet' (light pink), 'Iceland Queen' (white), 'Ivory Charm' (white), 'New Dawn' (white), 'Paul's Scarlet Climber' (medium red), and 'Viking Queen' (medium pink).

MINIATURE ROSES

Plants with small leaves and small flowers. To qualify as a miniature the plants are usually less than 1½ feet tall and the flowers are less than 1 inch across. Flower types range from singles to fully double. The following cultivars are recommended: 'Baby Betsy McCall' (light pink), 'Baby Darlin' (orange blend), 'Baby Masquerade' (red blend), 'Beauty Secret' (medium red), 'Bo-Peep' (medium pink), 'Chipper' (light pink), 'Cinderella' (white), 'Dwarf King' (medium red), 'Granata' (dark red), 'Judy Fisher' (medium pink), 'Kathy' (medium red), 'Little Buckaroo' (medium red), 'Marilyn' (light pink), 'Mary Marshall' (orange blend), 'Over the Rainbow' (red blend), 'Pink Cameo' (medium pink), 'Pixie' (white),

'Pumila' (deep pink), 'Red Imp' (dark red), 'Starina' (orange-red), 'Tinker Bell' (medium pink), 'Top Secret' (medium red), 'Toy Clown' (red blend), and 'Yellow Doll' (medium yellow).

TREE ROSES

Any cultivar of garden rose can be grown as a tree rose. The cultivar is budded at the top of a tall stem rather than at soil level. Because tree roses have long stems, it is difficult to protect them from winter cold. The "Minnesota Tip" is the most practical method of winter protection.

Chapter 19

Bulbs

In this book the term "bulb" includes any fleshy, underground storage organ capable of reproducing the plant. These storage organs are the true bulbs, corms, rhizomes, tubers, and fleshy roots. See Chapter 2 for definitions.

There are three general groups of "bulbs." The hardy spring-flowering bulbs are planted in the fall for bloom the following spring. The tender summer- and fall-flowering bulbs are planted in the spring and must be stored indoors over the winter. The hardy summer- and fall-flowering bulbs are left in the soil for a number of years and are considered in Chapter 16. This group includes the irises, lilies, and peonies.

Spring-Flowering Bulbs

These bulbs are offered for sale in the fall of the year and may be ordered through a mail-order catalog or purchased directly from a garden center. Most bulbs should be planted as soon as they become available, because they must form roots and become established before the ground freezes. Mulching with straw or marsh hay when cold weather sets in lengthens the period for rooting.

Buy only the best-quality bulbs. Bargain prices may not be a bargain at all. It takes the same amount of work to prepare for planting bargain bulbs as for planting first-class bulbs and the results can be vastly different.

Most spring-flowering bulbs like well-drained soil and full sunlight. The soil should be prepared to a depth of 1 to 1½ feet to allow deep penetration of the roots. Work in organic matter and a complete fertilizer high in phosphorus, such as a 5-10-10. Use the fertilizer at the rate of 2 pounds per 100 square feet of soil surface.

It is best to plant bulbs in clumps of a single variety. The size of the clumps depends on the effect desired. The depth of planting is also important. Usually the garden center or florist has charts that indicate the proper depth of planting. As a rule the depth is in direct proportion to the size of the bulb. Small bulbs like crocus and scillas should be planted 2 to 3 inches deep. Larger bulbs like tulips and daffodils should be planted 6 to 8 inches deep.

The following are the common spring-flowering bulbs:

Chionodoxa luciliae (Glory-of-the-Snow). Grows to 4 inches. This early, spring-flowering bulb is best grown in drifts. The pale blue flowers are about 1 inch across and have white, contrasting centers. The leaves are narrow and grasslike.

CROCUS (Crocus). A large genus of about 75 species mostly native to the countries bordering the Mediterranean Sea. Most bulbs sold for fall planting are of hybrid origin and grow about 6 inches tall. Colors range from white to yellow to blue. *C. chrysanthus* is the leading species in these garden hybrids. Bulbs should be planted in September for best results. They can be grown in the lawn, for plants come up early and bloom by late May. The first mowing of the lawn should be delayed until the leaves of the crocus die down.

Fritillaria imperialis (Crown-Imperial). The most striking *Fritillaria*, reaching a height of 1½ feet. It is commonly grown in Europe and England but seldom seen in our area. The upright, leafy stems are terminated in May with a crown of drooping, yellow, bell-shaped flowers and an upright tuft of green leaves above the crown. The soil must be deeply prepared with plenty of organic matter, and a winter mulch is needed. This plant is worth any effort required to grow it.

Galanthus nivalis (Common Snowdrop). Grows 4 inches tall. This is the earliest spring flower to bloom, flowering as early as mid-March but more often in early April. The nodding, white flowers rise above the leaves which are long and narrow.

Hyacinthus orientalis (Hyacinth). The Dutch, or florist's, hyacinths have evolved largely from this 10-inch-tall species, which is native to Turkey and Persia. The upright flower stem has numerous open, bell-shaped flowers ranging from white to purple that form a cylinder in April. The flowers have a delightful fragrance. There are named cultivars in white, pink, blue, red, and purple. The hyacinth is not fully hardy and may be short-lived. I have had best results by planting the bulbs close to the house foundation where they receive some heat from the basement during the winter months.

Muscari botryoides (Grape Hyacinth). Little (6 inch) bulb blooming in late April and early May. The erect spikes of blue or white flowers resemble clusters of grapes. This plant, after a summer rest, sends up grasslike leaves in the fall.

NARCISSUS (Daffodil, Jonquil). A large genus of over 60 species native to the Mediterranean region. The species hybridize in nature and plant breeders have developed thousands of named cultivars. The height of the plants, 6 inches to 2 feet, and the form and color of the flowers vary greatly. The flower has an inferior ovary, that is, the ovary is below the petals. The white or yellow petals and sepals are alike and constitute the perianth. These perianth segments spread to form a shallow saucer. Above the segments is a tubular structure called the trumpet, or corona, which may be short or long and which usually flares at the tip. The color of the corona may be the same as the perianth segments or a shade of orange.

Bulbs should be planted as soon as they are available in the fall. They must be planted by early October to allow sufficient time for roots to form before the ground freezes. Plant 6 to 8 inches deep in well-drained soil. Plants can be naturalized by planting in grassy areas. Delay mowing in the spring until the tops die down. The bulbs dislike excess moisture during the summer months. Avoid summer watering or dig the bulbs in early summer after the tops die down and store them in a dry, well-ventilated room until it is time to plant in the fall.

The classification of the species and hybrids is based on the form of the corona and on the number of flowers per stem. The following classification is that of the Royal Horticultural Society of England:

1. *Trumpet Narcissi.* One flower per stem; corona as long as or longer than the perianth segments.

2. *Large-cupped Narcissi.* One flower per stem; corona more than one-third but less than the length of the perianth segments.

3. *Small-cupped Narcissi.* One flower per stem; corona not more than one-third the length of the perianth segments.

4. *Double Narcissi.* Flowers are double with petaloid (petallike) stamens.

5. *Triandrus Narcissi.* Characteristics of *N. triandrus.* Flowers drooping, 3 to 9 per stem.

6. *Cyclamineus Narcissi.* Characteristics of *N. cyclamineus.* Solitary, deep yellow flowers with reflexed perianth segments and a long, tubular corona.

7. *Jonquilla Narcissi.* Characteristics of *N. jonquilla.* Bears 3 to 6 golden-yellow flowers per stem; corona cup shaped.

8. *Tazetta Narcissi.* Characteristics of *N. tazetta.* Bears 4 to 8 white flowers per stem; corona pale yellow, small; sweetly scented. The popular paper white narcissus belongs to this group.

9. *Poeticus Narcissi.* Characteristics of *N. poeticus.* One flower per stem; perianth segments white, 2 inches across; corona small, saucer shaped, pale yellow edged with red; sweetly scented.

10. *Species Narcissi.* A class containing species in cultivation other than those in classes 5 through 9.

Scilla sibirica (Siberian Squill). Grows to 6 inches. The drooping, bell-shaped flowers are porcelain-blue and formed in small clusters above the grasslike foliage in late April and early May. This is a long-lived perennial that increases in numbers each year.

TULIPA (Tulip). A large genus of over 100 species. Thousands of named cultivars have been developed and more people plant tulips than all other bulbs combined. Height varies from a few inches in some of the species tulips to over 2 feet in some of the hybrids. Plants have broad, strap-shaped leaves and an erect flower stalk terminated by a cup-shaped flower with 6 perianth segments (sepals and petals). Flower colors include every shade except blue. Flowering starts in early May with some of the species tulips and extends into June with the late-flowering hybrids.

Tulips grow best on well-drained soil in full sun. They do bloom when planted in light shade but the amount of bloom is decreased and the plants are short-lived. October is the best month to plant tulips, although satisfactory results will be obtained if planting must be delayed until November. Mulching is advised with late planting. Depth of planting is very important, for it affects the longevity of the bulbs. If the bulbs are too near the surface, the high soil temperatures cause the bulbs to divide and small flowers result. Plant 6 to 8 inches deep.

Fifteen classes of tulips are recognized. Eleven of these classes are of hybrid origin and the species characteristics have been lost in breeding. These are classified according to time of bloom and size and form of the flowers as follows:

Early

Single Early Tulips

Double Early Tulips

Midseason

Mendel Tulips. Chiefly the result of crossing 'DucVan Tol' with Darwin tulips. Flowers single; plants seldom over $1\frac{2}{3}$ feet tall.

Triumph Tulips. Chiefly the result of crossing single early tulips with late tulips. Flowers single; plants sturdier than the Mendel tulips and seldom more than $1\frac{2}{3}$ feet tall.

Darwin Hybrid Tulips. Chiefly the result of crossing Darwin tulips with *T. fosteriana* and other species. Flowers single.

Late

Darwin Tulips. Flowers single with lower part of each flower rectangular; plants over 1²/₃ feet tall.

Lily-flowered Tulips. Flowers single with pointed, reflexed perianth segments.

Cottage Tulips. Flowers single, often long and egg shaped.

Rembrandt Tulips. Perianth segments striped or spotted with brown, bronze, black, red, pink, or purple on red, white, or yellow background.

Parrot Tulips. Perianth segments with narrow lobes.

Double Late Tulips. Flowers double.

The four remaining classes are characterized by the dominant species used in breeding:

Kaufmanniana Tulips. Very early flowering, sometimes with mottled foliage. Flowers red or yellow.

Fosteriana Tulips. Very early flowering. Flowers large, brilliant red, with a black blotch in the center.

Greigii Tulips. Later flowering than the Kaufmanniana tulips. Foliage always mottled or striped. Flowers orange-scarlet with black blotch in the center.

Other Species Tulips. All other species that are grown.

Because of the many named cultivars and the limited availability of many of them, no attempt is made to give a recommended list. Visit collections of tulips in bloom and study illustrated mail-order catalogs and colored illustrations in garden centers to help you make your selections.

Summer- and Fall-Flowering Bulbs

A number of popular garden flowers are grown from "bulbs" that will not winter outdoors in our climate. The fleshy storage organs ranging from true bulbs to fleshy roots must be dug in the fall and stored over the winter in a frost-free place.

Begonia x *tuberhybrida* (Tuberous Begonia). Popular, summer-flowering begonia for outdoor hanging baskets and for planting in the shade. Several species have gone into the breeding of the tuberous begonia. Flowers are large, 3 to 4 inches across, in a variety of colors. Corms can be purchased in late winter and should be started in flats in March by partly embedding the fleshy corms in a soil mixture high in acid peat. Roots soon form and buds grow into leafy stems. As soon as the plants are well rooted, they should be potted in a soil mix high in organic matter. After danger of frost is past, the plants can be placed outdoors where they will receive some shade. They may be left in the pot or planted in soil high in organic matter. Plants should be brought indoors before danger of frost and allowed to die down. The corms can be carried over the winter in a cool, moist room; if the room is too dry, the bulbs shrivel.

Caladium x *hortulanum* (Fancy-leaved Caladiums). The fancy-leaved caladiums grow about 1½ feet tall and, although beautiful, are seldom planted outdoors in our area. They must be started indoors in pots and put outdoors in shaded and wind-protected areas after danger of frost has passed. Caladiums are grown for the delicate coloring of their leaves, which are variegated with red, rose, salmon, white, or green. The tubers are stored over the winter in a fairly dry, warm place like a furnace room.

Canna x *generalis* (Garden Canna). Most named cultivars of canna are of hybrid origin, and several species have been used in their breeding. The native home of the canna is South America. Plants grow to 5 feet and have large, colorful flowers produced on upright stems that rise above the foliage. The better cultivars are: 'King Hulbert' (red), 'King Midas' (yellow), 'Mrs. Alfred Conrad' (salmon-pink), and 'Mme. Butterfly' (yellowish-pink). Cannas require a long growing season; to produce bloom one must start the plants indoors in February or March. The rootstocks are divided and started in flats of sand. As soon as the divisions are rooted, they can be potted and grown until danger of frost has passed. Cannas are usually planted in beds for mass displays, or a few plants can be grown in the flower border. The fleshy, tuberous roots must be dug before killing frosts and stored in a cool, moist storage room with a temperature of 35° to 40°F.

Crocosmia x *crocosmiiflora* (Montebretia). Hybrid obtained by crossing *C. aurea* and *C. potsii*. The yellow to red, lilylike flowers are produced in open panicles on 2-foot-tall stems. The leaves are narrow, much like gladiolus leaves. Has the same cultural requirements as *Gladiolus* x *hortulana* (garden gladiolus).

DAHLIA (Dahlia). The numerous cultivars of dahlia have been developed largely from hybrids between *D. coccinea* and *D. pinnata*. The modern hybrids scarcely resemble their wild parents, which are native to Mexico. The modern garden dahlias have been bred for flower size, form, and color. Dahlia flowers are virtually every color except blue. The American Dahlia Society recognizes 12 groups based on the morphology of the flowers: Single, Anemone, Colarette, Peony, Formal Decorative, Informal Decorative, Ball, Pompon, Incurved Cactus, Straight Cactus, Semicactus, and Miscellaneous. Dahlias are also classified by size: A is over 8 inches; B, 4 to 8 inches; and M (Miniatures), under 4 inches.

Dahlias are grown by planting roots in the garden or from stem cuttings that are started indoors. Dahlias are frost tender and should not be planted until danger of frost has passed. Dormant roots can be planted about May 15, but rooted cuttings should not be planted much before Memorial Day. Dahlias are usually staked as soon as they are planted. Getting large, exhibition blooms requires special attention to pruning and disbudding. Roots should be dug in the fall as soon as the tops have been blackened by frost; they are stored in a cool, moist place over the winter. When separating the fleshy roots it is important not to break or injure the tapered upper part of each root, for this is stem tissue from which new buds develop.

Gladiolus x *hortulana* (Garden Gladiolus). The hundreds of named cultivars are the result of interspecies hybridization. *G. natalensis* has played a prominent role in the development of the gladiolus, a tender, 2- to 4-foot-tall perennial that develops a fleshy corm. Cormlets develop at the ends of short, lateral branches that arise from the base of the corm. These cormlets can be planted to produce flowering-size corms. The flower spikes are popular as cut flowers for interior decoration and for funeral arrangements.

The gladiolus is usually planted in rows to facilitate cultivation and weeding. It is best to keep named cultivars separate to avoid mechanical mixtures. The corms are harvested in the fall after the first killing frost. The tops are removed and the corms cured in a well-ventilated room. As soon as the old, basal corm separates with a clean break, the corms should be cleaned and put in winter storage. Keep the cultivars separate and label them. The corms are planted in the spring as soon as the soil starts to warm up, about mid-May. By staggering the planting dates, the blooming period can be extended. To select cultivars for your garden, visit a grower when the flowers are in bloom.

The gladiolus suffers from several soil-borne diseases. Diseased plants, which usually develop brown leaves, should be pulled and destroyed as soon as they are observed. The thrip must also be controlled both in the field and in storage. Red spider can also be a problem.

Hymenocallis narcissiflora (Peruvian Daffodil). Easily grown. Bulbs are planted after danger of frost has passed and in a few weeks the plants should be in bloom. Bulbs are dug in the fall and stored over the winter in a warm, dry room. It is best to keep the fleshy roots covered with soil during the winter so that they do not dry out. Failure to bloom can usually be traced to improper storage.

Polianthes tuberosa (Tuberose). A 1-foot-tall plant that usually blooms late in the fall, producing fragrant, white flowers. Bulbs should be started indoors and transplanted after danger of frost has passed. Failure to bloom may be the result of improper winter storage. Winter storage temperatures should not drop below 60°F.

Tigridia pavonia (Shell Flower). The large, cup-shaped flowers are produced on branched, 1½-foot stems that rise above the leaves. The colorful petals are scarlet-orange with purplish blotches near the base. Culture is similar to that for *Gladiolus* x *hortulana* (garden gladiolus).

Chapter 20

Annual Flowers

There is no surer way of having an attractive flower border in the summer and fall than to grow annuals. These can be planted in specially prepared beds each spring, or they can be mixed with perennials in the flower border. All annuals are grown from seeds started indoors or planted directly in the garden where the plants are to bloom. (A list of annuals that should be started indoors is presented on pp. 268-270.) Some gardeners prefer to plant their flower seeds with vegetables in rows in the kitchen garden; this works fine if the annuals are grown primarily for cut flowers.

This chapter provides descriptions of the most frequently grown annuals, including some tender perennials that are treated as annuals, and special lists designed to help you select annuals for the flower border and for other specific purposes.

Ageratum houstonianum (Floss Flower). Grows 6 to 10 inches tall. A number of cultivars of this Mexican plant are on the market. Breeding has emphasized compact, uniform growth and flower color, with white, blue, and pink prevailing. 'Summer Snow', 'Blue Angel', and 'Royal Blazer' are good cultivars. An excellent annual for edging the flower border and for mass effects.

Alcea rosea (Hollyhock). Also sold as *Althaea rosea*. A 3-foot-tall plant described in Chapter 16. Plant breeders have developed strains that bloom the first year from seed started indoors. 'Powder puff' received an All-America Award a few years ago. 'Indian Spring' is another annual hollyhock. The annual strains are not as tall as the biennial and perennial strains. Good for background plantings.

Amaranthus caudatus (Love-Lies-Bleeding). This tall annual grows to 3 feet and has coarse leaves with drooping, bright red spikes.

Amaranthus tricolor (Joseph's Coat). From 2 to 3 feet tall. This coarse annual is grown for its bright red leaves that are variously blotched. Improved strains such as 'Early Splendor' and 'Illumination' have made this a popular annual.

Anchusa capensis (Cape Forget-Me-Not). Grows to 1½ feet. Most *Anchusas* are biennials or perennials, but this species from South Africa can be grown as an annual if seeds are started early. The small flowers are blue or occasionally pink or white. Bloom peaks in July, but if the flowering stems are cut back, repeat bloom can be expected in the fall.

Antirrhinum majus (Snapdragon). Ranging from 6 inches to 2 feet tall, this popular greenhouse annual is available in a variety of colors and is now widely grown in the garden, thanks to the untiring efforts of the plant breeder. Plants with shorter stems to resist wind damage and more heat-resistant cultivars have been developed. The open, butterfly-type snap is another improvement. 'Madame Butterfly' (2½ feet), 'Little Darling' (1¼ feet), 'Pixie' (½ foot), and 'Rocket' (2½ feet) are popular cultivars. Start seeds indoors in early March for outdoor planting in late May.

Begonia x *semperflorens-cultorum* (Wax Begonia). This popular, bedding begonia is the result of much breeding effort. It is 8 to 10 inches tall and has little, green or bronze leaves. Flowers are small and white, pink, or red. Wax begonias do well in full sun or partial shade. Start seeds in February. The seeds and seedlings are very tiny and easily lost. Use a planting mixture high in acid peat. In the fall it is possible to dig plants and pot them for winter bloom. New plants for outdoor gardens can also be grown from cuttings.

Browallia speciosa (Browallia). Grows to 1 foot. The large, blue flowers bloom continuously after mid-July. This plant does best in partial shade. Seeds must be started indoors in March; they produce very small seedlings. Plants can be dug and potted for winter bloom.

Calendula officinalis (Pot Marigold). Growing 1½ feet tall, this cool-season annual is best grown for fall bloom. The yellow to orange, sunflowerlike blossoms are very attractive. Seeds can be started directly in the garden in June.

Callistephus chinensis (China Aster). This 1- to 1½-foot-tall annual would be more popular were it not for the six-spotted leaf hopper that transmits aster-yellows disease. Diseased plants are stunted, yellow, and form imperfect flowers. Some growers enclose their plants in a specially prepared frame covered with aster cloth to exclude the leaf hoppers. Healthy plants produce single and double, asterlike flowers in a variety of colors and make excellent cut flowers. Start seeds indoors in early April.

Catharanthus roseus (Madagascar Periwinkle). Also listed as *Vinca rosea*. An excellent annual for mass effects. It is 8 inches tall, its leaves are glossy green, and its saucer-shaped flowers range from white to rose. The flowers frequently have darker centers, or "eyes." Start seeds indoors in early April.

Celosia cristata (Cockscomb). This 1-foot-tall annual produces a tight head shaped like a cockscomb, with flower colors ranging from yellow to red. 'Fireglow' and 'Toreador' are good cultivars. A taller (to 2 feet) plumose group within this species produces upright plants that terminate in plumose panicles of small flowers ranging from yellow to red. These blend into a mixed flower border better than the crested type. 'Red Fox' and 'Golden Triumph' are popular cultivars of the plumose group. Start seeds in March.

Centaurea cyanus (Bachelor's-Button). Popular, 1½-foot-tall annual known for its profuse production of double, daisylike flowers in blue, purple, pink, rose, red, and deep wine colors. Once planted it generally self-sows, and volunteer seedlings are plentiful. The plant tends to sprawl. An excellent cut flower.

Centaurea moschata (Sweet Sultan). Growing 2 feet tall, this species is slightly larger than *C. cyanus* (bachelor's-button), with fringed, thistlelike blossoms up to 2 inches across. The flowers are in delicate shades of white, pink, lavender, and yellow. Another good cut flower.

Chrysanthemum parthenium (Feverfew). From 1½ to 2 feet tall. This tender perennial blooms the first year and can be grown as an annual. The flowers are produced in buttonlike heads in shades of white and yellow. Start seeds early for bloom in July and August.

Cleome hasslerana (Spider Flower). Often listed under the species name *C. spinosa*. Large (4 feet), shrublike annual best planted toward the back of the flower border. The pink and white flowers are produced in large, open clusters, and their long stamens give the plants a spiderlike appearance. Several cultivars are on the market; 'Pink Queen' has received an All-America Award. Seeds can be started indoors or planted where the plants are to bloom.

Coleus x *hybridus* (Coleus). Derived by hybridizing *C. blumei* with other species. The plants are 1 to 2 feet tall and are grown primarily for their foliage. Flowers that do form are usually removed. The leaves have various patterns, with colors ranging from light yellow to deep red. 'Rainbow' and 'Carefree' are popular strains. Seeds should be started in February, or plants can be grown from cuttings of selected parent plants.

Consolida orientalis (Annual Larkspur). Also listed as *Delphinium ajacis*. The height ranges from 2 to 3 feet, and the upright flower stalks are covered with flowers in early summer. Flowers resemble delphiniums and colors include blue, violet, dark purple, rose, light pink, scarlet, and white. It is best to seed this annual where the plants are to grow, since they do not transplant well. Seedlings must be thinned to a spacing of about 8 inches.

Coreopsis tinctoria (Calliopsis). Grows 1 to 3 feet tall, with finely cut foliage. This popular annual produces showy, daisylike flowers on slender stems. The ray flowers are golden-yellow, and each has a red spot at the base. The disk flowers are reddish-purple. Bloom peaks in August and September. Seeds can be started in the garden where plants are desired. An excellent cut flower.

Cosmos bipinnatus (Cosmos). Another popular annual with finely divided foliage. It is 2 to 4 feet tall and produces large, showy flowers in the fall. Flower colors include shades of white, pink, rose, lavender, purplé, and crimson. The ray flowers are toothed at the tips and quite wide, and their color is intensified toward the center of the flower. Seeds can be planted in the garden during early May, or plants can be started indoors.

Cosmos sulphureus (Yellow Cosmos). Similar to *C. bipinnatus* except the flowers are yellow.

Cynoglossum amabile (Chinese Forget-Me-Not). Grows to 1 foot. This biennial blooms the first year if seeds are started early. The erect, branched flower panicles rise above a basal rosette of leaves in midsummer. The small, blue flowers resemble those of *Myosotis scorpioides* (the true forget-me-not). Pink and white strains such as 'Blanche' are also available.

Dahlia merckii (Bedding Dahlia). Grown as an annual, reaching a height of 1 to 1½ feet. The single and double flowers come in a variety of colors. The 'Unwin' and 'Coltness' strains are popular. Seeds are started indoors in March and plants are set out about Memorial Day.

Dianthus x *alwoodii* (Hybrid Pinks). This hybrid was developed by crossing *D. caryophyllus* and *D. plumarius*. It is 6 inches to 2 feet tall, with bluish-green foliage. The flowers are larger than *D. barbatus* flowers and white to purple. The edges of the petals are fringed. An excellent plant for flower beds.

Dianthus barbatus (Sweet William). Normally a biennial but some strains flower the first year if plants are started early. The Sweet William is 1½ feet tall, with an interesting color range of white, pink, and red.

Dianthus chinensis (China Pink). Although this species was originally a perennial from Asia, breeding has created a number of annual strains. It grows to 1½ feet tall and has gray-green, grasslike foliage. The flowers are produced on erect stems in small clusters. Colors range from white to pink, rose, and lilac. 'China Doll' and 'Bravo' are excellent cultivars. By removing faded flowers, the blooming period can be lengthened.

Digitalis purpurea 'Foxy' (Common Foxglove). To 1½ feet. The foxglove is typically a biennial but the cultivar 'Foxy' flowers the first year from seed. The flowers usually form in late August and September. They are bell shaped, rose colored, and on upright stems. The throat of the flowers is spotted with dark specks. Start seeds indoors in March.

Eschscholzia californica (California Poppy). This state flower of California is a perennial but blooms the first year from seed. The native species, growing 1 foot tall, is golden-yellow with upfacing, cup-shaped flowers about 2 inches across. Plant breeders have widened the color range to include creamy-white, scarlet, and pink. Ballerina' has a mixture of colors. Sow the seeds early in the spring where you wish the plants to grow. Prefers sunny, well-drained soil.

Euphorbia heterophylla (Mexican Fire Plant). Reaches a height of 2 to 3 feet. The Mexican fire plant is not as showy as *Euphorbia pulcherrima* (the florist's poinsettia), but it is an attractive, compact bush with dark green foliage. Toward fall the upper leaves, or bracts, become red, and the flowers are inconspicuous above them. It is best to sow seeds where plants are to grow as soon as the soil warms up.

Euphorbia marginata (Snow-on-the-Mountain). Vigorous, 2-foot-tall annual grown for its variegated foliage. The leaves are edged with white, and the flowers are not showy. It is best to sow seeds directly since the plants are difficult to transplant. The juice of this annual may be irritating to some people's skin.

Gaillardia pulchella (Blanket Flower). This 1½-foot-tall plant, native from Missouri southward, is sold in both double and single forms. The colors range from white to red with various shades of yellow and orange. 'Tetra Fiesta' and 'Gaiety' have mixed colors. Seeds should be started indoors. Plant in full sun on well-drained soil.

Gomphrena globosa (Globe Amaranth). Grows to 1½ feet. This popular, branched annual is grown for its cloverlike flower heads in pink, red, magenta, purple, white, and orange colors. The flowers are excellent for arrangements and are used both fresh and dried. Soaking the seeds in hot water facilitates germination, which is slow. Allow 6 to 8 weeks to grow the plants before moving them to the garden.

Gypsophila elegans (Annual Baby's Breath). 1-foot-tall annual. The fluffy, flowering panicles of small, white to crimson flowers make excellent fillers in the flower border or in a mixed bouquet. Plants prefer full sun and well-drained soil. Sow the seeds directly in the flower border in early spring.

Helianthus annuus (Common Sunflower). Grows to 6 feet. This coarse annual is grown for its enormous, daisylike heads that may be single or double as in 'Sungold' and 'Teddy Bear'. Heads are usually solitary and turn toward the sun. The ray flowers vary from golden-yellow to bronze and may be twisted or frilled in various ways. The seeds are prized for bird food. It is best to plant sunflowers in rows in the kitchen garden or use them as a background for other flowers. Sow seeds directly about May 15.

Helichrysum bracteatum (Straw Flower). One of the better everlasting flowers for winter bouquets, growing 2 feet tall. The flower heads consist of papery, spreading ray flowers and overlapping, papery disk flowers that fold toward the center. Colors range from white to yellow, orange, pink, and red. After starting seeds indoors in early April, plant in full sun.

Heliotropium arborescens (Heliotrope). This annual is a garden favorite. It is 1½ feet tall, and its rich-purple flowers are produced in flat-topped clusters and are delightfully fragrant. Start seeds indoors in February.

Hunnemannia fumariifolia (Mexican Tulip Poppy). Tender perennial growing to 1½ feet. It flowers profusely from seed the first year and is grown in the North as an annual. The cup-shaped flowers are yellow with crinkled petals; the leaves are bluish-green and finely divided. Soak seeds before planting. Sow directly in the border, or if seeds are started indoors for early bloom, sow in individual containers to minimize the shock of transplanting.

Impatiens balsamina (Garden Balsam). Grows to 1½ feet. This favorite develops camellialike flowers close to the stem in axillary clusters. The flowers are soft pink to red and are partly hidden by the leaves. This is not a good cut flower. It grows best in partial shade.

Impatiens wallerana (Patience Plant). Also sold under the species name *I. sultanii*. It is an excellent flowering plant for shaded borders and ranges from 1 to 1½ feet tall. The flowers are usually single but double forms are known. The colors include scarlet, crimson, rose, pink, orange, and white. 'Elfin', 'Imp', and 'Zigzag' are popular cultivars. Other species of *Impatiens* are being used in hybrids with this species. Start seeds indoors in March.

Ipomoea purpurea (Common Morning Glory). This free-flowering vine grows rapidly to 10 or more feet tall and must have a support. The large, trumpet-shaped flowers are in a wide color range. Blue is the most popular color but white and red cultivars are available. 'Heavenly Blue', 'Pearly Gates', and 'Scarlet O'Hara' are recommended cultivars. The hard seed should be soaked overnight before planting. Sow seeds where the plants are to grow. Often planted on a fence to provide privacy.

Kochia scoparia var. *trichophylla* (Burning Bush). A dense, upright foliage plant that can be used for a temporary hedge. It is 2 to 3 feet tall and its green leaves are small and narrow. In the fall the plant turns brilliant red. Start seeds indoors in early April.

Lathyrus odoratus (Sweet Pea). This very popular flowering vine grows to 6 feet and has fragrant, pealike flowers in a variety of colors. It does not grow well in hot weather, so seeds must be planted very early to obtain bloom before hot weather comes. Some of the dwarf varieties are more heat tolerant. 'Bijou' is only 1¼ feet tall. Because sweet peas are susceptible to soil-borne diseases, it is best to rotate the plantings.

Linum grandiflorum (Flowering Flax). Grows 1 foot tall. This annual blooms from early June until frost. The saucer-shaped flowers are about 1 inch across and usually red. There are also rosy-pink forms, including 'Rubrum' and 'Roseum'. Sow outdoors as soon as the soil can be worked in the spring.

Lobelia erinus (Edging Lobelia). Popular, 6-inch-tall edging plant to be used in front of the flower border. The flowers are blue to red and cover the plants for the entire growing season. Start seeds indoors. Do not let the soil become dry. Good in both sun and shade.

Lobularia maritima (Sweet Alyssum). The most popular ar.nual for edging purposes. It is 6 inches tall and its small, mustardlike flowers are freely produced in flat-topped clusters. Flower colors range from white to violet. 'Carpet of Snow' and 'Violet Queen' are popular cultivars. By cutting back the plants after the first flush of bloom, they will continue to produce flowers all season. Seeds can be sown in the garden or started indoors for earlier bloom.

Matthiola incana (Ten-Weeks Stock). Grows 1 to 1½ feet tall. The color range of the double flowers includes shades of pink, rose, red, blue, purple, yellow, and white. The stocks are cool-season plants that are not commonly grown in this area. By starting the seeds indoors and setting the plants out by mid-May, blooms can usually be enjoyed before hot weather comes.

Mirabilis jalapa (Four-O'clock). A perennial in the South but grown as an annual in the North. Four-o'clock is 2 feet tall and has single, trumpet-shaped flowers that cover the plant from July to frost. The color range includes red, yellow, pink, salmon, lavender, and white. Flowers remain closed until late afternoon except on cloudy days. Start seeds indoors for earlier bloom.

Molucella laevis (Bell's-of-Ireland). Grows 2 feet tall. The green, cup-shaped bells are actually the calyxes of the flowers. The petals are rather inconspicuous and soon disappear, leaving the persistent green calyxes. Stems are often dried for winter bouquets. Start seeds indoors.

Nicotiana alata (Flowering Tobacco). This tender perennial from South America blooms the first year from seed and is treated as an annual. It grows 2 to 3 feet tall and its large, basal leaves have a velvety texture. The trumpet-shaped flowers, ranging from white to maroon, close in bright sunshine and open in the evening and on cloudy days. They are especially fragrant in the evening. Start seeds indoors in March.

Nierembergia hippomanica var. *violacea* (Cup Flower). Grows to 6 inches. The leaves are dark green and narrow. The mound-shaped plants are covered with blue, yellow-throated, cup-shaped flowers in late summer and fall. 'Purple Robe' is violet-blue and one of the more popular cultivars. Start seeds indoors.

Papaver nudicaule (Iceland Poppy). Short-lived perennial grown as an annual and reaching a height of 1 foot. Most of the deeply lobed leaves are basal, and the showy, white or yellow flowers are borne on slender stems. Seeds should be sown outdoors in early spring.

Papaver rhoeas (Shirley Poppy). Grows to 1½ feet. This annual poppy is common in Europe where it volunteers in cultivated fields. The saucer-shaped flowers are produced on slender stems in late spring and early summer. The flower colors include white, pink, scarlet, crimson, and salmon. Seed in the garden during early spring.

Pelargonium x *hortorum* (Bedding Geranium). Tender perennial popular as a houseplant and for outdoor planting. The height ranges from 1 to 1½ feet. Continuous bloom can be expected from well-grown plants from June until frost. Flower colors are white, pink, salmon, and red. Propagation is either by cuttings or from seed planted indoors in February. In recent years plant hybridizers have greatly improved seed-propagated strains.

Penstemon x *gloxinioides* (Beard Tongue). Most penstemons are perennial. The above hybrid (*P. hartwegii* x *P. cobaea*) blooms the first year from seed and is treated as an annual. It is 2 feet tall with tubular flowers ranging from white to crimson. Seeds must be started indoors in February for summer bloom.

Petunia x *hybrida* (Petunia). From 8 to 10 inches tall. Petunias have been greatly improved by hybridization. They are available in a variety of flower colors and sizes. Most are single but some are double. The multifloras produce many, medium-sized flowers. The grandifloras produce fewer but larger flowers. Double forms are present in both the multifloras and grandifloras. Petunia seeds should be started in March for summer and fall bloom. The most popular of all bedding plants.

Phlox drummondii (Annual Phlox). Very colorful annual, 8 inches to 1 foot tall, with flowers about 1 inch across. The flowers are saucer shaped with tubular bases and their colors include white, soft pink, rose, crimsom, scarlet, salmon, and violet, often with contrasting centers. The starred phlox such as 'Twinkle' have pointed corolla lobes. Seeds can be started indoors in early April or planted directly in the border. Grow in individual containers to reduce the shock of transplanting.

Portulaca grandiflora (Rose Moss). A 6-inch-tall plant. The large, showy flowers open only in full sun. There are double and single forms, and colors include white, yellow, crimson, orange, and rose. The rose moss likes full sunlight and grows in rather poor soils. Sow seeds directly in the garden in early spring.

Rudbeckia hirta var. *pulchella* (Gloriosa Daisy). An improved black-eyed Susan. The gloriosa daisies are 2 to 3 feet tall and bloom the first year from seed, producing a mass of large, colorful flowers in late summer. The single types have yellow, mahogany, and bicolored rays and dark-colored disk flowers. The double types are a rich, golden-yellow color. The plants self-sow and come up year after year. Seeds can be started indoors for earlier bloom.

Salpiglossis sinuata (Painted Tongue). Grows 2 feet tall. The velvety, petunialike flowers are produced on upright, branching stems from July to frost. The flower colors include shades of maroon, purple, blue, and scarlet. Seeds are very small and must be started indoors in March.

Salvia farinacea (Blue Salvia). This tender, 2-foot-tall perennial blooms the first year from seed and makes an excellent cut flower. The blue, mintlike flowers are produced on erect stems in late summer and fall. Start seeds indoors in March, or sow directly in the garden.

Salvia splendens (Scarlet Sage). A popular annual, 1½ feet tall, with fiery red flowers in late summer. There are many strains to choose from, such as 'Red Blazer' and 'Blaze of Fire'. Although red is the typical flower color, cultivars have rose, pink, salmon, and white flowers. *Salvias* must be started indoors during early March and grown at a warm temperature of between 70° and 80°F. Do not plant outdoors until the soil and air are warm in late May.

Scabiosa atropurpurea (Pincushion). Grows 2 feet tall. This attractive annual has a basal rosette of deeply divided leaves and erect flower stems terminated by fully double, pincushionlike flowers in a wide range of colors. Start seeds indoors by mid-March.

Senecio cineraria (Dusty-Miller). Tender perennial, 8 inches tall, grown for its finely divided, silvery foliage. The yellow flowers in late fall are not particularly showy. Start seeds in March.

Tagetes erecta (African Marigold). Large, usually fully double-flowered marigold. The height ranges from 1½ to 3 feet, and the leaves are finely divided. Plant breeders have done much to improve this species of marigold in recent years, and there are many cultivars to choose from, for example, 'First Lady' (yellow) and 'Orange Lady'. Colors are usually a shade of yellow or orange, and there is even a white marigold on the market. Seeds can be sown directly or started indoors in April for earlier bloom.

Tagetes patula (French Marigold). Like *T. erecta* (African marigold), this species has also been improved by plant breeders. The plants are much smaller, 10 inches to 1¼ feet tall, and both single- and double-flowered cultivars are available, for example, 'Naughty Marietta'. The ray flowers are typically golden-yellow but often marked with crimson and maroon-colored centers. Good for edging the flower border, these marigolds can also be planted in front of *T. erecta*. The culture is similar to that for *T. erecta*.

Tithonia rotundifolia (Torch Tithonia). A coarse annual growing to 5 feet tall. The daisylike flowers are very showy with orange-scarlet rays and tufted, yellow centers. An excellent cut flower and most colorful in the border. Start seed indoors in early April and plant only toward the back of the flower border.

Tropaeolum majus (Nasturtium). A trailing plant with orange-yellow flowers. This plant grows best in cooler parts of the area and reaches a height of 1 foot. Aphids can be a problem. Start seeds where you wish the plants to grow.

Verbena x *hybrida* (Verbena). This low (6 inch), spreading annual is covered in late summer with flat-topped clusters of small flowers in colors ranging from white to red with many intermediate shades of pink and blue. The verbenas like full sun and can grow on rather poor soil. Start seeds indoors.

Viola cornuta (Viola). Grows to 6 inches. A small-flowered, tufted pansy with blue or yellow blossoms. It flowers best in cool weather. There are several cultivars to choose from in colors ranging from yellow to blue; 'Monarch' has mixed colors. Start seeds indoors in February, and set plants outdoors early to obtain bloom before hot weather. Plants self-sow freely.

Viola x *wittrockiana* (Pansy). Sometimes listed as *V. tricolor* var. *hortensis*. The pansies are of hybrid origin and grow to 6 inches. Although they are short-lived perennials, it is best to treat them as annuals. There is a wide range of flower colors, and the petals are variously marked with different color patterns. There are many strains to choose from. Pansies prefer a cool site and tolerate some shade. Start the seeds indoors in February and set the plants out early to get bloom before hot weather. Plants usually bloom again in the fall if pruned back after the spring bloom.

Zinnia elegans (Zinnia). Zinnias are one of the three top annuals in seed sales. (The other two are petunias and marigolds.) The plant breeder has greatly modified the species. Plant size ranges from dwarf plants about 6 inches tall to large plants 3 feet tall. Flower form and size also varies from small, pompon blooms to giant flowers up to 5 inches in diameter, and every color but blue is represented in zinnia flowers. Seed catalogs are filled with descriptions of interesting cultivars. Except for powdery mildew, zinnias are free from insect and disease problems. Seeds can be planted outdoors as soon as danger of frost has passed, or for earlier bloom seeds can be started indoors in April.

Lists of Annuals

LOW ANNUALS FOR FOREGROUND PLANTINGS

Ageratum houstonianum	*Gypsophila elegans*
Anchusa capensis	*Impatiens wallerana*
Antirrhinum majus	*Linum grandiflorum*
Begonia x *semperflorens-cultorum*	*Mirabilis jalapa*
Catharanthus roseus	*Pelargonium* x *hortorum*
Chrysanthemum parthenium	*Petunia* x *hybrida*
Coleus x *hybridus*	*Phlox drummondii*
Coreopsis tinctoria	*Portulaca grandiflora*
Cynoglossum amabile	*Salvia farinacea*
Dahlia merkii	*Salvia splendens*
Dianthus x *alwoodii*	*Senecio cineraria*
Dianthus barbatus	*Tagetes erecta*
Dianthus chinensis	*Tagetes patula*
Eschscholzia californica	*Verbena* x *hybrida*
Gaillardia pulchella	*Viola* x *wittrockiana*
Gomphrena globosa	*Zinnia elegans*

TALL ANNUALS FOR BACKGROUND PLANTINGS

Alcea rosea	*Euphorbia heterophylla*
Amaranthus tricolor	*Helianthus annuus*
Cleome hasslerana	*Rudbeckia hirta* var. *pulchella*
Cosmos bipinnatus	*Tithonia rotundifolia*

LOW ANNUALS FOR EDGING

Ageratum houstonianum
Begonia x semperflorens-cultorum
Dianthum chinensis
Lobelia erinus
Lobularia maritima

Nierembergia hippomanica var.
   violacea
Portulaca grandiflora
Tagetes patula

ANNUALS FOR PARTIAL SHADE

Ageratum houstonianum
Antirrhinum majus
Begonia x semperflorens-cultorum
Browallia speciosa
Catharanthus roseus
Coleus x hybridus
Cynoglossum amabile

Impatiens balsamina
Impatiens wallerana
Lobelia erinus
Nicotiana alata
Petunia x hybrida
Viola cornuta
Viola x wittrockiana

ANNUALS FOR CUT FLOWERS

Antirrhinum majus
Calendula officinalis
Callistephus chinensis
Celosia cristata
Centaurea cyanus
Cosmos bipinnatus
Dianthus barbatus
Lathyrus odoratus

Matthiola incana
Rudbeckia hirta var. pulchella
Salvia farinacea
Tagetes erecta
Tagetes patula
Tithonia rotundifolia
Viola x wittrockiana
Zinnia elegans

FRAGRANT ANNUALS

Antirrhinum majus
Centaurea moschata
Cleome hasslerana
Dianthus barbatus
Heliotropium arborescens
Lathyrus odoratus

Lobularia maritima
Matthiola incana
Nicotiana alata
Petunia x hybrida
Tropaeolum majus
Viola wittrockiana

ANNUALS THAT SHOULD BE STARTED INDOORS

Annual	Indoor seeding	Transplant outdoors
Ageratum houstonianum	March 15	May 20
Alcea rosea	April 1	May 10
Amaranthus caudatus	March 15	May 20

Annual	Indoor seeding	Transplant outdoors
Amaranthus tricolor	March 15	May 20
Anchusa capensis	March 15	May 20
Antirrhinum majus	March 1	May 10
Begonia x semperflorens-cultorum	February 15	May 20
Browallia speciosa	March 1	May 20
*Calendula officinalis	April 1	May 20
Callistephus chinensis	April 1	May 20
Catharanthus roseus	April 1	May 20
Celosia cristata	March 15	May 30
Centaurea moschata	March 15	May 20
Chrysanthemum parthenium	March 1	May 20
*Cleome hasslerana	April 1	May 20
Coleus x hybridus	February 15	May 30
*Cosmos bipinnatus	April 1	May 10
*Cosmos sulphureus	April 1	May 10
Cynoglossum amabile	March 15	May 20
Dahlia merckii	March 15	May 30
Dianthus x alwoodii	March 15	May 20
Dianthus barbatus	March 15	May 20
Dianthus chinensis	March 15	May 20
Digitalis purpurea 'Foxy'	March 1	May 10
Gaillardia pulchella	April 1	May 20
Gomphrena globosa	March 15	May 20
Helichrysum bracteatum	April 1	May 20
Heliotropium arborescens	February 15	May 20
*Hunnemannia fumariifolia	March 15	May 20
Impatiens balsamina	March 1	May 20
Impatiens wallerana	March 1	May 20
Kochia scoparia var. trichophylla	April 1	May 20
Lobelia erinus	March 1	May 20
*Lobularia maritima	March 15	May 20
Matthiola incana	March 15	May 10
*Mirabilis jalapa	March 15	May 20
Molucella laevis	March 15	May 20
Nicotiana alata	March 1	May 20
Nierembergia hippomanica var. violacea	March 1	May 20
Pelargonium x hortorum	February 15	May 20
Penstemon x gloxinioides	February 15	May 10
Petunia x hybrida	March 1	May 20
*Phlox drummondii	April 1	May 20
*Rudbeckia hirta var. pulchella	April 1	May 20
Salpiglossis sinuata	March 15	May 20

Annual	Indoor seeding	Transplant outdoors
*Salvia farinacea	March 15	May 20
Salvia splendens	March 1	May 30
Scabiosa atropurpurea	March 15	May 20
Senecio cineraria	March 1	May 20
*Tagetes erecta	April 1	May 20
*Tagetes patula	April 1	May 20
Tithonia rotundifolia	April 1	May 20
Verbena x hybrida	April 1	May 20
Viola cornuta	February 15	May 10
Viola x wittrockiana	February 15	May 10
*Zinnia elegans	April 1	May 20

*Seeds can also be sown outdoors in the garden.

Index

Index

273